aspen grove in Santa Catalina Mountains

aspen grove in Santa Catalina Mountains

ARIZONA TRAILS
100 Hikes in Canyon and Sierra

David Mazel

Wilderness Press
Berkeley

Acknowledgements

Many people helped to create this book. My brother Mark Mazel drove me to and from innumerable backcountry trailheads. My wife Annie Mazel contributed her drawings and considerable moral support. Sanford and Jeannine Mazel supported me both morally and materially through much of the work. Janice Fryling and Christopher Nyerges printed the photographs. My sincerest thanks to them all.

I was assisted by many others, and I would like to thank them as well:

Julian Femath, Cliff Howard and Chris Law, of Phoenix;

Elissa Palma, Eric Nelson and the staff of the Child Educational Center in La Canada, California;

Ken Barnes of Pasadena City College;

Pat Sullivan of McCurdy Nature Center;

Paulette L. Claus of the National Geographic Society;

Dean L. Berkey, Bernard H. Brunner, Charles W. Denton, James L. Kimball, John McKelvey, William L. Russel Jr., Jerald D. Tower, Donald A. Van Driel and Johnny R. Wilson, of the United States Forest Service; and

Harthon L. Bill, Vicki H. Black, Karen Brantley, Richard W. Marks, John C. O'Brien and Bruce W. Shaw, of the National Park Service.

Copyright © 1981 by David Mazel

Photos by the author except as noted

Cover photo by Ed Cooper

Design by Thomas Winnett

Maps by Jeff Schaffer and Larry Van Dyke

Drawings by Annie Mazel

Library of Congress Card Catalog Number 80-53682

International Standard Book Number 0-89997-003-6

Manufactured in the United States

Published by Wilderness Press
2440 Bancroft Way
Berkeley, CA 94704

Write for free catalog

Contents

Introduction   1

Superstition Wilderness   13

The Southeastern Ranges   83

    Pusch Ridge Primitive Area
    Rincon Mountains
    Santa Rita Mountains
    Chiricahua Wilderness

The Eastern Highlands   179

    Blue Range Primitive Area
    Mt. Baldy Wilderness

Grand Canyon   225

Mazatzal Wilderness   267

Index   309

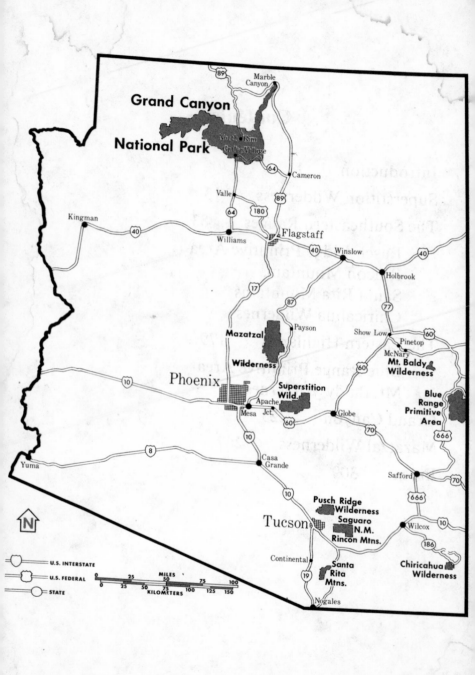

Introduction

To some people, the thought of hiking or backpacking in Arizona might seem ludicrous. After all, isn't the entire state just a vast, barren desert, bone-dry and choked with dust? Then, upon reflection, images come to mind that shatter the illusion: the awesome, terraced gulf of the Grand Canyon; the cool pine forests and soaring mountains near Flagstaff; the gleam of winter snow on the rugged peaks encircling Tucson. Suddenly it becomes obvious that, tucked away in the undeveloped recesses of the state, there must exist a wealth of beautiful hiking country.

And so there does. As of 1980, Arizona contained well over a million and a half acres of land officially classified as wilderness by either the state or the federal government. Closed to motor vehicles, forever spared the scourges of modern "development," and containing a wide range of ecosystems and landforms, these wildlands can provide the wilderness enthusiast with a variety of memorable hiking experiences. You can camp out beneath cool forests of pine and fir, where the wind sighs fretfully in the boughs, or on the sere desert flats, where the nights are warm and full of stars. You can scramble up twisting, forgotten canyons, where you might stumble across the remains of an ancient Indian dwelling or the fresh track of a cougar or a bear. Whatever you are looking for in the outdoors — rushing streams, jagged peaks, mountaintop vistas that stretch for a hundred miles, without a city in sight — you can find it in Arizona, along with plenty of peace and quiet, challenge and adventure, and that indefinable quality called wilderness.

The purpose of this guide is twofold: to introduce you to some of this magnificent country, and to insure that your visits to it are as safe, comfortable and informed as possible. Trails in nine separate wilderness areas are included, grouped according to geographical similarities into five regions (see map).

The *Superstition Wilderness* chapter covers hikes in the extremely rugged, relatively low-elevation Superstition Mountains near Phoenix. The *Southeastern Ranges* include the pine-topped Santa Catalina, Rincon and Santa Rita mountains, all near Tucson, as well as the Chiricahua Mountains in the extreme southeast corner of the state. The *Eastern Highlands* region takes in the White Mountains and the Blue Range, in east-central Arizona near the New Mexico border. The *Grand Canyon* chapter covers treks in the backcountry of Grand Canyon National Park. The *Mazatzal Wilderness* is a region of high peaks and rugged desert country northeast of Phoenix.

Each trip description contains a heading, which provides certain basic information at a glance. On a *round trip*, you hike to a specific backcountry destination, then return to the trailhead via the same route. The mileage given for such a trip represents the total distance you will have to hike, both going and returning. On a *loop trip* you do not have to retrace your steps to return to your vehicle; you enter and leave the wilderness by different trails. Some treks begin and end at different trailheads, necessitating a *shuttle*. Car shuttles can be handled in a variety of ways. You can talk a friend into dropping you off at your departure point, then have him or her pick you at your destination at a prearranged hour (or day). With two cars, you can park one vehicle at the destination, then transport the entire party to the jumping-off point in the other car (which will have to be picked up on the drive home). This is a very time-consuming and energy-inefficient method of handling long shuttles, though it works well for shorter ones. A more innovative approach is to split the party into two groups, which then hike the route in opposite directions, each ending up where the other began and returning with the other's vehicle. Car keys can be exchanged when the groups pass each other, though it is good insurance to provide each party with extra keys beforehand.

Public air and bus lines serve the South Rim area of the Grand Canyon. Compared to traveling by auto, this is an expensive way to go, but it has its advantages: you arrive fresh and relaxed, ready to enjoy your trip; then, following your trek, you can stretch back and snooze, rather than fighting to stay awake behind the wheel.

If, as a last resort, you decide to hitchhike between trailheads, it is best to leave your vehicle at your trip's destination, rather than its beginning; after a lengthy, tiring hike you will appreciate being able to head straight for the comforts of home. (Hitching is against

Introduction

the law in National Parks and Monuments, but legal elsewhere in the state, as long as you stand to the side of the roadway, well off the pavement. Hitching the interstate highways is illegal; you may stand on the on-ramps, but do not walk past the sign which says "pedestrians prohibited.")

Each trip has been graded for overall difficulty. *Leisurely* routes are generally under 5 or 6 miles long, and entail an elevation gain of less than 1000 feet. (The *elevation gain* listed for each trip takes into account all climbs of more than 40 feet, along the entire length of the route.) *Moderate* treks can be up to 12 or 14 miles long, with up to 2500 feet of elevation gain; anything harder than that is listed as *strenuous*. Many trips can be done either as dayhikes or backpacks. For example, a strenuous dayhike, when spread out over two or more hiking days, can become a moderate backpack. These numerical guidelines are only approximate; in borderline cases I have taken into consideration overall trail conditions, availability of shade and water along the route, and other, more subjective factors before making a classification.

Most of the trips fall into either the moderate or the strenuous category, but that does not mean this guide is only for athletic hikers — *nowhere is it written that you must hike a particular trip's entire length in order to have an enjoyable outing.* On many trips a saddle, a hilltop, or a stream crossing partway along the route makes a natural turnaround point for the more leisure-oriented backcountry explorer.

Because weather patterns fluctuate widely from year to year, it is difficult to recommend an ideal hiking season for many of the trips. The seasons given should be considered only rough guidelines; before setting out on a trip in an unfamiliar area it is always a good idea to check the regional weather summaries that appear in the newspapers.

Each trip heading has a water summary, which lists places where water is likely to be available during the trip's recommended season. To help you determine how much water you will need to carry, the distances of these points from the trailhead are given in parentheses. In most areas, streams and springs rely heavily on winter and summer precipitation for replenishment; during drier-than-normal years, all water sources not listed as "year-round" should be considered suspect, and should be checked out with the appropriate government agency (listed at the end of each chapter's preface). During wetter-than-normal years, water will generally be available at places other than just those listed in the summary.

In the text, the figures in parentheses indicate distance (in miles) from the trailhead, and elevation (in feet) of the point in question. These are usually given at readily recognizable places along the route — at passes, stream crossings, trail junctions, and so on. Campsites are listed as being poor, fair, good, or excellent, depending on such factors as the scenic value of the setting, availability of water and shade, and overall "feel." Most sites mentioned will have a small fire ring and cleared area, though in less frequently visited areas the term "campsite" or "tentsite" may be used simply to denote a good spot to bed down, even if it shows no evidence of previous use.

Trails in this guide range in condition from carefully constructed, frequently maintained "highways," such as the Grand Canyon's Bright Angel Trail, to routes that are almost entirely cross-country. If a given trail might prove too difficult for beginners, this is noted in the short introduction which precedes each trip description. On these fainter routes you will often find *ducks*, *cairns* and *blazes* to help guide you. A duck consists of one or two small stones placed conspicuously on top of a bigger rock. A cairn is a larger, more obvious pile of many stones. A blaze is a gash (usually in the shape of an "i") carved in the bark of a tree with an axe.

Junctions are listed as signed or unsigned, but bear in mind that trail signs are not fixed features of the landscape. (Unethical hikers sometimes use them for firewood, or cart them home as "souvenirs.") A "poorly signed" junction is one where a sign is in place, but is unreadable due to vandalism or weathering.

On this book's maps, described trails are indicated by a solid black line, cross-country routes by a dotted line. Other trails, not described in the text, show up as a faint, dashed line. Scales and contour intervals are clearly indicated on each map. On some trips, possible sidetrips are mentioned in the text but not described in detail; these are also shown on the maps.

Life Zones

Plants tend to form distinct communities whose nature depends on elevation and exposure. Hence any particular community will be found wherever the elevation and exposure are right. The concept of "life zones" — the notion that most plant species can prosper only within limited elevation ranges — is useful for grouping plants that are commonly found together. The most common trees and shrubs in Arizona in each zone, called "indicators" for that zone, are shown in the table below.

Life Zone	Elev. Range	Plant Community	Indicators
Lower Sonoran	2000–4000	Desert scrub	Saguaro, cholla, prickly pear, ocotillo, paloverde, creosote bush
"Lower" Upper Sonoran	4000–5000	Grassland Transition	Mesquite, gramagrass, nolina, sotol, amole
"Upper" Upper Sonoran	5000–7000	Oak-pinyon-juniper woodland	Emory oak, pinyon pine, Mexican blue oak, shrub live oak, cliff rose, point-leaf manzanita
Transition	7000–8500	Coniferous forest	Ponderosa pine, white oak, silverleaf oak, Gambel oak
Canadian	8500–10000	Coniferous forest	Engelmann spruce, subalpine fir, Colorado blue spruce

(Note: The altitude ranges given are only approximate, and will vary from area to area. In the Grand Canyon, which is geographically isolated from the rest of the state, certain indicator species are not found.)

Hikers who are familiar with Arizona's life zones can use the concept as a sort of crude "altimeter" when traveling in unfamiliar areas. When plants are mentioned in the text, it is not my intention to give an exhaustive account of the local flora, but merely to help you visualize the sort of country you will be hiking through. As for wildflowers, those mentioned in the text represent only those which I *saw* and *identified* during the particular *season* I did my field-checking. Other visitors, hiking in a different season, perhaps, or with sharper eyes than mine, will likely see other flowers as well.

Equipment

Since even the easiest trips in this guide venture into fairly rugged country, every hiker will want to wear a pair of sturdy, well-broken-in boots. A wide-brimmed hat and sunglasses are rarely amiss; even on cool winter days, the sun's glare can be uncomfortable. During the summer and winter rainy seasons you will need a poncho or parka. In the cooler months, or when hiking in the high country, always carry a windbreaker and a wool sweater. In general, clothing should be sturdy and loose-fitting; wear cotton for warm weather, wool for cold weather. All hikers should carry an emergency kit (containing matches, money, and a whistle in addition to first-aid items), a compass, extra food, road maps, and this book. On most trips you will have to carry water; make sure your containers are sturdy and leakproof.

Backpackers will find they need nothing unusual in the way of gear, aside from extra water containers. Those unfamiliar with the joys and disciplines of backpacking may wish to consult Thomas Winnett's *Backpacking Basics*, an excellent guide for the novice.

Hazards and Precautions

Dehydration   Anytime you are not sure of water availability along your route, carry *at least* ½ gallon of water per person per day — 1 gallon or more during hot weather. It is better to store your water in several small containers than in a single large one — it is easier to handle, and a single leak will not endanger your whole supply.

If you entertain paranoid visions of dying of thirst on any of these hikes, remember that most of this book's trips are short enough that you could reach one trailhead or another in a forced march of less than a day. (Many of the trailheads, however, have no water supplies, so it is wise to keep a few gallons in your car.) If for some reason you find yourself out of water and more than a day's walk from help, the best thing to do is probably to walk *out* the same way you came *in*. To conserve your body's water, maintain a moderate, "no sweat" pace, and wear longsleeved clothing. In moderate temperatures you will not die of thirst in two days' time, which is long enough to get out of any area reached by this book's hikes. In extreme cases, dehydration might begin to impair your judgment by that time; this is the reason for turning around and hiking out on a familiar trail (unless, of course, you are well past your trip's halfway point). *Do not* go off willy-nilly in search of water. You probably won't find any, and will only confuse the efforts of those who may eventually have to come looking for you. Always let someone back in town know your planned route and schedule, and then *stay on that route.*

Weather   In many areas of the state, between mid-June and early September, hardly a day goes by without a spectacular afternoon thunderstorm. If you see cumulus clouds building up nearby, avoid ridges, hilltops and flat, open areas. Remember that thunder heard in the distance may be right on top of you in a matter of minutes, so move *quickly* to the nearest safe place.

Which spots are safest during an electrical storm? Best of all is the base of a steep slope or cliff. In open country, head for any sort of depression and squat down, after ditching any metal gear a safe distance away.

Summertime is also flash-flood season, and washes and canyon bottoms should be abandoned if a heavy storm appears to be brewing. Backpackers are similarly advised to resist the temptation to bed down in the luxuriously soft sand of dry streambeds. (Sand is very hard to sleep on anyway because it compacts.)

Though not the norm, heavy rain (and snow at higher altitudes) is possible throughout the winter months. Occasionally a low-pressure system will stray in from the Pacific coast and sit over the state for several days, causing thoroughly miserable hiking conditions (but also replenishing springs and streams, and preparing the land to explode with spring wildflowers). Such storms can sometimes mire access roads so badly that hikers may find themselves stranded for several days at their trailhead. Such occurrences can usually be avoided by checking the local weather forecast before leaving home.

Extreme heat and cold are best avoided by hiking a trip within its recommended season. Should you feel an irresistible urge to hike during hot weather, there are several ways to increase the safety and enjoyment of your trip:

1. Choose a hike that is both physically easy and easy to follow.
2. Carry at least 1 gallon of water per person per day, if none will be available en route.
3. Wear a hat, and light-colored, loose-fitting, long-sleeved cotton clothing. (This helps reduce water loss through sweating. Many hikers will prefer to wear little more than a pair of shorts; this is fine, but *only* if plenty of water is available for drinking.)
4. Hike early in the morning or late in the afternoon. If the moon is near full, try hiking at night — the desert can be enchanting by moonlight.
5. Take it easy — rest and drink frequently, *before* you feel you need to.

Venomous Creatures

Rattlesnakes are found in nearly every corner of the state, but are not aggressive and will not strike unless they feel cornered. Should you be bitten, *remain calm* — adrenalin may compound the toxicity of the venom, and a quickened pulse only serves to spread it faster. Have a member of the party go for help immediately, unless it is only an hour or two to the trailhead, in which case the victim can be carried out by companions. In many cases, he or she will be able to walk out unassisted. Someone should still precede the main party, to arrange for help to be available at the trailhead.

Cut-and-suck snakebite kits are available at sporting-goods and some drug stores, and should be carried if you will be hiking alone or far from civilization. For short trips they are not necessarily recommended, as the do-it-yourself surgery required may be riskier than any rattler's venom. If you elect to carry one, know how to use it. Before cutting, remember that the victim's chance of survival is very high, even with no treatment at all.

Scorpions   Only two species of Arizona scorpions — each attaining a length of no more than 2″ — are potentially fatal to humans, and these have so far killed only a few small children. The larger, more common species of scorpion can inflict a painful wound, but if stung you need hardly say your prayers.

Coral Snakes This beautifully banded, venomous serpent is rarely seen, and has never been known to bite a human, much less kill one. It can be distinguished from the similar false coral snake by noting the arrangement of the colored bands: red adjoins black in the false coral, whereas red adjoins cream in the true.

The *Gila monster*, one of only two venomous lizards known to science, is a chubby, stub-nosed fellow who grows to be about a foot long. Gila monsters may be identified by their beaded, black-and-tan splotched skin. Although their venom is potentially fatal, they are too sluggish to be of concern to humans. (Only people who actually pick them up and handle them have been known to be bitten.)

Centipedes and *tarantulas* can also muster up a painful bite, but are never fatal.

Any bite, whether poisonous or not, carries with it the possibility of bacterial infection, and should always be washed thoroughly, disinfected, and bandaged. The surest way to avoid these creeping and slithering hazards is to watch where you place your hands and feet. Be particularly careful when stepping over rocks and logs or when walking through brush. At night, zip your tent doorway up a few inches. If you have no tent, prop up the perimeter of your groundcloth with small branches or stones.

Rules, Regulations and Backcountry Courtesy

The days are long past when one could go into the wilderness, cut down trees and branches to build shelters and feed roaring bonfires, and in general do as one pleased. Today's wilderness is too scarce and fragile a resource to be treated cavalierly; as backcountry use increases, it becomes increasingly crucial that all visitors heed the following common-sense rules and regulations:

1. Camp at least 100 feet from streams, farther from springs (to avoid spooking the shy wildlife which depends on them for water). Avoid sleeping in meadows or on soft vegetation; bedding down on pine duff is almost as comfortable and far less destructive.
2. Bury human waste under at least 6 " of soft, biologically active soil, far from water sources, trails, and popular campsites.
3. Soap (including biodegradable soap) must be kept out of streams and springs. If you must use soap, carry a pot of water to your camp and do your washing there.

4. Fishermen will need a valid Arizona state fishing license. Special limits and regulations apply in Grand Canyon National Park; inquire about these at the park visitor centers.

5. On National Forest lands, smoking is not permitted while traveling through vegetated areas; you may, however, stop and smoke in a safe place.

6. Cutting switchbacks eventually destroys trails, and is illegal in national forests and parks.

7. If you intend to build a fire outside of an officially designated wilderness area, you will need a campfire permit, obtainable at local Forest Service offices.

8. In any wilderness area, you are required to *pack out* what you *pack in.*

9. Pack and saddle stock have the right-of-way on trails; hikers should move a few feet off the trail and stand quietly until the animals pass.

10. Cutting plants and trees (including dead but standing snags), tormenting wild animals, chopping down signs and painting rocks are all prohibited.

11. In national forests, group size is limited to 25 persons; the stay limit is 14 days.

12. As of this writing, wilderness permits are not needed to enter Arizona's national forest wildernesses, but they may be in the future. In Saguaro National Monument and Grand Canyon National Park, backpackers must obtain a Backcountry Use Permit (available at park and monument visitor centers).

Ultimately, the only protection which our wildlands enjoy lies not in rules such as those above, but in the attitudes of people who visit them. All of us who love this magnificent wilderness country would do well to remember that we have not inherited it from our parents, but have only borrowed it from our children. Let's return as much of it as we can to them.

Further Reading

Flowers of the Southwest Mountains (5th edition), by Leslie P. Arnberger (Southwest Parks and Monuments Association, Globe, Arizona 1974)

Flowers of the Southwest Deserts (9th edition), by Natt N. Dodge and Jeanne R. Janish (Southwest Parks and Monuments Association, Globe, Arizona 1976

Desert Wildlife, by Edmund C. Jaeger (Stanford University Press, Stanford, California 1961)

Desert: The American Southwest, by Ruth Kirk (Houghton Mifflin, Boston, Massachussetts 1973)

The Desert Year, by Joseph Wood Krutch (Penguin Books, New York, New York 1977)

Voice of the Desert: A Naturalist's Interpretation, by Joseph Wood Krutch (William Morrow and Co., New York, New York 1955)

Woody Plants of the Southwest, by Samuel H. Lamb (Sunstone Press, Santa Fe, New Mexico 1977)

Desert Survival, by Dick Nelson and Sharon Nelson (Tecolote Press, Tecolote, New Mexico 1977)

Flowers of the Southwest Mesas (5th edition), by Pauline M. Patraw and Jeanne R. Janish (Southwest Parks and Monuments Association, Globe, Arizona 1977)

Desert Tree Finder: A Pocket Manual for Identifying Desert Trees, by May Theilgaard Watts and Tom Watts (Nature Study Guild, Berkeley, California 1974)

Rocky Mountain Tree Finder: A Pocket Manual for Identifying Rocky Mountain Trees, by Tom Watts (Nature Study Guild, Berkeley, California 1972)

Backpacking Basics, by Thomas Winnett (Wilderness Press, Berkeley, California 1979)

Weavers Needle, from the head of Needle Canyon

Area 1:
The Superstition
Wilderness

Comparatively low in elevation, arid, and exceptionally rugged and beautiful, the 124,000-acre Superstition Wilderness affords some of the finest desert hiking to be found anywhere. Elevations range from under 2000 feet, in the canyons of the west end, to over 6000 feet in the eastern uplands. This is less vertical relief than is found in the other regions covered by this guide, but don't be fooled—this is extremely rugged country, ringed with cliffs, studded with thorny cacti, and shot through with steep-walled, deeply eroded canyons. The fact that these mountains have survived as wilderness, in spite of their proximity to the sprawling Phoenix metropolitan area, is a testament to their harshness and inaccessibility. The periphery of the wilderness area is in fact visible from within the city limits, but once one enters the more remote parts of the backcountry, the city could just as well be a thousand miles away.

The highest point in the western part of the wilderness is 5077-foot Superstition Mountain. A number of narrow canyons drain northwestward from here, slicing through a once-rolling landscape of mesas and hills before emptying into the Salt River. To the south, the land falls abruptly away along a steep escarpment to the floor of the Arizona desert. The vegetation in this western area consists primarily of a typical Lower Sonoran mixture of paloverde, saguaro, prickly pear and hedgehog cactus, jojoba and creosote bush, with some Upper Sonoran plants such as agave, mountain mahogany, and shrub live oak showing up at

higher elevations. A smattering of single-leaf pinyon pines are
found in the Pinyon Camp area near Fremont Saddle, and small
copses of cottonwood, sycamore, netleaf hackberry, sugar sumac,
velvet ash, and Arizona walnut grow near springs and along canyon bottoms. Except for the fairly common collared peccary, or
javelina, the local mammalian life is mostly nocturnal; the largest
animal you are likely to see (by moonlight, probably) is a striped or
spotted skunk, a raccoon, a woodrat or a ringtail cat. In the
daytime you will almost surely be able to spot a Cooper's or a red-
tailed hawk, possibly a golden eagle as well. In the spring, a host of
smaller birds can be identified in forested, well-watered areas.

The eastern half of the wilderness is considerably higher than
the western, with dense chaparral cloaking its sunnier slopes, and
pockets of pinyon pine, one-seed juniper, alligator juniper and
ponderosa pine growing in shadier, more sheltered places. Stream-
courses are more likely to have water here than in the west, and
their serene, oak- and sycamore-shaded banks can provide
delightful camping. Being harder to reach from Phoenix, this area
is also less frequently visited; hence hikers here have a greater
chance of finding genuine solitude, and of glimpsing such man-shy
animal residents as the cougar, the desert mule deer, and the black
bear.

Both halves of the Superstitions are uncomfortably hot between May and October, but summer hiking can be feasible in the
eastern area *if* you begin your trip very early in the morning, early
enough to reach your destination before the hottest part of the
day. Violent thunderstorms are quite common in July and August,
and often provide a measure of relief from the midday heat.
Winter temperatures are generally pleasant, but visitors should be
prepared for an occasional downpour. In the higher elevations, be
equipped for cold weather and the possibility of light-to-moderate
snowfall.

The Superstitions contain no perennial streams, and even the
most reliable springs have been known to become unpotable during drought years. For dayhikes and short backpacking trips it is
advisable to carry all the water you need; this is not only the safest
policy, but it also frees you of the necessity of camping near
springs. (Please remember that many wildlife species depend on
these springs for their water, too, but will not use them if they see
humans nearby — try to make your camp at least a few hundred
yards away.) Lengthy backpacking trips should be attempted only
after rains, when springs and streams are likely to have water.

Under provisions of the Wilderness Act of 1964, some cattle grazing is currently allowed within the wilderness area. This grazing does not cause *too* much of a disturbance ecologically, we are assured by the Forest Service, but the sight of a decidedly tame heifer in otherwise wild country detracts mightily from the area's wilderness aura. Cows can also foul springs, leave their droppings in otherwise attractive campsites, and in myriad other small ways make nuisances of themselves. One can only hope that existing grazing allotments will be gradually phased out over the next several years.

The geological history of the Superstition Mountains is complex. During the mid-Cenozoic era, about 30 million years ago, this was gently sloping, open country, located between the geologically stable Colorado Plateau region and the far more active Basin and Range province. About 29 million years ago, in response to forces not yet fully understood, hot lava bubbled up from deep within the earth, forming a cluster of mountains rising 2-3000 feet above the surrounding level. This activity was later followed by a series of more violent eruptions, which spread a thick carpet of volcanic ash over a wide area. As this layer thickened, the hot ash was compressed by its own weight and welded together to form the rock known as "tuff." So much magma was ejected in these tremendous eruptions that the surface rocks caved in for lack of support, forming a gigantic pit, or "collapse caldera," about 9 miles in diameter. Another siege of volcanic activity pushed up the center of this caldera to form the present steep-walled Superstition Mountain area. The debris from these explosions was not hot enough to fuse into tuff; instead it formed the pale yellow rock which is now exposed at Palomino Mountain and on top of Battleship Mountain and Geronimo Head. Some 18-15 million years ago, black lava oozed out of the caldera, hardening into the dark basalt layer which presently caps Black Mesa and Black Top Mesa. The current rugged relief of the Superstition Mountains' interior is due mainly to water erosion, particularly the scouring action of repeated flash floods. Weaver's Needle, the single most dominant landmark in the wilderness, is a tall spire of dark lava that apparently hardened in the neck of a volcano and was subsequently exposed by erosion. (The Needle, by the way, was named for Pauline Weaver, a (male) frontier scout. The local Indians are said to have referred to it with a far more apt noun—the word that meant, in their language, "stallion's penis.")

The human history of the region goes back at least 700 years; ruins of the Hohokam and Salado Indian cultures have been found and dated at 1200–1300 AD. (Trips 17, 19, and 23 visit the site of one Salado dwelling.) After the abandonment of these sites (an unexplained event, presumably related to the wholesale abandonment of hundreds of similar dwellings across the Southwest), Apache raiders found the rugged range to be a secure base from which to conduct forays against Papago and Pima Indians, and later against white settlers.

Many readers will recognize the Superstition Mountains as the (alleged) home of the (equally alleged) Lost Dutchman Gold Mine. In all probability this mine never existed, but the legends concerning it are interesting enough to be touched on lightly here. Many variations exist, the most commonly told story being that, in the early 1800's, one Don Miguel Peralta discovered a fabulously rich vein of gold somewhere in the inaccessible reaches of what was then northern Mexico, on land that had been awarded to the Peralta clan by the Spanish Crown. The lode was named "El Sombrero," after a distinctive, hat-shaped peak which loomed within sight of the mine. (The yarn-spinners invariably equate this peak with Weaver's Needle.) Following the Mexican-American War, the Peraltas hurried northward to milk their mine one last time, before the land surrounding it should be ceded to the United States. In its haste, the party purportedly left itself open to Indian attack, and was almost completely wiped out by a band of Apaches.

Some 30 years later, the legend goes on, a man named Jacob Waltz — the Dutchman — saved the life of one of the survivors of the Peralta massacre, who divulged the mine's location out of gratitude. Waltz furtively worked the mine for years; those who tried to follow him to his treasure either got lost in the Superstitions' labyrinthine canyons or were ambushed and killed outright by the wily Waltz. The Dutchman died in 1891, without ever revealing the location of the mine — though he left behind enough "hints" that a small army of rainbow riders has been searching for it to this day.

Hikers should be aware that this legend has absolutely no basis in verifiable fact. The "Peralta Grant" never existed, but was merely a fabrication perpetrated as part of James Addison Reavis' infamous land fraud scheme of the late 1800's. Contemporary newspapers never mentioned a man named Waltz as having a mine of any value; if the Dutchman did show up in Phoenix from time to time, loaded down with gold about which he kept rather quiet, he may have simply been acting as a fence for dishonest laborers who were "high grading" (filching) ore from nearby mines. To the professional geologist, the idea that there could be gold in these mountains is ludicrous on its face, a volcanic field being the last place one would expect to find precious metals. The Superstition region has in fact been investigated by the U.S. Bureau of Mines, whose report states flatly that it is a "non-mineralized area."

Unfortunately, so powerful is the Lost Dutchman legend that such disclaimers have failed to prevent the aforementioned self-styled "prospectors" from digging around in search of the mythical treasure; several of the hikes in this chapter lead past the ugly scars they have left behind. And they are still looking — there are today at least twenty active (but legally suspect) "claims" being "worked" in the area. Wilderness enthusiasts will be glad to know that no new claims may be filed after December 31, 1983. Then, one hopes, with the veiling glitter of gold removed from before their eyes, visitors to this beautiful, wild region will be more prone to appreciate its fabulous scenery, curious wildlife and challenging trails. It is these things, after all, which constitute the *real* treasure of the Superstition Mountains.

Managing Agencies

Forest Supervisor's Office
Tonto National Forest
102 S. 28th Street
P.O. Box 29070
Phoenix, AZ 85038
(602) 261-3205

Mesa Ranger District
26 N. MacDonald Street
Mesa, AZ 85201
(602) 261-6446

Globe Ranger District
Route 1, Box 33
Globe, AZ 85501
(602) 425-7189

Tonto Basin Ranger District
P.O. Box 647
Roosevelt, AZ 85545
(602) 467-2236

Further Reading

Tales of the Superstitions, by Robert Blair (Arizona Historical Foundations, Tempe, Arizona 1975)

The Treasure of the Superstition Mountains, by Gary Jennings (W.W. Norton and Company, New York, New York 1973)

Superstition Wilderness Management Plan (1972). Available for inspection at local Forest Service offices

Approaches/Trailheads

Canyon Lake   From Apache Junction drive northeast on State Highway 88 to Canyon Lake, about 14 miles. As the highway skirts the south side of this reservoir it crosses two narrow bridges; the trailhead is on the right-hand side of the highway just past the second bridge, 15.4 miles from Apache Junction. This approach is paved all the way.

First Water   From Apache Junction drive northeast on State Highway 88 for 5.3 miles, then turn right onto First Water Road (Forest Road 78). Follow this dirt road (OK for passenger cars) 2.6 miles to the parking area at its end. The Dutchman's Trail begins just beyond the Superstition Wilderness boundary sign.

Kings Ranch   From Apache Junction follow U.S. 60/80/89 for 6.7 miles to Kings Ranch Road. Turn left onto the latter and follow it 2.8 miles to an intersection, then turn right onto Kings Way and proceed 0.8 mile farther to the trailhead at its end. This is private property; please do not act so as to disturb the nearby residents. As of 1980, the last mile or so of this approach was unpaved, but easy for passenger cars.

Peralta   From Apache Junction drive southeast along U.S. 60/80/89 approximately 9 miles, then turn left onto Peralta Road (Forest Road 77). Follow this northeast for 5.4 miles to a fork, turn left, and continue 2.0 miles farther to the parking area at road's end.

JF Ranch   From Florence Junction drive east on U.S. 60 for 2 miles to Queen Valley Road (paved). Follow this north 1.7 miles, then veer right onto Forest Road 357. Follow the latter 3.0 miles and turn left onto Forest Road 172. Follow it north 8.1 miles to a fork, where Forest Road 172 goes left and Forest Road 172A goes right. Turn left here and proceed 1.9 miles to the point where

Forest Road 172 enters Fraser Wash, just before it terminates at JF Ranch. The trail to Tortilla Pass and Rogers Canyon begins on the north side of the road just southeast of the wash, and the trail to Dripping Spring starts near the ranch entrance.

The last 14 miles of this approach are over dirt roads, and may not be negotiable by some passenger vehicles (or by any vehicles immediately following a heavy rain).

Rogers Trough (limited to 4-wheel-drive vehicles)   Follow the directions for JF Ranch to the point where Forest Road 172A branches off of Forest Road 172 (8.1 miles from Forest Road 357). Turn right here, onto 172A. As you proceed you will come to two forks; turn right at the first, left at the second. The trailhead is at the end of the road, 4.0 miles beyond Forest Road 172.

Upper Horrell Place (limited to 4-wheel-drive vehicles)   From Florence Junction follow U.S. 60 approximately 36 miles to a junction, then turn left onto State Highway 88 and follow it 22 miles farther to Forest Road 449. Turn left onto the latter and proceed south, turning left at a fork near a ranch house. The dirt road follows the wash of Campaign Creek much of the way beyond here, and may be impassable to all vehicles after a heavy rain. At a second fork keep to the right, and continue a short distance to a corral (7.7 miles from State 88). Park on the far side of the corral and walk along the road the remaining ¼ mile or so to the trailhead near another ranch house. Upper Horrell Place is privately owned; please ask for permission to park here, and be sure to close any gates you may happen to open on the drive in.

Reavis Trailhead   From Apache Junction follow State Highway 88 approximately 30 miles to a Highway Department maintenance yard opposite Apache Lake. Continue east along State 88 from here for 0.9 mile, then turn right onto Reavis Ranch Road (Forest Road 212) and follow it uphill 3.1 miles to the barricades which mark the beginning of the Reavis Ranch Trail. The last 3.1 miles of this approach might be troublesome for some passenger cars.

Trip 1
Canyon Lake Trailhead to Indian Paint Mine

6.6 miles round trip; 1640´ elevation gain

Moderate dayhike or backpack (2 hiking days)

Season November to April

No permanent water along route; La Barge Creek (mile 3.0) and Boulder Creek (near mile 3.3) have water during rainy periods only

Features

Indian Paint Mine is the primary destination of this fine trip, but hardly its sole *raison d'etre*. For en route to the mine the hiker encounters magnificent vistas at almost every turn—views of rocky, saguaro-studded hillsides, of the rugged Mazatzal Range rising above Salt River Canyon, and of the famous landmark of Weaver's Needle embedded deep in the Superstition backcountry. An added bonus is the opportunity to linger or camp in La Barge Canyon or Boulder Canyon, either of which is a good bet to contain a clear, running stream during the rainy season.

Description

From the trailhead at Canyon Lake (0.0; 1680), follow the Boulder Canyon Trail as it leads east a short distance, then turns left at an unsigned fork and begins climbing. As soon as we gain a little elevation a nice view opens up across the placid waters of Canyon Lake, backgrounded by the swelling foothills of the Mazatzal Mountains. The ground cover along this first part of the trail is rather sparse, consisting chiefly of yellow paloverde, buckhorn cholla, jojoba, brittlebush, pale green prickly pear, some medium-sized saguaros and a smattering of agave. A few faint side trails branch off here and there; look for cairns to guide you at confusing forks.

After negotiating a few very steep sections we arrive at the top of a small hill (0.9; 2360). This is a good place to get acquainted with some of the more prominent landmarks of the western Superstitions, such as Geronimo Head (the high, rugged line of cliffs to the southeast), Battleship Mountain (the square-cut formation sitting atop the ridge which divides Boulder and La Barge canyons), the obvious, slender pinnacle of Weaver's Needle, and

Superstition Mountain, the high point of the dark, massive ridges far to the south.

From the hilltop the trail drops slightly to a small saddle and crosses temporarily to the northeast side of the ridge it has been following. After passing through another gap a short distance farther along, we drop again and wind through a rocky, craggy drainage studded with saguaros. At a small saddle beyond this picturesque area it is possible to look down into La Barge Canyon and see whether there will be water available on the route ahead. A ¾-mile-long, switchbacking descent from this overlook then brings us to an unsigned fork at the bottom of the canyon. The right-hand path leads down to La Barge Creek, which usually has running water from the beginning of the winter rainy season until April or so. (As with all streams in these arid mountains, the "live" season of this creek varies greatly from year to year, depending on weather conditions. Hikers who will not be packing in all of their water should contact the Forest Service and get an up-to-date report on the water situation before starting their trip.)

The trail that branches left here is the continuation of our route, which leads upcanyon 0.3 mile to a Superstition Wilderness boundary sign and then crosses the stream. Hikers with time on their hands can make a worth-while sidetrip from this point: leave the trail at the crossing, and boulderhop 1.3 miles directly up La Barge Creek to a fabulously spooky "box," or narrows, in the canyon. At its narrowest point this bottleneck is only a few dozen yards across, with walls that rise almost vertically some 500' on either side. (Caution: do not enter this area if a heavy storm seems imminent.)

Beyond this crossing the trail leads gradually away from the creekbed into an area of red rocks stained with blotches of bright green lichens. Some nice saguaros and teddy-bear chollas grow along this section, as well as a few doughty scrub oaks. After a short, gentle climb we reach Paint Mine Saddle (3.3; 1970), just beyond which, on the left, is Indian Paint Mine. Here you will find a vertical mineshaft and a few ruins. (Use caution if you approach the shaft closely.) Apparently nothing of any value was ever taken from the ground at this old site; like all the other "mines" which dot the Superstitions, this working was almost certainly a will-o'-the-wisp, a deadend for some diehard prospector who felt sure he'd at long last ferreted out the legendary Lost Dutchman lode. At least the deluded fellow was able to do his digging in a spectacular setting—the saddle affords magnificent views of Bat-

tleship Mountain, looming almost directly above, and of the cliffs
of Geronimo Head, rising a sheer 1500 ' above La Barge Creek.

Backpackers looking for campsites would do well to continue
downhill from Paint Mine Saddle about 200 yards to Boulder
Creek, which has more water and more comfortable tentsites than
La Barge. If for some reason you find yourself without water, and
both Boulder and La Barge creeks are dry, water *may* be available
at Second Water Canyon (see Trip 5).

Return the way you came.

See Map 1

Canyon Lake

Trip 2
First Water Trailhead to Garden Valley and Black Mesa

6.6 miles round trip; 670' elevation gain

Leisurely dayhike

Season November to April

No reliable water available along route

Features

Black Mesa affords a superb view of Weaver's Needle, in addition to many other, less famous landmarks which it behooves the hiker to learn to recognize before venturing further into this rugged backcountry. Along the way the route passes through dense fields of mesquite and paloverde, thickets of spiny cholla, and a "forest" of tall saguaros. All in all, this trip is an excellent introduction to the magnificent desert country of the western Superstitions.

Description

From the parking area at the end of the First Water Road (0.0; 2240), walk southeast along an old dirt road a few hundred yards to a signed junction. Continue straight ahead here and follow the Second Water Trail as it crosses First Water wash, then proceeds across a rather confusing area laced with use trails (stay on the most distinct-looking of these paths). At a low saddle (0.8; 2280) a spur trail branches left; ignore this and walk gently downhill to the right. After crossing a small drainage the trail swings left and begins climbing north up the canyon of a tributary. About 0.5 mile later this rocky ascent tops out at the brink of Garden Valley, a large flat between Hackberry and Black mesas. The trail strikes off northward across this pretty area, threading dense stands of foothill paloverde, honey mesquite and jumping cholla. Doves, cactus wrens, curve-billed thrashers and Gambel's quail are all common here, and observant hikers might also spot some woodrat nests tucked away in the impenetrable cholla thickets, safely beyond the reach of inquisitive predators.

Soon the trail reaches the signed turnoff to Black Mesa (1.9; 2410), where we turn right and resume climbing, almost imperceptibly at first, then moderately. The dark, basaltic cap of Black

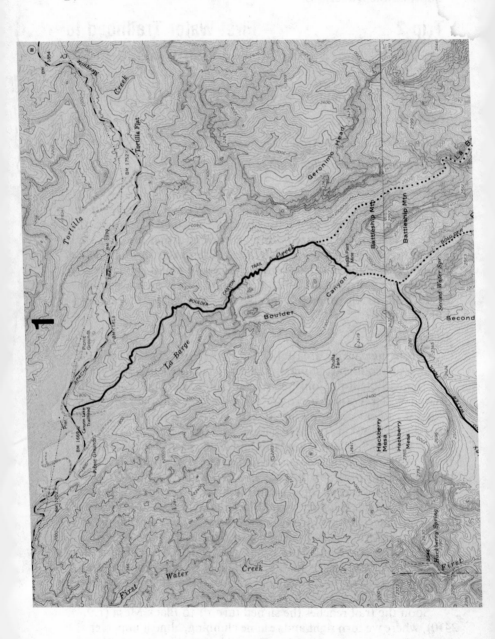

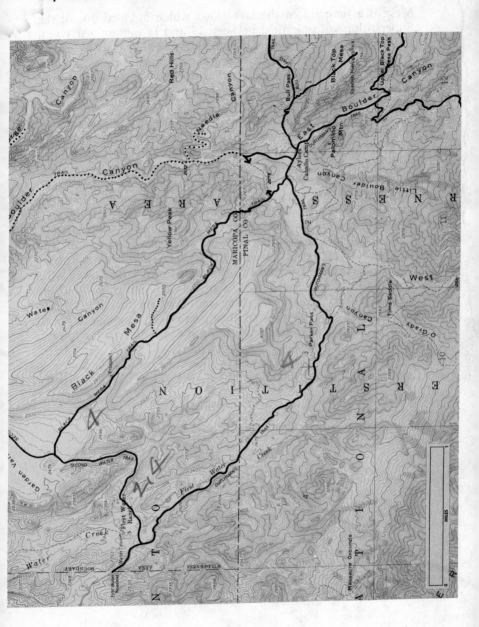

Mesa is a remnant of the lava flows which bubbled out of the Superstition volcanic field between 15 and 18 million years ago. Before huge parts of it were breached and carried away by stream erosion, this basalt layer covered a much larger area; today only portions of it remain, such as at nearby Hackberry Mesa and at Blacktop Mesa, near Palomino Mountain on the far side of Boulder Creek.

The gradient continues to steepen as we exit some nice stands of teddy-bear cholla and work our way up a rocky draw planted with stout saguaros. A mile later the route levels off again, this time at Black Mesa. The view of Weaver's Needle rising up from far beyond the flat expanse of this cholla-thicketed plateau is un- forgettable. This vista can be especially enchanting on winter mornings, when the sun, hanging low in the southeastern sky, suf- fuses a fuzzy yellow glow across the foreground of spiny chollas.

About ¼ mile beyond the edge of the mesa, where the trail begins to descend gently toward the far side, there is a small clear- ing in the cholla. From here it is possible to work one's way left a few hundred yards, out of the cacti and up to a high point of the low ridge (3.3; 2850) north of the trail. With its fine views of Bat- tleship Mountain, Geronimo Head, and high, swelling Supersti- tion Mountain, this spot makes a good destination for today's trek.

Return the way you came, or continue on to Boulder Basin and return via the Dutchman's Trail (9.1 miles total; see Trip 4).

See Map 1

Trip 3   First Water Trailhead to Parker Pass, Boulder Basin and Black Top Mesa

11.2 miles round trip; 1870' elevation gain

Moderate dayhike; leisurely to moderate backpack (2–3 hiking days)

Season November to April

Water available at West and East Boulder Creeks (miles 3.6 and 4.4) during rainy periods only

Features

The Dutchman's Trail over Parker Pass offers the quickest access to the Superstition backcountry in the vicinity of Boulder Basin. Hikers can use this relatively easy entry route to save energy for greater endeavors — such as the stiff, 1,000-foot climb up to Black Top Mesa. This ascent is steep and laborious, but the fabulous view from Black Top's strategically located summit fully justifies the effort.

Description

From First Water Trailhead (0.0; 2240), walk southeast along an old dirt road a few hundred yards to the signed junction with the left-branching Second Water Trail. Turn right here, following the Dutchman's Trail (still a road at this point) as it proceeds gently uphill, crosses First Water wash a few times, and then climbs more steeply toward a saddle on the left. The road narrows to a trail as we drop slightly and then pass through another gap. Several spur trails branch off to either side through here; stay on the most worn pathway, which presently brings us to Parker Pass (2.5; 2630). Here there are good views back across the Goldfield Mountains, and forward to Palomino Mountain, Black Top Mesa and Weaver's Needle. Just to the north are the basalt cliffs of Black Mesa, and it is not hard to mentally extend this layer of solidified lava through space to meet the similar dark cap atop Black Top Mesa. These two formations were indeed once connected, part of the same lava flow; in the millennia since the Superstition volcanoes ceased erupting, erosion has carried away all but a few disconnected fragments of this once-extensive basalt layer.

From Parker Pass the trail winds gently downhill toward

Boulder Basin, the flat at the base of Palomino Mountain. During this descent the route is again confused by a profusion of use-trails; at forks where there is some doubt as to which is the "most worn pathway," stay left. After the trail levels off on the basin floor, it crosses the wash of West Boulder Creek (which does not generally flow until after a few good winter rains have replenished the water table), and then proceeds eastward to a signed junction with the left-branching Black Mesa Trail (4.1; 2280). (*Black* Mesa, the destination of Trip 2, should not be confused with *Black Top* Mesa, the goal of this trek.) There are some nice, but unshaded, campsites in this area, amid a smattering of mesquites and paloverdes. At the junction we continue straight ahead, climb up to a low ridge, and drop a short distance to the floor of East Boulder Canyon. Beyond here the trail leads past several faint, left-branching spurs (variants of the Boulder Canyon Trail), bring-ing us in less than ¼ mile to a junction marked by a signpost (4.4; 2300). Here, at the mouth of the deep gorge from which East Boulder Creek issues, the Bull Pass Trail branches left. This route begins faintly, but its continuation is plainly visible cutting up a hillside to the north.

Turning onto the latter, we cross East Boulder Creek (about as likely to have running water as its twin, West Boulder Creek), then climb steeply through a jumble of gigantic boulders which have spalled off the cliffs looming directly above. Beyond here the very rough trail veers to the right, then makes two switchbacks before arriving at Bull Pass (5.0; 2750). To reach Black Top Mesa from this sometimes windy gap, turn onto the faint pathway that can be seen branching off to the right. This climbs quite steeply at first, but the gradient eases as we gain the surprisingly grassy shoulder of the mesa. Soon the path grows very obscure, then peters out completely, leaving us to scramble where we will the re-maining few hundred feet to the top (5.6; 3354). From this central-ly located summit one can pick out virtually every prominent land-mark of the western Superstitions. Most obvious of these is Weaver's Needle, standing off to the southeast. Turning counter-clockwise from this spire one next sees Needle Canyon, with Bluff Spring Mountain rising beyond it; then comes La Barge Canyon, backgrounded by the cliffs of Black and Malapais mountains, followed by Battleship Mountain, capping the divide between La Barge and Boulder canyons. Black Mesa rises beyond Boulder Basin; just to the left, and considerably closer, are the buff-colored cliffs of Palomino Mountain. To the southwest, in the distance, lie the massive, swelling ridges which culminate in 5057-foot Superstition Mountain.

The "Spanish Hieroglyphics" indicated on the topo as being nearby are neither Spanish nor hieroglyphics, but apparently just some nonsense associated with one of the many fruitless searches for the legendary Lost Dutchman treasure. These old graffiti are not easy to locate, and not particularly worth the trouble.

After soaking up the vista, return the way you came. Or return via the Black Mesa and Second Water Trails (12.0 miles total; reverse the steps of the first half of Trip 4.)

See Map 1

saguaros, paloverdes and teddy-bear chollas above Garden Valley

Trip 4 First Water Loop (First Water Trailhead to Black Mesa, Boulder Basin and Parker Pass)

9.1 mile loop trip; 920 ' elevation gain

Moderate dayhike or leisurely backpack (2 hiking days)

Season November to April

Water available at West Boulder Creek (mile 4.7) during rainy periods only

Features

After sampling the interesting desert-plant communities of Garden Valley, and the spectacular views to be had from atop Black Mesa, this route drops down to Boulder Basin, where backpackers will find good campsites and ample sidetrip opportunities. The Dutchman's Trail provides for a change of scenery on the return route; this is, in fact, one of the few Superstition loop trips which is both highly scenic and short enough to appeal to most dayhikers.

Description

From First Water Trailhead (0.0; 2240), follow the route of Trip 2 to the cholla clearing atop Black Mesa (3.0; 2750), then continue along the Black Mesa Trail as it leads gently downhill in the general direction of Weaver's Needle. About 0.5 mile later the gradient steepens abruptly, and the trail soon swings left into a well-defined canyon. After we cross back and forth across a small wash, this canyon bends to the left; here our route veers right and climbs gently a short distance to a minor saddle (4.4; 2590). As the trail leaves this gap and works its way downhill, we are treated to some fine views of buff-colored Palomino Mountain, a heavily eroded remnant of the tuff layers laid down by the primordial Superstition volcanoes. Behind Palomino Mountain rises the graceful volcanic plug of Weaver's Needle.

The occasionally steep descent from Black Mesa soon ends, and the trail eases out onto the floor of Boulder Basin. At West Boulder Creek (dry except for periods following heavy rains) a spur path branches left; here our route continues straight ahead and crosses the streambed. Beyond this point the Black Mesa Trail is very indistinct. To reach the Dutchman's Trail, our return route, walk cross-country (or follow any of a number of faint use trails) toward the cliffs of Palomino Mountain. In 0.2 mile you will intersect the relatively obvious Dutchman's Trail within a few hundred feet of a sign (4.9; 2280) indicating the "official" terminus of the Black Mesa Trail. This sign is just west of the low saddle which would have to be crossed if one were to keep walking toward Palomino Mountain. There are many good campsites in the vicinity, but little shade (except for that provided by an occasional large mesquite or paloverde) and no water (except when West Boulder Creek is running). A variety of interesting explorations can be made from this central location — up East and West Boulder Canyons, down Boulder Creek to Needle Canyon, or up to Black Top Mesa (see Trip 3).

When ready to return to the trailhead, turn right, onto the Dutchman's Trail, and follow it over Parker Pass (6.6; 2630) and on to First Water Trailhead (9.1; 2240) (reverse the steps of the first 4.1 miles of Trip 3).

See Map 1

Weavers Needle, from near Terrapin Pass

Trip 5   First Water Trailhead to Canyon Lake via Garden Valley and Indian Paint Mine

7.5 miles one-way (13-mile car shuttle required); 820′ elevation gain

Moderate dayhike or leisurely backpack (2 hiking days)

Season November to April

Water is usually available at Second Water Spring (near mile 3.4) from the beginning of the winter rainy season until April or May; Boulder Creek (mile 3.7) and La Barge Creek (mile 4.5) have water only during rainy periods

Features

In spite of its moderate length, this trek traverses a surprisingly varied stretch of terrain, and affords a veritable kaleidoscope of fine vistas. Overnighters will find the itinerary just right for filling a leisurely winter or spring weekend, and backpacker and dayhiker alike will appreciate the relatively short car shuttle involved.

Description

From First Water Trailhead (0.0; 2240), follow the route of Trip 2 to the signed trail junction in Garden Valley (1.9; 2410). Turn left here, and proceed along the Second Water Trail north, then northeast, past a cattle tank off to the left. Soon the trail begins dropping, almost imperceptibly at first, into the canyon that separates Black Mesa from Hackberry Mesa. As we begin to drop more steeply, through an area of angular, black basalt boulders (remnants of the lava flow which once covered much of this area), a nice view opens up to the northeast, across Boulder Canyon to Battleship Mountain, Geronimo Head, and, in the far distance, the Four Peaks of the Mazatzal Range. One can also catch an occasional glimpse of Weaver's Needle, just poking over the shoulder of Black Mesa.

Shortly after passing an unsigned, left-branching spur trail, the Second Water Trail cuts to the right, across a low ridge, and then drops into another drainage. A second spurious path branches to the right here; we ignore it and descend steeply past an im-

typical Sonoran Zone vegetation near Canyon Lake

pressive stand of saguaros to a nice campsite with a good view. Just below here, Second Water Canyon comes down from the right and joins our drainage. Second Water Spring, a short scramble up this side canyon, generally flows throughout the rainy season (but check it out with the Forest Service if you will be depending on it for water).

Below the confluence of Second Water Canyon, we pass a few more campsites, then descend more and more gently to a signed junction (3.7; 1940) just above Boulder Creek. Here we turn left onto the Boulder Canyon Trail, which promptly disappears among the sand and rocks of the wash. The next section of our route can be tricky: rockhop ¼ mile downstream, to a point where a small drainage drops directly down from the gap (Paint Mine Saddle) between Battleship Mountain and the next peak to the north. Scramble up this drainage a few yards, until you spot the continuation of the Boulder Canyon Trail leading uphill to the left. A short climb up the newfound trail now brings us to Indian Paint Mine and Paint Mine Saddle (4.2; 1970). To complete your trek from here, reverse the steps of Trip 1 the remaining 3.3 miles to Canyon Lake (7.5; 1680).

See Map 1

Trip 6   First Water Trailhead to Peralta Trailhead via Parker Pass, Bull Pass, La Barge Canyon and Bluff Spring

15.0 miles one-way (24-mile car shuttle required); 1790′ elevation gain

Moderate dayhike; leisurely to moderate backpack (2–3 hiking days)

Season November to April

Water is usually available at Charlebois Spring (mile 8.0), La Barge Spring (mile 9.2), and Bluff Spring (mile 11.4) (check with Forest Service during dry periods); West and East Boulder creeks (miles 3.6 and 4.4) have water during rainy periods only

Features

La Barge Canyon, with its almost-always-reliable springs and its small, rainy-season-only creek, is the chief attraction of this route. The springs support small islands of vegetation that stand in sharp contrast to the stark aspect of the surrounding country; these oases are as attractive to the native wildlife as they are to the human visitor, making this trip a good choice for one who would observe the many birds and mammals which manage to eke out a living in these sere mountains.

Description

From the trailhead at the end of First Water Road (0.0; 2240), follow the route of Trip 3 to Bull Pass (5.0; 2750). Those who wish to make the strenuous but worthwhile sidetrip to Black Top Mesa should turn right here and follow the rudimentary pathway that leads steeply up to the top (see Trip 3). Otherwise, continue straight ahead, and descend moderately across a series of grassy hillsides to a minor saddle. Passing through this, the route next drops steeply into Needle Canyon, crosses a wash, and climbs gently to a signed junction (6.1; 2480) in an open area offering a beautiful view of Weaver's Needle. Here we turn left, rejoining the Dutchman's Trail (which we abandoned back in East Boulder Canyon, in order to take the scenic "short cut" over Bull Pass), and then proceed across a sparsely vegetated flat before dropping into La Barge Canyon. In the canyon bottom is a signed junction with the Cavalry Trail (6.5; 2370), where we turn right, staying on Dutchman's, and ascend gently along the right-hand side of La Barge Creek. A few hardy cottonwood trees grow in this area, and the creek generally has running water after the first few winter rains.

A mile or so upcanyon from the last junction, the trail crosses a tributary wash, then swings left and climbs north a short distance to meet the signed spur path (8.0; 2500) to Charlebois Spring. The spring, 0.2 miles up the spur, *almost* always has water; check it out with the Forest Service during spells of dry weather. This is one of the nicest springs in the western Superstitions, all the more so to those who arrive with parched throats and empty canteens. There are several good campsites in the area, beneath a comparatively lush overstory of cottonwoods and sycamores. The Forest Service asks that you not camp right on top of this spring. Black phoebes, bright red cardinals, Scott's orioles and robins are among the many birds you may hear singing in the trees here. Most of the larger mammals which frequent this oasis are nocturnal; venture out of your sleeping bag on a moonlit night and you might come upon a family of skunks, a raccoon, or possible a rare kit fox.

From the junction with the Charlebois Spring spur, the Dutchman's Trail cuts back to the right, climbs moderately a short distance to a low ridgetop, and then meets the Peters Trail at a signed fork. Here our route stays right, drops back into La Barge Canyon, and proceeds gently upstream, crossing the bouldery wash from side to side on occasion. After about a mile we enter a small copse of trees near the signed terminus of the Red Tanks Trail (9.2; 2610). La Barge Spring, which is nearly as reliable as Charlebois Spring and has a few nice campsites, is a short distance upcanyon from here.

To complete your trek, turn right at this junction and follow the Dutchman's and Bluff Spring trails the remaining 5.8 miles to Peralta Trailhead (15.0; 2420) (see Trips 12 and 10).

See Maps 1 and 2

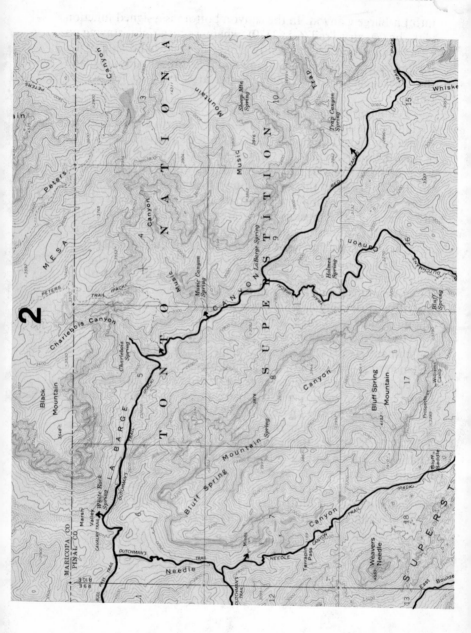

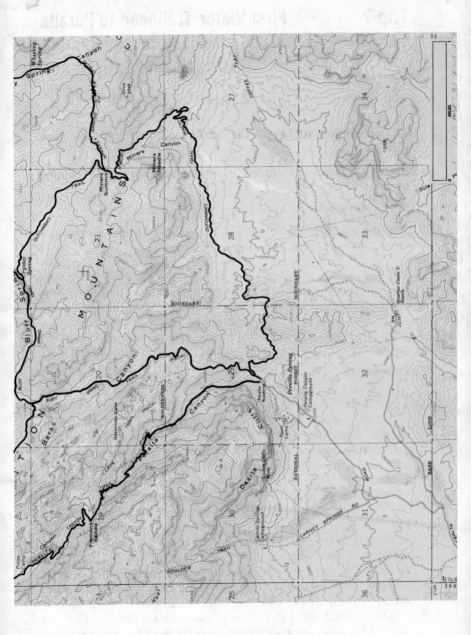

Trip 7
First Water Trailhead to Peralta Trailhead via Black Mesa, Boulder Basin, Needle Canyon and Bluff Saddle

12.3 miles one-way (24-mile car shuttle required); 2240 ' elevation gain

Moderate dayhike; leisurely to moderate backpack (2–3 hiking days)

Season November to April

Water available at West Boulder Creek (mile 4.7) and East Boulder Creek (miles 5.2 to 6.0) during rainy periods only

Features

Piercing the heart of the rugged western Superstitions, this route offers a succession of vistas which are among the finest in the range. Particularly impressive are the many views of spectacular Weaver's Needle. With several nice campsites located at about the halfway point, this trip is a "natural" for an overnighter.

Description

From First Water Trailhead (0.0; 2240), follow the route of Trips 2 and 4 across Black Mesa to the end of the Black Mesa Trail in Boulder Basin (4.9; 2280). (One can also follow the slightly shorter, slightly less scenic Dutchman's Trail to this point; see Trip 3.) Backpackers will find plenty of level tentsites in this mesquite- and paloverde-dotted valley, but shade is scarce, and water is generally available only following heavy rains. Somewhat more sheltered campsites can be found in nearby East Boulder Canyon.

At the Black Mesa Trail/Dutchman's Trail junction we turn left onto the Dutchman's Trail, climb eastward over a low ridge separating West and East Boulder Creeks, then drop a short distance to a sign which indicates the start of the left-branching Boulder Canyon Trail. Our route continues straight ahead at this fork, as it does at the junction with the Bull Pass Trail a few hundred feet beyond, and climbs gently past an outcropping of dark, graffiti-scarred rocks in the lower end of East Boulder Canyon. High cliffs loom to either side of us as we thread our way through this deep cleft—those of Palomino Mountain to the right, Black Top Mesa's to the left. After passing beneath a natural "hole in the wall" high up on the Palomino massif, the gradient steepens a bit, and presently we arrive at a signed junction with the right-branching Peralta Canyon Trail (5.9; 2470). Here we turn left, and follow the route of the second half of Trip 10 the remaining 6.4 miles to Peralta Trailhead (12.3; 2420). (It is also possible to turn *right* at this fork, and reverse the steps of the *first* half of Trip 10 to the same trailhead—12.2 miles total. Because Pinyon Camp makes such a nice overnight stop, backpackers may prefer this routing.)

See Map 2

alligator-juniper bark above Reavis Headquarters

Trip 8   Kings Ranch to Hieroglyphic Canyon

3.6 miles round trip; 650′ elevation gain

Leisurely dayhike

Season November to April

Water available at Hieroglyphic Canyon (mile 1.8) except during extremely dry periods

Features

On its way to some interesting Indian petroglyphs this short, leisurely route climbs through a pretty desert area at the base of rugged Superstition Mountain. It is a fine choice for the hiker seeking to "warm up" for longer, more strenuous excursions.

Description

From the trailhead at the end of Kings Way (0.0; 2020) you pass through a gate and follow the wide Hieroglyphics Trail toward Superstition Mountain, the high, cliff-banded peak visible in the north-northeast. The abrupt line of precipices which forms the northern skyline in this area is the southern edge of the pushed-up center of the ancient Superstition caldera — the huge crater formed by the volcanic upheavals that witnessed the birth of these mountains some 20–30 million years ago. The trail climbs gently at first, through healthy stands of yellow paloverde, red-blossoming ocotillo, creosote bush, saguaro, prickly pear, and staghorn, teddy bear, and jumping cholla. A few tesotas, or desert ironwood trees, grow down in the depression to the right. The wood of the tesota, one of the densest woods known, does not float in water and quickly dulls even the sharpest tools. A variety of wildflowers carpet this area during the spring, including the beautiful desert mallow, fleabane, bright yellow brittlebush, desert dandelion and Indian paintbrush. During favorable years the creosote bushes and paloverdes contribute exuberant sprays of yellow blossoms to the general panoply of color.

The way steepens a bit as we climb onto the backbone of a low ridge, and as we gain elevation, pleasant vistas open up to the south and west — at least on days when there is no wayward Phoenix smog creeping across the valley floor. At the combined Tonto National Forest/Superstition Wilderness boundary sign (0.7; 2210) we pass through another fence, then continue climbing to a small saddle of sorts (1.5; 2510). From here the trail traverses into Hieroglyphic Canyon, petering out as it approaches a narrow spot in the canyon where there are a few low cliffs and, possibly, a few pools of water (1.8; 2670). Most of the "hieroglyphics" — petroglyphs, actually, since these pictures do not seem to stand for any definite words, ideas or events — are to be found in this area, on the dark rocks just across the creekbed. Most of the etchings are of bighorn sheep, but there are also some human figures, a centipede, and a few forms not readily identifiable. There is also, sad to say, a growing amount of modern vandalism mixed in with the more ancient artwork.

If there is no water here, it can usually be gotten at Hieroglyphic Spring, a short distance up the drainage bottom. All water from this area should be purified before drinking; on such a short trip as this, it is probably easier just to pack your own.

Return the way you came.

See Map 3

Along the trail to Hieroglyphic Canyon

Trip 9   Peralta Trailhead to Fremont Saddle
and Pinyon Camp

4.6–6.6 miles round trip; 1350–1800′ elevation gain

Moderate dayhike or backpack (2 hiking days)

Season November to April

No water available along route except after heavy rains

Features

The short, steep watercourse of Peralta Canyon provides one
of the quickest and most scenic routes into the backcountry of the
central Superstitions. This trip takes the hiker to the threshhold of
that country at lofty Fremont Saddle, which offers magnificent
views over a large portion of the range. Backpackers have the option of continuing on to Pinyon Camp, a delightful campsite near
the base of spectacular Weaver's Needle.

Description

From the parking area at the end of the Peralta Road (0.0;
2420) follow the wide Peralta Trail north through a dense and
varied vegetative cover of jojoba, scraggly mesquite trees, yellow-
blossoming creosote bush, teddy-bear cholla, and some foothill
paloverde. During the spring months this area is brightened by a
number of wildflowers, including brittlebush, delicate yellow
paperflower, tiny white eriophyllum, orangish globe mallow,
fleabane and narrow-leaf aster. The path quickly grows narrower
as it enters Peralta Canyon, and we pass occasional patches of
shade provided by sugar sumacs and shrub live oaks. The trail
stays near the canyon bottom for the first 1.5 miles or so, climbing
gently to moderately and crossing usually-dry Peralta Creek a few
times. Beyond here we abandon the creekside for the shadeless
canyonsides above it, gaining good views down the throat of
Peralta Canyon and of the many short pinnacles (reminiscent of
the mysterious stone sculptures found on Easter Island) which
seem to grow out of the slopes nearby.

Above here the trail returns briefly to the wash, crosses it, and
then switchbacks steeply uphill. These switchbacks have been
shortcutted in many places, and the resulting erosion has made it
difficult in spots to distinguish the real trail from the spurious

ones. Please try to stay on the "official" pathway as best you can, because the only way to eliminate these destructive — and confusing — shortcuts is to concentrate use onto a single trail.

At length the switchbacks cease and we arrive at Fremont Saddle (2.3; 3766). This is the highest point reached by trail in the western Superstitions, and the views it affords are correspondingly extensive. To the north and northwest, parts of the Goldfield and Mazatzal mountains are visible far beyond the nearby, double-peaked crest of Weaver's Needle, while to the southeast the vista stretches across parts of the eastern Superstitions and the rows and rows of low desert ranges that wrinkle the earth between the 'Stitions and the Santa Catalinas. You may see a Cooper's hawk or a golden eagle soaring high above the canyons which fall away to either side of the saddle.

This spot is a good destination for dayhikers. Backpackers who wish to continue on to Pinyon Camp should follow the Peralta Canyon Trail as it drops down the slope north of the saddle, makes a few well-graded switchbacks, and then swings out onto the left-hand wall of East Boulder Canyon. A mile later, where the trail approaches East Boulder Creek, there is a nice flat with some fair-sized sugar sumacs and a few single-leaf pinyons. This is Pinyon Camp (3.3; 3320). There are good campsites here, as well as a superb, close-up view of Weaver's Needle, but no water except after a heavy rain.

Return the way you came, or continue on to Black Top Pass and return via Bluff Saddle (see Trip 10).

See Map 2

Trip 10
Weaver's Needle Loop (Peralta Trailhead to Fremont Saddle, Blacktop Pass, Needle Canyon and Bluff Saddle)

12.7 mile loop trip; 2850′ elevation gain

Strenuous dayhike or moderate backpack (2–3 hiking days)

Season November to April

No permanent water along route; during rainy periods water is generally available at Pinyon Camp (mile 3.3), East Boulder Creek (mile 6.3), and possibly in other drainages

Features

This fine trip makes a complete circuit of Weaver's Needle, allowing the hiker to view this most famous of all Superstition landmarks from virtually every angle. The four passes crossed en route command a variety of far-reaching vistas, making this one of the most scenic, if strenuous, routes in the entire range.

Description

Follow the directions for Trip 9 to Pinyon Camp (3.3; 3320). From there continue gently down East Boulder Canyon, past some excellent campsites right in the shadow of Weaver's Needle. About a mile beyond Pinyon Camp, East Boulder Canyon falls off to the right, while the trail stays high on the canyonside and soon cuts left through a minor saddle (5.0; 3050). After dropping a short distance from here we meander across a small flat, then descend a few rocky switchbacks and swing across a hillside to another saddle, where we have a good view across East Boulder Canyon to distinctive-looking Black Top Mesa. The dark basalt layer atop this mesa is a solidified remnant of the lavas that oozed out of the Superstition volcanoes some 15–18 million years ago. It is most likely a part of the same formation found on nearby Black Mesa, though the intervening portion of the frozen lava flow has long since been carried away by erosion.

The trail does not pass through this saddle, but cuts back to the left and crosses the ridge ¼ mile farther along. Once we are on the Boulder Canyon side of this ridge a few unsigned spur trails branch off to the left and right; the correct path is for the most part visible below as it descends to the bottom of East Boulder Canyon via two long switchbacks. The fork at the bottom of the lower switchback can be confusing — be sure to go left here.

At a sign in East Boulder Canyon we meet the Dutchman's Trail (6.3; 2480). Backpackers will find a few fair campsites here, where there is generally running water during rainy periods. To continue on our loop back to Peralta Roadend, we turn right onto the Dutchman's Trail. In about 200 yards, after crossing East Boulder Creek, the trail passes a steep shortcut trail branching right, then turns sharply left and climbs one long switchback up to Blacktop Pass (7.0; 2790) ("Upper Black Top Mesa Pass" on the topo map). Bluff Spring Mountain, Weaver's Needle, Palomino Mountain and Black Top Mesa are all visible from this point.

From Blacktop Pass we drop a short distance into a basin with comparatively gentle contours. Where a small drainage comes down from the right is an unsigned trail junction (7.4; 2640); here our route turns right, onto the Terrapin Trail (which may be incorrectly signed "Needle Canyon Trail"), and begins climbing again. The view of Weaver's Needle from this area is exceptionally fine. Following a short, steep rise, the trail drops suddenly to a good campsite in a comparatively lush copse of netleaf hackberry and shrub live oak. Shortly beyond here, at a spot marked by a metal post, a use-trail branches left and proceeds up the bottom of Needle Canyon; our route swings right and makes a few very steep climbs up to the crest of a low ridge. Fortunately for the hiker, the remainder of the ascent to Terrapin Pass (8.3; 3180) is considerably easier than the preceding passages. The pass offers nice, long vistas to the north and west; Superstition Mountain, Black Top Mesa and Palomino Mountain are visible, as are parts of the distant Mazatzal and Goldfield mountains. Weaver's Needle, of course, continues to dominate the view to the south.

Beyond Terrapin Pass the trail makes a few steep ups and downs as it works its way past the base of the Needle. After passing a brushy, overgrown section (and an inviting campsite beneath a large sugar sumac off to the right of the trail) the route reunites with Needle Canyon wash, whose gentle course is then followed to its head at Bluff Saddle (9.7; 3420). This is a picturesque area, with a complex array of rhyolite bluffs and pinnacles framing vistas of the distant mountains to the east and south. (To get the best views it is necessary to scramble up a short distance among the rocks on either side of the saddle.)

From Bluff Saddle we walk gradually downhill, winding between rock outcroppings and passing a couple of fair campsites among mesquite, agave, some medium-sized saguaros and lots of prickly pear. The trail grows rather obscure as it negotiates a low gap and begins dropping into a canyon — look for ducks to stay on the right track. At the bottom of this descent we cross a wash and meet the Bluff Spring Trail at a signed junction (10.4; 3160), where we turn right and proceed down-canyon, staying a little above the creekbed at first, then dropping down to the bottom. About ¾ mile later the trail disappears temporarily in the wash. Here we rockhop directly down the streambed, passing through a sort of narrows and ignoring a side trail which can be seen leading up a ravine on the right, until the Bluff Spring Trail reappears and begins climbing up the right-hand canyonside. About 0.3 mile later we reach a small saddle (11.6; 3000), where we catch one last glimpse of Weaver's Needle before beginning the descent back to Peralta Trailhead.

At the saddle, the trail swings to the right, then crosses a small drainage, and proceeds gently downhill to the south. After passing the Superstition Wilderness boundary sign, we round a ridge and soon meet the Cave Trail branching off to the right. Our route stays left here and drops steeply toward the flatlands, passing a side trail to an old prospect hole on the right, until it intercepts the Dutchman's Trail coming in from the left. The combined Bluff Spring/Dutchman's Trail continues southwest a short distance to a crossing of Peralta Creek; the trailhead (12.7; 2420) is just beyond.

See Maps 2, 3 and 1

Weaver's Needle, from Pinyon Camp

Trip 11   Peralta Trailhead to Crystal Spring

9.3 mile loop trip; 1260' elevation gain

Moderate dayhike or backpack (2 hiking days)

Season November to April

Water usually available at Crystal Spring (mile 5.8); check with Forest Service first

Features

This loop route skirts the base of the Superstition Mountains, passing a variety of pleasant vistas across open desert country, then climbs over Miners Summit and drops into the backcountry. With nice campsites located just beyond the halfway mark, backpackers will find this trip ideal for an overnighter.

Description

From the end of Peralta Road (0.0; 2420) follow the combined Bluff Spring/Dutchman's Trail across Peralta Creek, then to a signed junction just beyond. Here the two trails part; we turn right, onto Dutchman's, and climb moderately across a hillside planted with foothill paloverde, ocotillo, yellow-blossoming brittlebush, canyon ragweed, jojoba, creosote bush and some tall saguaros. The trail, rather wide up to this point, narrows as it swings across a drainage and contours into a low saddle (0.5; 2540). After 0.4 mile of gentle descending we cross the Superstition Wilderness boundary, just beyond which is an unsigned junction at the foot of a tall saguaro. Our route swings left here and winds along the fringe of Barkley Basin, gradually climbing up onto the "bajada," or debris-slope, at the foot of the Superstition Mountains.

After passing beneath craggy Miners Needle we drop slightly into the shallow wash which drains Miners Canyon (2.6; 2550), then begin a moderate-to-steep, switchbacking ascent of the hillside beyond. As we gain elevation a good view opens up across Barkley Basin to Buzzard's Roost, standing guard over the Coffee Flat area to the east-southeast, and an unnamed, oddly sculptured pinnacle just east of the trail. Presently the switchbacks cease and the route climbs steadily northwest. The old Miners Trail is visible far below. After circling around the head of Miners Canyon we meander up through a rocky area to Miners Summit (4.4; 3260),

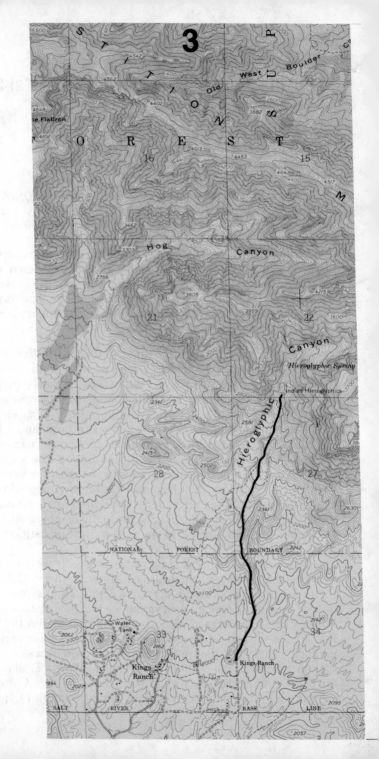

where the trail splits into three branches. The right-hand fork goes to Whiskey Spring, the middle path is the continuation of the Dutchman's Trail, and the left-hand branch is a steep shortcut of Dutchman's. We take the central fork and descend moderately via a single long switchback into the open basin to the north. After crossing a small drainage the trail climbs back up a bit, then drops into a tributary of Bluff Spring Canyon. In a comparatively lush area, featuring a nice stand of scrub oak, sugar sumac and netleaf hackberry, we cross a wash and meet the Bluff Spring Trail at an obscure, unsigned junction (5.8; 3020). Crystal Spring, off in the trees near this junction, usually has water; if not, try nearby Bluff Spring, located a few hundred feet left of an old corral which will be found just north of here. Neither of these springs is completely reliable, and during dry periods backpackers should check them out with the Forest Service before planning to spend the night here.

To return to Peralta Trailhead, turn left onto the Bluff Spring Trail and follow it west gently uphill. Shortly after you pass through a narrow section of Bluff Spring Canyon a spur branches off to the left; ignore it and continue gradually uphill to a low saddle, beyond which the route swings south to meet the signed, right-branching Terrapin Trail (7.0; 3160). Here we go left and follow the Bluff Spring Trail the remaining 2.3 miles to Peralta Trailhead (9.3; 2420) (see Trip 10).

See Map 2

Pine Creek, Superstition Wilderness

Trip 12   Peralta Trailhead to Whiskey Spring, La Barge Canyon, and Crystal Spring

14.4 mile loop trip; 1980 ' elevation gain

Strenuous dayhike or moderate backpack (2–3 hiking days)

Season November to April

Water usually available at Whiskey Spring (mile 5.8), La Barge Spring (mile 8.6), and Bluff Spring (mile 10.8); check with Forest Service first

Features

The highlight of this trip is La Barge Canyon, a major drainage which slices across the heart of the western Superstition backcountry, and which is a good bet to contain a clear, running stream during winter and early spring. With water and good camp-sites generally available at convenient intervals, backpackers who like to take their time and really *see* the country through which they pass can draw this excursion out over 3 or 4 hiking days — just right for a holiday weekend.

Description

Follow the directions for Trip 11 to Miners Summit (4.4; 3260). Here we turn right, onto the Whiskey Spring Trail, and make a rough, steep climb to an unnamed saddle (4.9; 3380). The trail now drops quickly down a minor drainage, then swings left in-to Whiskey Spring Canyon and descends more gradually to the ce-ment tank which catches the effluent of Whiskey Spring (5.8; 2940) (reliable except during dry seasons). There are a few nice campsites in this area, scattered beneath a spotty forest cover of medium-sized cottonwoods and netleaf hackberries.

At an unsigned trail fork 0.5 mile below Whiskey Spring we stay right, then climb a short distance and drop down to La Barge Creek, which generally contains at least a trickle of water during the winter rainy season. Immediately after crossing the creek to its north side we meet the Red Tanks Trail at a signed junction (6.6; 2800). If the creek is running high and the day is warm, you may wish to make a sidetrip to some sparkling swimming holes in Up-per La Barge Box, approximately 1 mile up-canyon. If not, turn left here and proceed down-canyon.

After climbing over a low ridge in order to "straighten out a bend" in the canyon, the trail tends to stay close to the streambed, disappearing now and then in the rather barren, bouldery floodplain and crossing from side to side frequently. After about a mile, a faint, unsigned spur trail branches right to Trap Canyon Spring (situated at the mouth of the narrow cleft which disappears between the steep bluffs to the north; water during rainy periods only). Continuing straight downcanyon here, we presently arrive at La Barge Spring (8.6; 2610), just off to the right of the trail in a lovely grove of tall cottonwoods and sycamores. Backpackers will find delightful camping here, and reliable water (except possibly during very dry years — check with the Forest Service first). A variety of birds congregate in this area of La Barge Canyon during the spring months, including kinglets, black phoebes and bright red cardinals. The spring and the creek attract a number of mammals as well, most of them nocturnal; overnighters may be awakened in the dead of night by the noise of a raccoon, a ringtail cat or a woodrat investigating their foodstores.

A short distance beyond La Barge Spring the Red Tanks Trail ends at a signed junction with the Dutchman's Trail. To complete our loop to Peralta Trailhead we now turn left and begin climbing moderately up the right-hand side of Bluff Spring Canyon. A mile later, after dropping steeply back down to the canyon bottom, the trail swings right at a split in the drainage, then climbs gently to an open flat containing an old corral (10.8; 2980). Just beyond this enclosure a side trail branches right to Bluff Spring (there is generally water here, and at nearby Crystal Spring, except during very dry periods). A few hundred yards past this turnoff, at Crystal Spring (where there is a nice campsite shaded by comparatively large scrub oaks and netleaf hackberries), the Dutchman's Trail forks left at an unsigned junction. Here we continue straight ahead, following the Bluff Spring Trail up-canyon past a spurious, left-branching sidepath. After tracing Bluff Spring Canyon to its head, the route tops out at a low saddle, then drops gently a short distance to a signed junction with the Terrapin Trail (12.1; 3160). Go left at this fork and follow the Bluff Spring Trail the remaining 2.3 miles to Peralta Trailhead (14.4; 2420) (see Trip 10).

See Map 2

Trip 13   Peralta Trailhead to Miners Summit, La Barge Spring, Charlebois Spring and Bluff Saddle

18.0 mile loop trip; 2580 ' elevation gain

Moderate backpack (2–3 hiking days)

Season November to April

Water usually available at Whiskey Spring (mile 5.8), La Barge Spring (mile 8.6), and Charlebois Spring (mile 9.8); check with Forest Service during dry periods

Features

This lengthy loop route, a fine choice for backpackers looking for a fairly challenging weekend outing, climbs into the Superstition backcountry via Miners Summit. After passing several cottonwood- and sycamore-shaded seeps down in La Barge Canyon (where rainy-season trekkers might also find a clear, running stream), the trail climbs past classic vistas of Weaver's Needle to scenic Bluff Saddle, a fitting climax to this varied excursion.

Description

From Peralta Trailhead (0.0; 2420), follow the Dutchman's Trail to Miners Summit (4.4; 3260) (see Trip 11), then proceed along the Whiskey Spring and Red Tanks Trails to La Barge Spring (8.6; 2610) (see Trip 12). At a signed junction just beyond the spring we turn right, onto the Dutchman's Trail, then continue gently down La Barge Canyon, crossing the wash at frequent intervals and passing through sparse stands of oak, mesquite, sycamore and cottonwood, and an occasional Arizona walnut. Soon after passing the short, right-branching lateral to Music Canyon Spring (water during rainy periods only), the trail climbs moderately up the right-hand canyonside to meet the signed Peters Trail atop a minor ridge (9.7; 2580). We stay left at this junction and descend a short distance to a sign pointing out the spur trail to Charlebois (locally pronounced "Charley-boy") Spring (0.2 mile up Charlebois Canyon to the right). Water is *almost* always available here, but during dry periods it should be checked out first with the Forest Service. There are several nice campsites in this area, shaded by some large sycamores and cottonwoods. (The Forest Service asks that you do not camp right at this spring.)

Continuing from here along the Dutchman's Trail, we soon recross La Barge Creek and resume descending gently down-canyon. Shortly after we pass a drift fence, a nice view opens up across the canyon to the steep basaltic cliffs of Black Mountain and, in the distance, the yellow rhyolite bluffs of Geronimo Head. At the head of Marsh Valley the signed Cavalry Trail comes in on the right (11.3; 2370); our route goes left here, and begins climbing gently away from La Barge Creek. Soon we reach a signed junction with the Bull Pass Trail, where we stay left again. There is a fabulous, head-on view of Weaver's Needle from here.

As we climb into Needle Canyon the route is temporarily con-fused by use-trails; the correct path trends steadily south along the left side of Needle Creek wash. When the track becomes once again unambiguous, we cut over to the right side of the creekbed and soon meet the Terrapin Trail at a junction marked only by a signpost (12.7; 2640). To complete our loop back to Peralta Trailhead, we turn left onto the latter and follow the directions for the second half of Trip 10 back to the parking area (18.0; 2420). (It is also possible to turn *right* here, reverse the steps of the *first* half of Trip 10, and return via Blacktop Pass and the Peralta Trail — 20.1 miles total.)

See Map 2

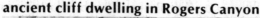

ancient cliff dwelling in Rogers Canyon

Trip 14   Peralta Trailhead to Canyon Lake via Fremont Saddle, Boulder Canyon and Indian Paint Mine

14.4 miles one-way (31-mile car shuttle required); 2010' elevation gain

Strenuous dayhike or moderate backpack (2–3 hiking days)

Season November to April

Water is generally available along Boulder Creek (miles 7.1 to 10.9) during rainy periods only

Features

This transmontane trek climbs into the Superstition back-country via Fremont Saddle, then traces Boulder Creek for virtually its entire length — from its eastern headwaters near Pinyon Camp, in the shadow of Weaver's Needle, to within a mile of its end at La Barge Creek. Dayhikers will have little time to linger along this long, sometimes rough route, but backpackers with a layover day (or two) will be able to make a number of fascinating side trips along the way.

Description

From Peralta Trailhead (0.0; 2420) follow the Peralta Canyon Trail across Fremont Saddle to the signed trail junction in East Boulder Canyon (6.3; 2480) (see Trips 9 and 10). Here we turn left, onto the Dutchman's Trail, and proceed down-canyon, past occasional fair tentsites shaded by small hackberries and sugar sumacs. When East Boulder Creek has running water (a likelihood after a good, soaking winter rain or two), the music of a number of riffles and cascades accompanies the hiker through this delightful section, the comparative lushness of which is attributable partly to the presence of the creek, and partly to the morning and evening shade provided by the high cliffs looming to either side. As you pass beneath the buff-colored precipices of Palomino Mountain (on your left), look for the small natural arch which has formed near its summit.

Where East Boulder Canyon begins to open up a bit, the Bull Pass Trail branches right at an unsigned fork. If you wish to make the strenuous but worthwhile sidetrip up to Black Top Mesa (1.2 miles one-way; see Trip 3), turn right here. Otherwise, continue straight ahead along the gently descending Dutchman's Trail, arriving in 0.1 mile at a signed junction with the Boulder Canyon Trail (7.1; 2480). Here we turn right and proceed down the rocky, brushy wash of East Boulder Creek, ignoring the occasional use-paths branching off to either side. After about 0.5 mile, West Boulder Creek comes in from the left and joins our wash. Beyond here the Boulder Canyon Trail, which was never really all that distinct to begin with, disappears into the boulders and sand of what is now Boulder Canyon. The next 3 miles of our route consist essentially of boulder-hopping cross-country down the canyon, though if you wish you may try to follow the disconnected snatches of use-trail that appear now and then on either side of the watercourse. These typically fade out after leading only a few hundred yards, but they make the going easier in many places. It is necessary to cross Boulder Creek several times in the miles ahead, and when the water is exceptionally high the route may be impassable.

A little less than a mile after leaving the Dutchman's Trail, Needle Canyon wash can be seen emerging from a steep-walled slot on the right. The spooky, twisting gorge of lower Needle Canyon is well worth an exploratory visit (unless a heavy storm seems imminent). About 2.5 miles downstream from this point, Second Water Canyon will be seen coming down from the left (west); the Second Water Trail joins our route at a signed junction on a rocky bench near the confluence of Second Water and Boulder creeks (10.6; 1940). Second Water Spring (which generally has water from the first winter rains until April or May) is about 0.5 mile up Second Water Canyon (see Trip 5).

The next section of our route is crucial: rockhop ¼ mile downstream from the preceding junction, to a point where a minor drainage drops directly down from the gap (Paint Mine Saddle) between Battleship Mountain and the next peak to the north. Scramble up this drainage a few yards, until you spot the continuation of the Boulder Canyon Trail leading off to the left. A short climb up this now brings us to Indian Paint Mine and Paint Mine Saddle (11.1; 1970). To complete your trek from here, reverse the steps of Trip 1 the remaining 3.3 miles to Canyon Lake (14.4; 1680).

See Maps 2, 3 and 1

Trip 15   JF Ranch to Dripping Spring

5.6 miles round trip; 500' elevation gain

Leisurely dayhike or backpack (2 hiking days)

Season November to April

Water available at Dripping Spring (mile 2.8) following rainy periods only

Features

Fraser Canyon, with its groves of hackberry, mesquite and cottonwood, provides the shortest and most pleasant route to Dripping Spring, a leafy oasis that attracts a wide variety of bird and animal life. This is a fine "warm-up" trip; not too taxing, yet providing enough exercise to prepare the hiker for more strenuous outings in the future, and offering a degree of solitude and wilderness "feel" that is more than commensurate with the modest effort involved.

Description

Just after crossing Fraser Wash, Forest Road 172 intersects a fence delineating the JF Ranch property. Just to the right of the ranch entrance is a gate with a Forest Service trail sign. The Coffee Flat Trail starts here (0.0; 3120), and we follow it first westward, then southward, as it circumvents a series of corrals and fences. Shortly after winding through a grove of mesquites this trail drops into shallow Fraser Wash (0.4; 3080) and promptly disappears among the boulders and sand of the creekbed. Here we turn right and boulder-hop our way downstream, past an exceptionally large cottonwood tree which serves as a helpful landmark for locating the trail again on the return trip.

Occasional stretches of trail can be found on either side of the wash as we proceed down-canyon, but unless the creek is running exceptionally high (it usually does not run at all), there is little reason for the foot-traveller to seek them out — it is just as easy to walk cross-country directly down the streambed. Fraser Canyon gradually grows deeper and better defined, and soon we must thread a narrow, cliffy bottleneck, or "box." (Those who are religiously tracing out the trail at this point may pick it up again on the right — north — side of the stream after passing through here.)

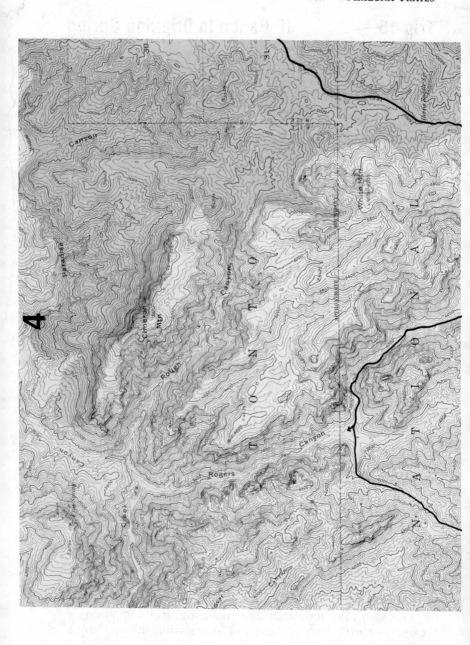

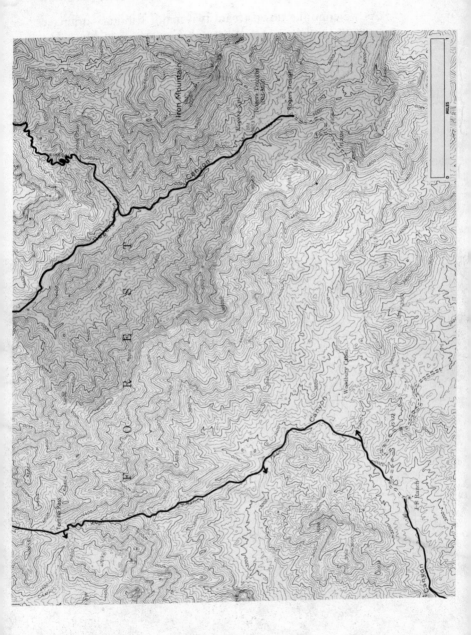

As we continue downstream two major tributary drainages open up on the left — first Whetrock Canyon, then Musk Hog Canyon. About 0.6 mile below the confluence of the Musk Hog drainage, Fraser Canyon ends at Randolph Canyon, the large defile heading up to the right. The Coffee Flat Trail is on the north side of Fraser Wash at this point; just before it crosses Randolph Creek a signpost marks a junction with the right-branching Red Tanks Trail (2.8; 2620). There are nice campsites in the vicinity, scattered among groves of sycamore, mesquite and netleaf hackberry. Dripping Spring is at the base of the south canyon wall a hundred yards or so downstream.

Return the way you came.

See Maps 4 and 5

riparian forest in Rogers Canyon

Trip 16   JF Ranch to Peralta Trailhead via Dripping Spring, the Red Tanks Trail, Upper La Barge Box and Whiskey Spring

15.7 miles one-way (33-mile car shuttle required); 2160' elevation gain

Moderate backpack (2–3 hiking days)

Season November to April

Water is usually available at Whiskey Spring (mile 9.9) and, during rainy periods only, at Dripping Spring (mile 2.8) and along La Barge Creek (miles 8.0 to 9.1)

Features

Faint, twisting, at times perplexing and exasperating — the Red Tanks Trail is one to test the route-finding prowess of even the most experienced wilderness traveler. Those with the patience and skill to trace this rarely trod route will find their efforts amply rewarded, however, for the solitude and the desolate beauty of the backcountry it traverses are commensurate with its difficulty. An added bonus is the delightful spring-season swimming that, during wet years, is to be had in the potholes of Upper La Barge Box.

Remember — this is no route for beginners.

Description

From JF Ranch (0.0; 3120), follow the route of Trip 15 to the trail junction near Dripping Spring (2.8; 2620). Here we turn right, and follow the Red Tanks Trail as it climbs gently along the right-hand side of Randolph Canyon wash, which sometimes contains running water during the rainy season (but not always — check with the Forest Service first). Where Red Tanks Canyon branches off to the left, the trail veers right and proceeds up Randolph Canyon a very short distance, to an exceedingly obscure junction marked with a cairn (3.4; 2720). Turning left here, we drop down a few yards, cross Randolph Canyon wash, then climb up and over a low, cholla-covered ridge into Red Tanks Canyon.

The trail stays mostly to the left of Red Tanks wash as it proceeds up-canyon, sometimes winding through shady glens of oak and sugar sumac (nice camping), other times climbing high up on the grassy canyonsides, where early-morning and late-evening hikers might spot a herd of collared peccaries, or javelinas, feeding upon the prickly pear of which they are so fond. At a major split in Red Tanks Canyon we cross the creekbed to the right, walk up the right-hand fork a few dozen yards, then cross back to the left and clamber over a low ridge to intersect the left fork. The quickly steepening trail then follows this northwestward-trending drainage to its head at Red Tanks Divide (5.8; 3660), a wide saddle affording fine views of the long cliffs of Coffee Flat Mountain and across the pinyon- and juniper-forested headwaters of La Barge Creek.

From the divide we wind westward through a maze of small rock outcroppings, then swing right and drop into a canyon. After passing a drift fence the trail becomes quite obscure, (even more obscure than it has been heretofore), and ducks appear on occasion to help us keep our bearings. At doubtful forks, remember that the route tends to keep to the left of the drainage as it descends. Just before reaching a small basin visible below, we contour to the left across a broad ridge, following ducks, then drop down to and recross the drainage near its confluence with a tributary of La Barge Creek. From here the path strikes off westward, past the site of an old corral, then swings left and descends gently to the edge of a spacious, juniper-dotted basin. The trail grows considerably more distinct as it heads across the northern fringe of this basin.

Next to a northward-trending tributary of La Barge Creek we meet the signed, right-branching Hoolie Bacon Trail (7.6; 3220), at which junction we stay left and proceed across relatively level terrain toward Upper La Barge Box, the cliff-edged narrows visible down-canyon. A number of faint sidetrails branch off to the left through here, leading to nice campsites along nearby La Barge Creek. Beyond this area the trail climbs up onto the north canyonside, preparing to avoid the more difficult passages of Upper La Barge Box. This routing unfortunately misses the many fine swimming holes which pool up in the Box when the water is high, and skilled cross-country travelers may prefer to temporarily abandon the trail and scramble directly down the bouldery throat of the narrows.

After emerging from the west end of Upper La Barge Box, we drop down to creek level, then continue about 0.5 mile down-canyon to a signed junction with the Whiskey Spring Trail (9.1; 2800). To complete your journey from here, turn left and walk part of the route of Trip 12 (in reverse) to Miners Summit (11.3; 3260). Then reverse the steps of the first part of Trip 11 the remaining distance to Peralta Trailhead (15.7; 2420).

See Maps 4, 5 and 2

Trip 17   JF Ranch to Rogers Canyon Cliff Dwellings

11.4 miles round trip; 2940 ' elevation gain

Strenuous dayhike or backpack (2 hiking days)

Season November to April

Water is generally available at Rogers Creek (mile 5.3) from the beginning of the winter rainy season until April or May

Features

This trip features a special destination: a set of ancient cliff dwellings tucked away beneath the precipitous walls of Rogers Canyon. But these ruins, fascinating as they are, are not the sole attraction of this route, for Rogers Canyon is a delight as well — threaded by a clear, sparkling stream (in season), shaded by leafy groves of oak and sycamore, as wild and serene today as it was in the time of the cliff dwellers themselves.

Description

From the signed trailhead just before the end of Forest Road 172 (0.0; 3160) follow the JF Trail as it heads northeast along the right side of Fraser Wash (which may have running water after a heavy rain). After ¼ mile, near where a small tributary drainage enters Fraser Wash on the left, the trail crosses the creekbed and begins climbing up the left-hand canyonside. Stay left at an unsigned fork just beyond here, and continue uphill to a saddle (0.7; 3480). Now we drop slightly, veer left, and enter Randolph Canyon near a Superstition Wilderness boundary sign. After crossing and recrossing the wash, the trail climbs up the left bank to a low ridge, which offers an unobstructed view of the rugged southern flanks of 5077-foot La Barge Mountain, off to the northwest. Presently we drop back down to a signed junction (1.4; 3250),

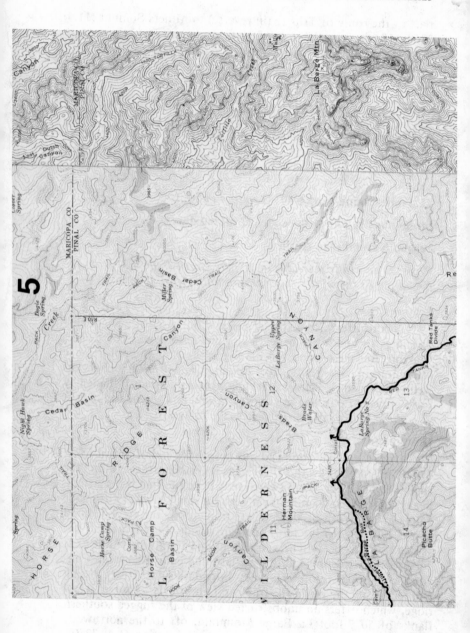

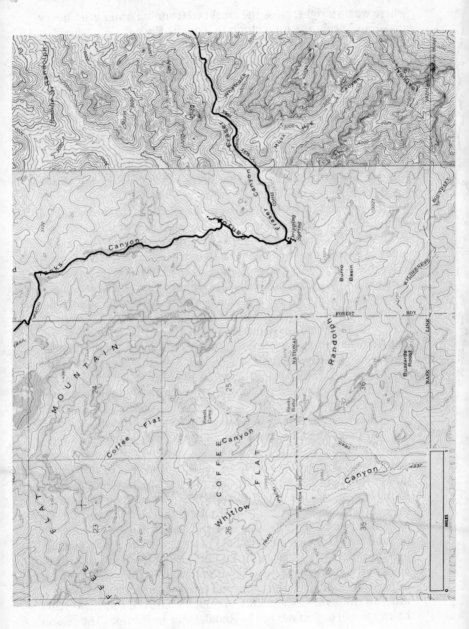

where we turn right, cross the creekbed (running water after heavy rains) and begin the long climb to Tortilla Pass.

The ensuing climb is very rough and steep in places. Part way up, the trail grows more distinct and passes Palmer oaks, shrub live oaks, and some tenacious one-seed junipers — signs of our increasing elevation. Near the top of the climb we cross a wash that may contain a trickle of water during the wet season.

At Tortilla Pass (3.3; 4480) there is a small corral. The trail passes to the right of it, then turns left to a poorly signed fork. Here we turn right onto the Rogers Canyon Trail and climb a short distance farther to a second, unnamed pass (3.6; 4600). On a clear day the broad backbone of the Sierra Ancha range, far to the north, can be seen from this point.

From this saddle the trail drops steeply down to the head of a tributary of Rogers Canyon Creek. The first part of this descent is exceptionally steep and rough. After threading a narrow, rocky gateway in this canyon the route swings right and levels off considerably. As it does so, the tenor of the landscape grows more congenial — the canyon walls are higher and they provide a measure of shelter from the winds which often whip across the highlands; there is occasionally running water down in the creekbed; and single-leaf pinyons, Emory and Arizona white oaks, and tall Arizona sycamores appear in larger and larger groves. By the time we cross Rogers Canyon Creek in a small, grassy basin and meet the Frog Tank Trail at a signed junction (5.3; 3680), we are likely to blink our eyes and wonder if we are still in the same arid mountain range we started in. There are a number of excellent campsites here, and fair swimming when the water is high.

To reach the cliff dwellings, continue east along the Rogers Canyon Trail, boulderhopping across the stream several times. After 0.4 mile the trail should be on the right (south) side of the creek; just before it climbs up into an oak thicket beyond here, look for a sign on the left (5.7; 3800). The ruins are directly across the canyon from here, on the north side at the base of an overhanging cliff about 100 feet above Rogers Canyon Creek. Not a great deal of the old settlement remains, just a few walled-off rooms set here and there in recesses in the cliff. Yet their antiquity is immediately apparent, even to the most casual observer, and they are impressive enough if viewed in the proper perspective. They are, after all, thought to date back to about 1300 AD, some 200 years before the first glimmer of the Renaissance in Europe. The reason for their abandonment — and for the abandonment of hundreds of similar sites scattered across the Southwest — remains a mystery. We may never know precisely why the inhabitants of this particular set of dwellings left their lovely home, but the visitor who lingers awhile in Rogers Canyon, with its singing, crystalline creek and its serene groves of oak and sycamore, will readily understand why they chose to settle here in the first place.

The ruins are legally guarded by the Federal Antiquities Act, but the only real protection they have lies in the respect and common sense of visitors. Please do not damage or alter them in any way.

Return the way you came, or via the trail up Rogers Canyon to Rogers Trough (9.9 miles; 10-mile car shuttle required; see Trip 19).

See Map 4

Trip 18   Rogers Trough to Reavis Grave

4.8 miles round trip; 660 ' elevation gain

Leisurely dayhike

Season all year; best in spring and fall

Water available in Rogers Canyon (miles 0.0 to 1.8) during rainy periods only

Features

The destination of this fine, leisurely excursion is the gravesite of Elisha Reavis, a remarkable recluse who, during the late 1800s, almost singlehandedly homesteaded 60 acres of land on nearby Reavis Creek. Along the way we pass through the quiet, shady defile of upper Rogers Canyon, whose serene groves of sycamore and walnut help put the hiker in the proper frame of mind to visit the final resting place of the man who probably knew these mountains better than any other.

Description

From the end of Forest Road 172A (0.0; 4840) the trail proceeds gently downhill along the banks of Rogers Creek. A few hundred yards from the start an indistinct spur trail branches off to the right; we stay left here, and continue down-canyon through a delightful riparian forest of hackberry, sycamore and walnut. About 1.5 miles later, after winding back and forth across the rocky creekbed a number of times, the trail swings northward toward a side canyon which can be seen opening up on the right. At a signed junction here the Rogers Canyon Trail branches left (1.8; 4400); we stay right and follow the Reavis Ranch Trail as it passes a fence and climbs moderately up the tributary canyon. The surroundings here are less congenial than in Rogers Canyon — the few large trees are confined to widely spaced pockets down in the wash, and the shadeless stretches between them are bouldery and throttled with brush. (This entire area burned in the Iron Fire of 1966.)

About 0.6 mile beyond the preceding junction, immediately after crossing the tributary creekbed from its right to its left side, we arrive at an unsigned junction (2.4; 4620) marked with a cairn. The right-hand fork here is the continuation of the Reavis Ranch Trail, which leaves the streambed at this point and climbs up the canyonside to the north; to reach Reavis Grave we follow the left fork as it cuts steeply up a rocky hillside. After proceeding only a few dozen yards this rough pathway peters out between clumps of shrubbery; the grave is in an inconspicuous clearing just to the left of this area.

The cause of Reavis' death was never determined. When his remains were found here in 1896 the head was located some distance away from the rest of the body, and thus was born many a grisly legend concerning the "Curse of the Superstition Mountains." But probably coyotes or other scavengers were responsible for this "beheading."

Return the way you came.

See Map 4

Trip 19   Rogers Trough to Rogers Canyon
Cliff Dwellings

8.4 miles round trip; 1040 ' elevation gain

Moderate dayhike or leisurely backpack (2 hiking days)

Season all year; best in spring and fall

*Water is generally available along entire route from the beginning
of the winter rainy season until April or May (check with Forest
Service first)*

Features

This route provides the easiest access to the ancient cliff dwellings in Rogers Canyon. Along the way it stays close to Rogers Canyon Creek, one of the leafiest and most congenial watercourses in
all the Superstitions. With its lack of steep, tiring climbs, this trip is
a good choice for the beginning hiker or backpacker, yet its
beautiful setting and intriguing destination make it worthwhile for
more experienced trekkers as well.

Description

From the parking area at the end of Forest Road 172A
(0.0; 4840) our route proceeds gently down the right-hand side of
Rogers Canyon Creek. After a few hundred yards a faint spur trail
branches right; we stay left at this junction and continue down-
canyon, crossing the creekbed frequently. Where a major side canyon opens up to the northeast we swing right, away from the
stream, and meet the Rogers Canyon Trail at a signed junction
(1.8; 4400). If you wish, you may go straight ahead here and make
the side trip to Reavis Grave (1.2 miles round trip; see Trip 18).
Otherwise we turn left, cross a rocky area back to Rogers Canyon,
and continue downstream. Soon after we pass an old corral and
stock fence, the canyon walls begin to steepen considerably, providing enough shelter to foster a fairly dense forest cover of stately
sycamores, sturdy alligator junipers, Emory and white oaks and a
few Arizona walnuts and velvet ashes. During late winter and early
spring there is usually enough running water to permit some brisk
swimming in the pools which, for the next mile or so, decorate the
stream like beads on a necklace.

After skirting the base of a steep cliff the trail swings to the

left, then drops down to a sign on the left (south) side of Rogers
Canyon Creek (4.2; 3800). The cliff dwellings are just across the
creek from here, 100 feet or so up the hillside at the base of a high,
overhanging cliff. (For a description of these ruins, see Trip 17.)
There are a few fair campsites in this area, but backpackers will
find far better ones at the Rogers Canyon/Frog Tank Trail junction, 0.4 mile down the canyon from here.

Return the way you came, or via the trail to Tortilla Pass and
JF Ranch (9.9 miles total; 7-mile car shuttle required; see Trip 17.)

See Map 4

Trip 20   Upper Horrell Place to Pine Creek

8.6 miles round trip; 1840 ' elevation gain

Moderate dayhike or backpack (2 hiking days)

Season all year; hot in summer

Water available at Pine Creek (mile 4.3) during rainy periods only

Features

Tucked away in the uplands of the eastern Superstitions is the
delightful basin of Pine Creek. This is more mountain country
than desert country — browsed by mule deer, forested with oaks
and tall pines, and threaded by a cold, clear creek during the rainy
months. To those who have visited only the western side of the
mountains, it hardly seems like the Superstitions at all.

Description

From the trailhead at Upper Horrel Place (0.0; 3280) follow
an old road west toward Campaign Creek. This road quickly deter-
iorates into a foot trail and begins crossing and recrossing the
stream, which often contains at least a little water and supports a
nice riparian growth of walnuts, sycamores and Fremont cottonwoods. Shortly after passing the Superstition Wilderness boundary sign we reach an unsigned junction at a fork in the creek. Our
route stays left here, and continues upstream to a signed junction
with the left-branching KRN Trail (0.7; 3420). Here we turn right
and climb a short distance onto a ridge which affords a nice view of

Two Bar Mountain to the northwest. Ignoring a faint spur trail which drops down to the right from here, we proceed along the backbone of this ridge until it melts into a larger hillside. At this point the trail veers to the right and climbs gently, paralleling the course of a drainage visible below.

Presently we cross this drainage, then climb steeply up a hillside to a flat area which contains some curiously arranged rocks — possibly an Indian ruin. Beyond here the trail continues climbing, steeply at times, to the head of the wash at Reavis Gap (3.3; 4820). Just downhill from this pass the Two Bar Ridge Trail branches right at a signed junction; we stay left and descend gently through a grassy area, then climb back up a short distance to a saddle between small hills. The forested headwaters of Pine Creek finally come into view as we drop first gently, then more steeply, down a pinyon- and juniper-studded slope. At Pine Creek itself (4.3; 4630) there are a few sycamores, some tall ponderosas and excellent camping. The creek generally runs only during rainy periods and for a short time thereafter.

Return the way you came.

See Map 6

Trip 21 Upper Horrell Place to Rogers Trough via Pine Creek, Reavis Headquarters, and Reavis Grave

14.6 miles one-way (80 mile car shuttle required); 3190′ elevation gain

Strenuous dayhike or moderate backpack (2–3 hiking days)

Season all year; hot in summer

Water is generally available along Reavis Creek (miles 7.1 to 7.7) and Rogers Canyon Creek (miles 12.8 to 14.6) from the beginning of the winter rainy season to April or May (check with Forest Service first); Pine Creek (mile 4.3) has water only during rainy periods

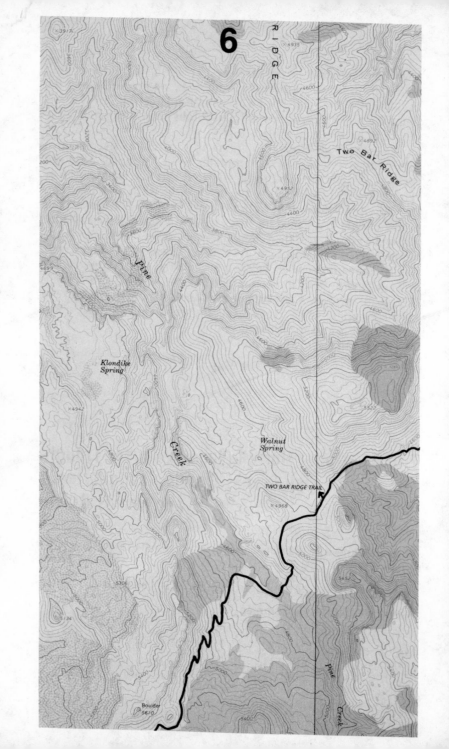

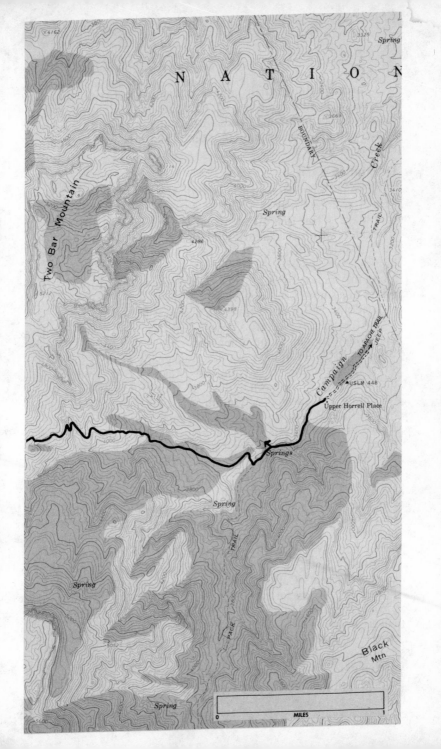

Features

After climbing stiffly up from Campaign Creek, this trip samples a healthy portion of the pine-and-chaparral-cloaked eastern Superstition highlands. En route, hikers can visit the homestead and gravesite of pioneer Elisha Reavis, and camp in three separate drainages.

Description

From Upper Horrell Place (0.0; 3280), follow the route of Trip 20 to Pine Creek (4.3; 4640). When the creek is flowing, this spot makes a fine first night's camp for backpackers. To continue from here, we proceed across a relatively flat area, past a few more fair campsites, then cross a wash and begin climbing steeply up a hillside. Some sparkling crystals of quartz may catch your eye along this section of trail; a little searching will also turn up a few pieces of a smooth-surfaced variety of the same mineral, known as chalcedony, which often takes on a pretty, bubblelike form.

After passing beneath a series of bluffs and broken pinnacles, the trail tops out at an unnamed saddle (5.8; 5280) beneath Boulder Peak. From here we descend, gently at first, then more steeply, toward the valley containing Reavis Creek, gaining some nice vistas across the basin to the 6000-foot-plus summits of White Mountain and Mound Mountain, the two highest peaks in the Superstition Wilderness. At times the metal-roofed ranchhouse at Reavis Headquarters is visible far below. The descending trail continues to steepen until it brings us to Reavis Creek, which usually has running water from the beginning of the winter wet season until well into spring (but check it out with the Forest Service first). From here our route crosses the creek, heads downstream alongside a fence for a short distance, then cuts left and parallels a second fence to a signed junction with the Reavis Ranch "Trail" (an old road, now closed to motorized travel). We turn left onto the latter, and proceed gently uphill about 0.5 mile to Reavis Headquarters (7.5; 4860). The ranchhouse here, built in the late 1930's by the Clements Cattle Company and subsequently used by the Forest Service as an "administrative site," is an architectural melange, consisting mostly of adobe and sandstone walls and covered with a metal roof. A variety of fairly modern construction materials and techniques have been thrown in since its original construction. You may "camp" in the house if you wish; if you prefer more natural surroundings, a number of good campsites can be found along the creek.

When ready to continue your trek, follow the route of Trip 23
to Reavis Grave (12.2; 4620), then reverse the steps of Trip 18 to
the end of Forest Road 172A at Rogers Trough (14.6; 4840).

See Maps 6, 7 and 4

Trip 22   Reavis Trailhead to Reavis Headquarters

19.6 miles round trip; 1640 ′ elevation gain

Moderate backpack (2 hiking days)

Season all year; hot in summer

*Water available at Reavis Creek (mile 9.8) from the beginning of
the winter rainy season until April or May (check with Forest Service first)*

Features

From 1872 until his death in 1896, Elisha M. Reavis homesteaded 60 acres of land in the pine-and-juniper-forested highlands
of the eastern Superstitions. He was the perfect picture of a hermit, living and working alone, letting his hair and beard grow to
prodigious lengths, appearing in town only at rare intervals to sell
his home-grown vegetables. This trip follows an abandoned road
up to his old ranch site, where backpackers can get a taste of the
serene, undisturbed life which Reavis enjoyed for nearly a quarter
of a century. (The homestead was purchased by the Forest Service
in 1967, and has been open to the public since then.)

Description

From the parking area at Reavis Trailhead (0.0; 3660), walk
gently uphill, past the barricades that block the Reavis Ranch
Road to vehicular traffic. The corridor surrounding this road,
which knifes deeply into the backcountry, is presently excluded
from the Superstition Wilderness area, though it may be reclassi-
fied as wilderness sometime in the future. For the first few miles
the trail-road ascends at an easy grade, staying on or near the crest
of a winding ridge, crossing from one side to the other frequently.
Views are excellent from the start, both northward, across Apache

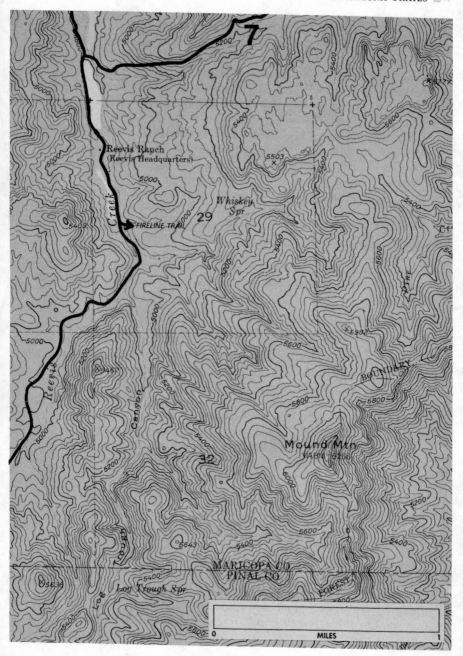

MILES

Lake to the beautiful Four Peaks of the Mazatzals, and westward, across the maze of peaks and ridges surrounding Fish Creek and the Salt River Canyon. Vegetation is mostly sparse along this section, consisting chiefly of yucca, snakeweed, treacherous mats of agave and sotol, and a few hardy shrubs such as mountain-mahogany and shrub live oak. After we pass through a major saddle (4.0; 4620) and begin traversing beneath the high northeast face of Castle Dome Mountain, the plant cover grows noticeably denser, and hoptree and single-leaf pinyon appear.

After passing through another saddle, the trail (actually still very much a road in appearance) drops a slight distance to Windy Pass (6.1; 4900), which offers an excellent view westward, across the central Superstitions of the seemingly ever-present landmark of Weaver's Needle. From this gap we drop downhill along a minor drainage (a section of the road has washed away here, but the route is clear) to Plow Saddle, a broad, grassy notch containing a corral. Here the route resumes climbing, topping out at a small ridgecrest affording another good view of Weaver's Needle. After dropping a bit to a signed junction with the Frog Tank Trail (8.0; 4820), the trail-road swings gradually onto the east slope of a long ridge and traverses southward, paralleling Reavis Creek, down in the canyon some distance below. At a sycamore-shaded corral we meet the Reavis Gap Trail, branching left at a signed junction. Here we continue straight ahead on the old road, past some rusting, abandoned farm machinery and an apple orchard, relics of a bygone era which presage our arrival at Reavis Headquarters (9.8; 4860).

Reavis' original cabin no longer exists. The present ranchhouse was built by the Clements Cattle Company in the 1930's and is now used by the Forest Service as an "administrative site". Architecturally this structure is quite a hodge-podge, with walls that are variously of adobe and stone, covered by a metal roof. An assortment of other building techniques and materials, some of them incongruously modern-looking, have been applied over the years. You may "camp" in the house if you wish; those who prefer more natural surroundings will find a number of good tentsites nearby. This valley is one of the most pleasant areas in the Superstitions, sporting a spotty cover of ponderosa pine, single-leaf pinyon, some tall sycamores near the creek, and Palmer and white oak. Reavis Creek, which flows only after the winter rainy season has gotten well under way, is apparently the only source of water.

A number of tall tales revolve around Reavis, known to contemporaries as the Hermit of the Superstitions. One writer reports that his cabbages grew to a phenomenal size, often weighing as much as ten pounds. Another rumor has it that he ran about naked at night, shouting and shooting bullets at the stars, and was thus never bothered by the local Apaches, who supposedly feared the evil spirits by which he was possessed. He died in 1896 on the other side of Reavis Saddle (to visit his grave, see Trip 23), and by the time his remains were located the head had been chewed off of the body by scavengers; this perfectly natural occurrence, widely reported as a "beheading," immediately got hitched onto the legend of the Lost Dutchman Mine as "The Dutchman's Revenge," the "Curse of the Superstition Mountains," and so on. In reality, one supposes, Reavis was nothing more than a harmless old recluse — a bit antisocial, no doubt, but neither a raving madman nor a victim of some fanciful curse.

Return the way you came.

See Maps 8 and 7

Trip 23   Reavis Trailhead to JF Ranch via Reavis Headquarters, Reavis Grave, and Rogers Canyon

23.2 miles one-way (80-mile car shuttle required); 2960′ elevation gain

Moderate backpack (3 hiking days)

Season all year; hot in summer

Water is generally available along Reavis Creek (miles 9.8 to 10.4) and Rogers Creek (miles 15.1 to 17.8), from the beginning of the winter rainy season until April or May (check with the Forest Service first)

Features

After climbing up to the old ranchhouse at Reavis Headquarters, this route continues uphill and crosses the pine-topped, mile-high crest of the eastern Superstitions. Once over the top, we pass the site of Reavis' grave and visit the ancient cliff dwellings in Rogers Canyon before climbing out of the backcountry and dropping down to JF Ranch.

With excellent campsites located along Reavis Creek and in Rogers Canyon, this route is tailor-made for a 3-day trek.

Description

From Reavis Trailhead (0.0; 3660), follow Reavis Ranch Road (closed to vehicle traffic) to Reavis Headquarters (9.8; 4860) (see Trip 22). Here the road narrows to a trail, which we follow past the ranchhouse and across a grassy, fenced-in clearing. Shortly after dropping down to Reavis Creek we meet the signed Fireline Trail coming down from the left (east). Our route continues straight ahead here, climbing gently for the most part and staying close to the creek, which generally has a good flow during late winter and early spring.

A half mile or so beyond the Fireline Trail junction we veer to the right, away from the creek, and continue to climb gently, through a gradually thickening forest cover of ponderosa pine, some stout alligator junipers, single-leaf pinyon and a few Arizona cypresses. In places along this section of trail, where the pines grow tall and thick and pile their needles in luxurious, soft carpets on the ground, it is possible to stretch out beside the gurgling creek, listen to the chattering of squirrels, and completely forget that one is surrounded by thousands of square miles of sere desert country.

Beyond here we pass through an area scarred by the Iron Burn of June 1966, a lightning-ignited blazed that blackened over 10,000 acres before it was put out. (Nowadays, in recognition of wildfire's important role in many natural ecosystems, such a fire might be allowed to burn itself out.) Temporarily leaving the burn area, we soon pull up alongside the stream again. At a point roughly between White Mountain and Point 5636 the drainage makes two forks in quick succession (12.3; 5100). A short distance up the right-branching drainage is Honeycutt Spring, which is not completely dependable, but which often has water when upper Reavis Creek is bone dry. The trail continues due south from here, and follows the central drainage fork to its head at Reavis Saddle (13.2; 5330), where we are treated to a fine view of 6056-foot Iron Mountain, and of the chaparral-cloaked ridges rising beyond Rogers Canyon. Reavis Saddle Spring, shown on the topo, may be dry.

From Reavis Saddle the trail drops steeply across a south-

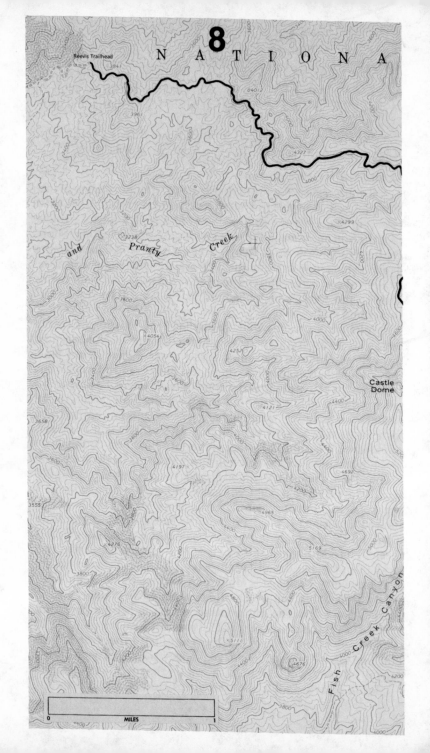

8

NATIONA

Reevis Trailhead

Pranty Creek

Castle Dome

Fish Creek Canyon

0   MILES   1

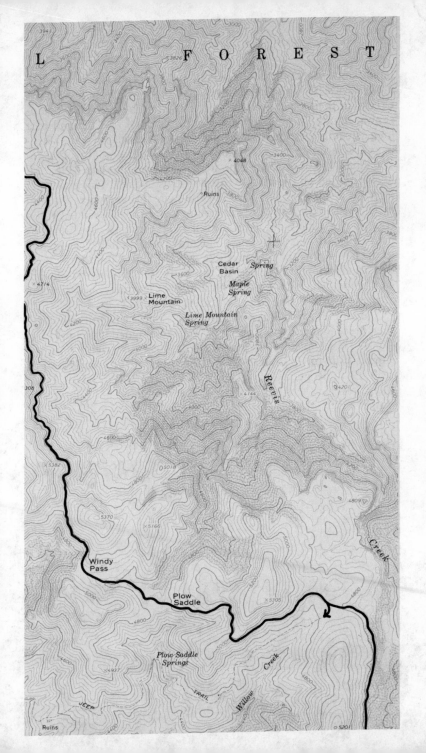

facing slope that contrasts markedly with the gentler country north
of the divide. Gone are the junipers and pines which shaded Reavis
Creek; in their place we find a rough, scrubby stubble of manzanita, mountain mahogany and shrub live oak. At the end of a
long, steadily descending traverse we drop down several switchbacks, bottoming out at a tributary (usually dry) of Rogers Canyon Creek (14.5; 4620). Elisha Reavis died near here in 1896, and
he was buried on the hillside just above us. To reach his gravesite,
look for a cairn at the bottom of the switchbacks, where the trail
meets the tributary streambed. Follow a steep, badly eroded gully-
trail up the slope from here, until it fades out between clumps of
brush a few dozen yards later. The grave is in a small clearing just
to the left of this spot. Before Reavis' corpse was found, the head
was separated from the rest of the body, presumably by scavengers, a fact which gave rise to a number of legends concerning the
alleged "Curse of the Superstition Mountains."

Below Reavis' Grave we cross the Rogers Canyon tributary,
then descend moderately about 0.5 mile to a signed junction (15.1;
4400). To complete your journey from here turn right, onto the
Rogers Canyon Trail, and follow the route of the second half of
Trip 19 to Rogers Canyon Cliff Dwellings (17.5; 3800). From
there, reverse the steps of Trip 17 the remaining 5.7 miles to JF
Ranch (23.2; 3160).

See Maps 8, 7 and 4

ranch house at Reavis Headquarters

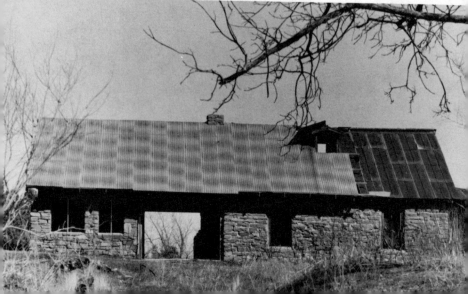

Area 2: The Southeastern Ranges

Arizona's southeastern ranges, for the purposes of this guide, consist of the Santa Catalina, Rincon, Santa Rita and Chiricahua Mountains. Each of these is an "island" range, rising out of a surrounding sea of desert and grassland to heights in excess of 8-9000 feet. With their broad altitudinal sweep, some parts of these mountains provide enjoyable hiking during every month of the year. Lower elevations are warm (hot in summer), dry, studded with cacti and, in spring and fall, awash with colorful wildflowers. In the middle regions you will find pretty forests of silverleaf oak, pinyon pine and alligator juniper, while the heights are crowned with ponderosa pine, Mexican white pine, Douglas-fir, quaking aspen and, in the Chiricahua Mountains, Engelmann spruce.

Trips in the Santa Catalina and Chiricahua mountains lie within the Pusch Ridge Wilderness and the Chiricahua Wilderness, respectively, while those in the Santa Rita Mountains explore the proposed Mount Wrightson Wilderness. The Rincon Mountains backcountry lies within Saguaro National Monument, and has been set aside as wilderness by the National Park Service. Hikers will be glad to learn that cattle grazing is no longer permitted in any of these areas.

When hiking the higher trails in July or August, remember that afternoon thundershowers are an almost daily occurrence. Carry raingear even if the morning weather is clear, and plan your itinerary so as to avoid exposed peaks and ridges (prime targets for lightning) during the afternoon. You may wish to visit the high country during dry periods in the winter; if you do, be prepared for subfreezing nighttime temperatures and unexpected snowstorms. Trips with very wide elevation ranges have no "ideal" hiking season; you will have to decide if you wish to be hot down low or cold up high. Temperature extremes can be avoided somewhat by hiking in spring and fall.

Wildlife is still plentiful in these ranges. The huge herds of pronghorn antelope that once roamed the surrounding grasslands may be gone, but the mountains themselves still boast healthy populations of mule deer and Coues white-tailed deer, coati-mundis, cougars and bobcats. A few black bears either inhabit or visit each area, and some 50 or so desert bighorn sheep — exceedingly man-shy creatures — cling to existence in a rugged corner of the Santa Catalina Mountains. A variety of colorful, subtropical birds migrate northward each spring from Mexico and Central America, to nest in the hardwood-forested canyons of the Chiricahua and Santa Rita ranges. There have even been rumors that jaguars — long extinct in the United States — occasionally stray into the Chiricahuas from the fastnesses of the Mexican Sierra Madre.

The present rugged relief of this section of the state is the result of massive thrusting and faulting that has been going on since at least the beginning of the Cenozoic era some 70 million years ago. Structurally, that relief is even greater than it appears to be, since eons of erosion have filled the valleys between the mountains with thousands of feet of alluvial deposits; today, some of the ranges are so deeply awash in this alluvium that they barely manage to poke up out of their own debris.

The areas covered in this chapter are essentially devoid of valuable mineral deposits. There is no particular geological reason for this, however — it merely reflects the sad fact that only those few areas that *were* mineral-free have survived as official wilderness. An exception to this is the Santa Rita Mountains, where there are quite a few active mines. (The proposed Mount Wrightson Wilderness, however, contains only a few, presently inactive workings.)

The southeastern ranges have long played an important role in the history of the region. In pre-Columbian times they provided the local Indians with plentiful game, reliable water, and relief from the sweltering heat of lowland summers. Later, following the invasion of the whites, they served as virtually impregnable wartime citadels. In Arizona's first "Indian uprising," a band of Pimas led by Luis Oacpicagua killed several Spanish settlers, then fled to the Santa Catalina Mountains. As a result of this revolt an army was stationed in the area, and a general escalation of hostilities promptly ensued. The Pimas were soon brought under military control, but not before the Apaches had joined the fray, and *they* were not to be so quickly conquered. For the next 80 years, in one of the longest wars in history, these hardened, highly skilled, and vastly outnumbered guerrilla fighters harassed first the Spaniards, then the Mexicans, and finally the Americans, holding continuous sway over vast tracts of disputed land, until the decimation of their ranks broke their resistance. Perhaps the most feared of the Apache bands were the Chiricahuas, who operated out of the mountains of the same name and, under the leadershop of the likes of Cochise, Juh, and Golthlay (Geronimo), were the last to surrender to the whites.

Visit the ranges today and you will find not a trace of these bloody, protracted battles. What you *will* find is a penetrating sense of stillness and serenity, the excitement of storms, vistas that know no bounds, skies of the deepest blue. And you will come away feeling that these mountains are just as much worth fighting for today as they were during they heyday of the Apache.

Managing Agencies

Santa Catalina Ranger District
2500 N. Pantano Road, Suite 126   Pusch Ridge Wilderness
Tucson, AZ 85715
   (602) 296-6245

for Sabino Canyon Visitor Center, dial (602) 749-3223

Saguaro National Monument
Box 17210   Rincon Mountains
Tucson, AZ 85731
   (602) 298-2036

Nogales Ranger District
1410 Rio Rico Drive   Santa Rita Mountains
Rio Rico, AZ 85621
   (602) 281-8424

Douglas Ranger District
1925 A Avenue, Drawer Y   Chiricahua Wilderness
Douglas, AZ 85607
   (602) 364-3231

Further Reading

Watch for Me On the Mountain (biography of Geronimo) by Forrest Carter (Delacorte, New York, NY, 1978)

Guide to the Santa Catalina Mountains of Arizona, by Edgar G. Heylmun (Treasure Chest Publications, Tucson, Arizona, 1979

Apaches, Eagles of the Southwest, by Donald E. Worcester (University of Oklahoma Press, Norman, Oklahoma, 1979)

Southern Arizona Wildflower Guide (Tucson Daily Citizen, Tucson, Arizona, 1974)

See also the Pusch Ridge and Chiricahua wilderness management plans, available for inspection at local Forest Service offices

Approaches/Trailheads

Pusch Ridge Wilderness

Rancho Romero   From Tucson, drive north along U.S. 89 (Oracle Road). Approximately 7 miles beyond Ina Road (1.2 miles after crossing the bridge over Canada del Oro), turn right onto a dirt road (OK for passenger cars) and proceed a few hundred yards to a junction near the ranch headquarters. Turn left here, and continue 1.8 miles to a clearing in a forest of mesquite trees (stay on the most-travelled road at all forks). Park here; the jeep road which can be seen heading east across Canada del Oro is the start of the Romero Canyon Trail. This is private property; please act accordingly.

Magee Roadend   From the intersection of Ina and Oracle roads in Tucson, drive north on Oracle Road for 1 mile, then turn right onto Magee Road and follow it to a parking area at its terminus, 1.5 miles from Oracle Road. This trailhead, presently on private property, may be moved in the future a short distance onto National Forest land.

Cactus Picnic Ground   From the intersection of Sabino Canyon and Sunrise roads in Tucson, drive northeast on Sabino Canyon Road for 0.8 mile, then veer left onto a spur road to the picnic ground. The signed *Espero Trail* begins just beyond here, on the right-hand side of the spur. Backpackers should leave their vehicles at the Sabino Canyon Visitor Center parking lot, 0.7 mile back down the road, as overnight parking is not permitted here.

Sabino Canyon Roadend   From the intersection of Sabino Canyon and Sunrise roads in Tucson, follow signs a short distance to the Sabino Canyon Visitor Center. The upper portion of Sabino Canyon Road is closed to private cars, so park here and ride the Sabino Canyon shuttle the remaining 4 miles to the trailhead at road's end. (Inquire at the Visitor Center for current fare and schedule information.)

Lower Bear Canyon   From the intersection of Sabino Canyon and Sunrise roads in Tucson, drive northeast along Sabino Canyon Road. 0.5 mile after passing the Sabino Canyon Visitor Center, turn right and follow signs the remaining 1.6 miles to the trailhead at the north end of the Lower Bear Picnic Area loop. Overnight parking is not permitted here; backpackers should leave their cars at the Visitor Center parking lot. At some time in the future, the Sabino Canyon shuttle may be expanded to serve this area.

Showers Point Campground   From the intersection of Catalina Highway and Snyder Road in Tucson, follow Catalina Highway (which just beyond here is called Mount Lemmon Highway) about 25 miles to Palisade Ranger Station, then turn left onto a dirt road (OK for passenger cars) and proceed 0.5 mile farther to the signed spur road to the campground. Turn right here; the trailhead is just beyond.

Mt. Lemmon Highway   To reach the start of the *Box Camp Trail* on Mount Lemmon Highway, follow the preceding directions to Palisade Ranger Station, then continue along Mount Lemmon Highway 2.3 miles farther, to a point where the signed trailhead can be seen at the base of a hill to the left of the highway.

Marshall Gulch Picnic Area   Follow the Showers Point Campground approach as far as Palisade Ranger Station, then continue on Mount Lemmon Highway approximately 5 miles to a junction. Go straight ahead here, and proceed past Summerhaven a little over 1 mile to the picnic ground at road's end. Note: As of 1980, the last part of this approach was impassable due to flood damage. (Before then this section had been closed off anyway, owing to water-pollution problems associated with the local summer homes.) Until this area is reopened, hikers will have to park their cars at the road closure point (about 0.5 mile below Summerhaven) and walk the remaining 0.5 mile to the trailhead.

Rincon Mountains

East Speedway Trailhead   From the intersection of Country Club Drive and Speedway Boulevard in Tucson, proceed east on Speedway approximately 14 miles to the end of the public road at a turnoff to a guest ranch. There is a parking area off to the right here; a National Park Service interpretive sign marks the start of the Douglas Spring Trail.

Javelina Picnic Ground   From Tucson, follow Old Spanish Trail to the Saguaro National Monument visitor center. Just beyond the visitor center, turn right and proceed 1.8 miles farther to the picnic ground. Park here, then walk back down the road a short distance to a sign indicating the start of the trail to Juniper Basin and Tanque Verde Peak.

Miller Creek   From Tucson, drive southeast on Interstate 10 about 45 miles, then turn off at the Mescal/J-6 Ranch exit. Proceed directly north past Mescal, then continue northwestward along Ash Creek. After the road climbs over a saddle and drops into Happy Valley (about 16 miles from I-10), you will see two small ranch houses off to the left. Continue beyond these, cross a cattle guard, and then bear left at a sign indicating the trailhead.

The last 14 miles of this approach are over a dirt road which may prove troublesome for some passenger cars.

Santa Rita Mountains

Bog Springs Campground   From Tucson, drive south on Interstate 19 for about 25 miles and turn off at the Continental exit. Proceed east past Continental, then curve right (south) at a junction 7 miles from I-19 (stay on the paved road). Five miles beyond this junction a sign indicates the turnoff to the campground; turn left here and drive up a winding but still paved road 0.5 mile farther. Once in the campground, look for an old road that branches off to the right just beyond the third campsite. This is the start of the trail to Bog Springs. Hiker parking is available a short distance up the main campground road from here.

Madera Canyon Roadend   From the Continental exit on I-19, 25 miles south of Tucson, drive east, then south, to Santa Rita Lodge in Madera Canyon, about 13 miles. (Stay on the main, paved road at all forks.) Proceed up-canyon from here 0.9 mile to a fork, then turn left and continue a short distance farther to a parking area at road's end.

Florida Canyon Experimental Range Headquarters   From the Continental exit on I-19, about 25 miles south of Tucson, drive southeast along the road toward Santa Rita Lodge and Madera Canyon. Seven miles from I-19 this paved road turns 90 degrees to the right; leave the pavement here and proceed straight ahead on Forest Road 62A (OK for most passenger cars). Go straight ahead at another junction 0.3 mile beyond here, and continue 2.9 miles farther to a point where the road crosses Florida Canyon wash. Just beyond this crossing, before the road enters the Experimental Range Headquarters, you will see the signed trailhead off to the left.

Chiricahua Wilderness

Rustler Park   From Willcox drive southeast along Highway 186 for 33 miles to a junction with Highway 181. Turn left (east) onto the latter and follow it 3 miles to Pinery Canyon Road (Forest Road 42). Turn right onto this good dirt road and continue 12 miles to Onion Saddle, then turn right onto Forest Road 42D. The signed trailhead is 3 miles farther.

Snowshed Trail   Four miles southeast of Portal, Forest Road 42 (see above) crosses Cave Creek; just east of this crossing a sign indicates the start of the trail.

Turkey Creek   From the junction of U.S. 666 and Highway 181 drive 12 miles due east along Highway 181, then turn right onto Forest Road 41. Nine miles along this well-graded dirt road is a sign indicating the short spur to the *Saulsbury Canyon Trail* (turn left and drive 0.5 mile to the parking loop at the end of the road). Several hundred yards up the main road, another sign points out the bottom of the *Mormon Ridge Trail*. The *Morse Canyon Trail* begins about a mile and a half beyond, at the very end of the road.

Rucker Forest Camp   From the junction of U.S. 666 and Highway 181 drive south along U.S. 666 for 8 miles to a junction. Turn left (east) here and follow a well graded dirt road 27 miles to its terminus a short distance beyond Rucker Lake.

South Fork Forest Camp   From Portal drive southwest along Forest Road 42 for 3 miles to the junction with the South Fork Road. Turn left onto the latter and follow it a little over one mile to the signed trailhead at its end.

Trip 24   Rancho Romero to Romero Canyon

5.6–12.4 miles round trip; 1120–3340' elevation gain

Moderate to strenuous dayhike or backpack (2 hiking days)

Season November to April

*Water always available at Romero Creek (mile 2.8); also from mile
5.0 to 6.2 during rainy periods only*

Features

A fine introduction to the "front range" of the western Santa
Catalinas, this route passes alternately along wildflower-dotted
hillsides and through leafy, intimate forest cloisters on the way to
the head of Romero Canyon. En route we gain excellent views
across the rough-cut skyline of Pusch Ridge, beneath which
sprawls some of the wildest and most inaccessible country left in
southern Arizona.

Description

From the parking area at Rancho Romero (0.0; 2720) follow a
dirt road east as it crosses sandy Canada del Oro and swings up onto a low bluff just beyond. A mile later this road ends at a point
overlooking Montrose Canyon wash on the right (1.1; 2960).
(With a four-wheel drive vehicle it might be possible to drive to this
point.) Here we turn onto a foot trail which can be seen heading
off to the left, and climb up to a fence at the Coronado National
Forest boundary. Above here the trail climbs rather steeply,
switchbacking occasionally and soon rising high above rugged
Montrose Canyon. The vegetative cover here is dense and varied,
consisting chiefly of statuesque saguaros, sprawling ocotillos,
yellow (or foothill) paloverde and prickly pear. During the spring
months there are bright patches of wildflowers all through this section, including yellow-blossomed brittlebush and paperflower, as
well as some narrowleaf aster. Views are excellent to the south,
sweeping across the cliffy foothills of Pusch Ridge to steep-walled,
square-topped Table Mountain. With luck you might spot one of
the 50 or so bighorn sheep which inhabit the inaccessible fastnesses
of Pusch Ridge, particularly during the winter, when fierce
snowstorms occasionally drive them off the heights.

After winding up and down through a jumbled, rocky area,
the trail threads a narrow notch atop a ridge (2.4; 3640). From here

we climb a short distance eastward along the ridge, gaining good views up the long defile of Romero Canyon, and then drop rather steeply down to Romero Creek (2.8; 3600). A series of potholes just downstream from here always have water, and provide enjoyable swimming during warm weather. A few poor-to-fair campsites are located nearby.

For the next 0.5 mile we proceed up-canyon, crossing the creek on occasion but mostly staying on the dry flats to either side. Sycamore, walnut and velvet ash grow near the stream, while Mexican blue oaks and mesquites are predominant in the drier areas away from the water. The canyon quickly grows narrower and rougher, and the trail soon begins a steep, switchbacking ascent up the left-hand canyon wall. As we gain elevation there are good views of the craggy headlands surrounding 7952-foot Cathedral Rock.

After gaining some 800 feet the trail levels off and begins traversing high above the canyon floor. Approximately 0.5 mile later, after crossing a brushy flat (the site of an old corral), we drop down a few steep switchbacks to a poorly signed junction with a spur trail to Romero Spring (5.0; 4680). Here there is an old campsite featuring a couple of large stone fireplaces and a considerable collection of discarded cans, bottles and other trash. Nicer, less "improved" campsites can be found just up- or down-stream. Romero Creek, which runs only during the rainy season (and often intermittently even then), is just beyond the trail junction. Romero Spring is a short distance down-canyon, at the confluence of a tributary wash which comes down from the south. It is apparently not a reliable source of water during the dry months.

To continue to the head of Romero Canyon, follow the trail as it proceeds moderately up-canyon, crossing the bouldery streambed frequently. About 0.5 mile later we switchback a short distance up the north canyonside, through a light forest cover of pinyon pine and alligator juniper, then drop back down to creekside. There are excellent campsites in this area, beneath a shady overstory of silverleaf and Arizona white oaks, velvet ash, walnut, and an occasional cypress or ponderosa. During the spring, delicate yellow columbines bloom in moist pockets by the water.

A few hundred yards above here the trail swings to the right and enters a side canyon (6.2; 5320), preparatory to beginning the ascent to Romero Pass. Here, at the end of today's excursion, there is one final campsite (water during rainy periods only).

Return the way you came.

See Maps 9 and 10

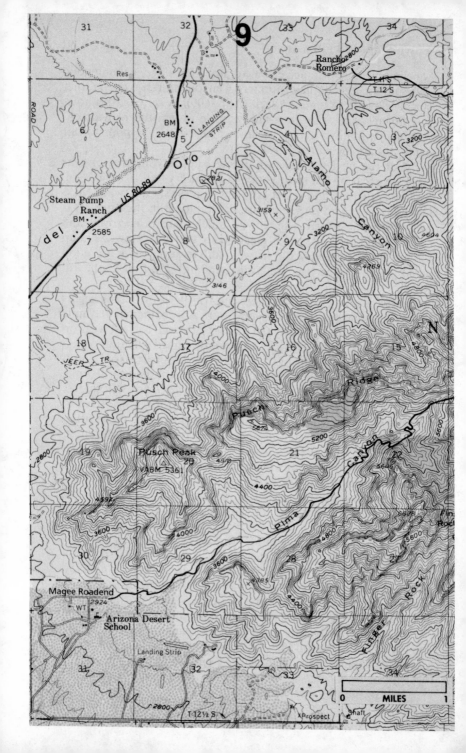

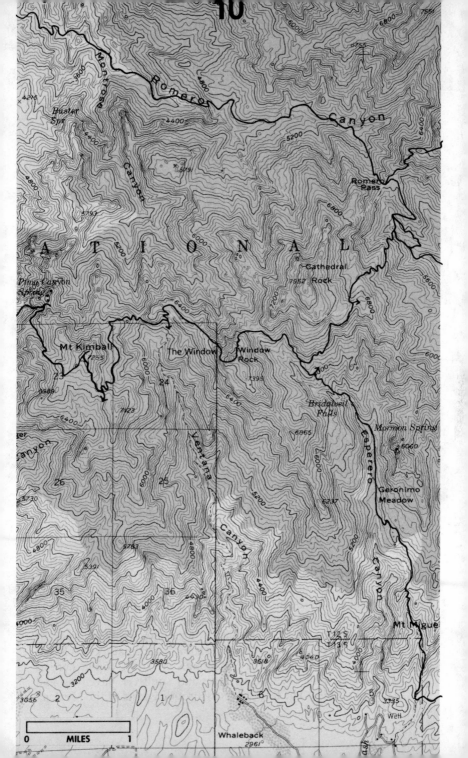

Trip 25   Magee Roadend to Pima Canyon

6.4 miles round trip; 1020′ elevation gain

Leisurely dayhike or backpack (2 hiking days)

Season November to April

Water available intermittently in Pima Canyon (miles 1.1 to 3.2) during rainy periods only

Features

Pima Canyon, draining the "back side" of rugged Pusch Ridge, provides the easiest access to the front range of the Santa Catalinas. A good midwinter warmup, this leisurely trip samples the interesting desert country along the lower part of the canyon, reserving the high, forested region beyond for later, more strenuous excursions.

Description

From the parking area at the end of Magee Road (0.0; 2940) walk east along a dirt road. Immediately after crossing a wash this road forks; stay left and proceed a few dozen yards farther to where a foot trail can be seen climbing up a small embankment on the right. We follow the latter across the rocky slopes at the south base of Pusch Peak. After dipping in and out of a small drainage, the trail passes through a fence at the Coronado National Forest/Pusch Ridge Wilderness boundary, then contours to the left into Pima Canyon. The ground cover here is a typical Lower Sonoran mixture of gangly ocotillos, tall saguaros, foothill paloverdes and prickly pears. Bright yellow brittlebush blossoms carpet the area in the spring.

Presently the trail switches back to the right and drops down to Pima Canyon wash (1.1; 3180) (generally dry except during rainy periods). Above here we work our way gradually up-canyon, winding in and out among large boulders and frequently crossing the creekbed. Here and there in the smooth bedrock you may see metates, small pits in which the Indians once ground acorns into meal. A wide variety of birdlife congregates in this canyon at various times of the year, including robins, cardinals, kestrels and black phoebes. A number of mammals are to be found here as well: desert mule deer, Harris ground squirrels, javelinas and blacktail rabbits. The large, debris-shrouded nests of the Mexican woodrat are sometimes found in brushy thickets by the creek, though the architects themselves are not so frequently seen.

Near where a major, northward-trending tributary joins the wash there is a nice campsite beneath some robust cottonwoods. Above here the trail gradually grows steeper and harder to follow, but even those hikers who are unsure of their route-finding skills can generally make it up as far as a point where another, steeper tributary drainage (3.2; 3960) comes down from cliffy Point 6628 (off to the right, or southeast). Here there are a few stunted Mexican blue oaks, fair camping, and a nice view of Tucson through the deep "V" of Pima Canyon.

Return the way you came, or continue up the trail (which soon becomes even steeper and more difficult to follow) to the high country at Mount Kimball (see Trip 26).

See Map 9

"horned toad" in Santa Catalina Mountains

Trip 26   Magee Roadend to Mount Kimball

14.2 miles round trip; 4320' elevation gain

Strenuous dayhike or backpack (2–3 hiking days)

Season all year, except after snowstorms

Water is almost always available at Pima Canyon Spring (mile 5.3) (check with Forest Service during dry weather periods)

Features

Standing like a sentinel above the western end of the Santa Catalina front range, 7255-foot Mount Kimball commands a fine view of some of the roughest, most beautiful country in Arizona. Because the latter half of the Pima Canyon Trail up to the peak is exceptionally steep and difficult to follow, this trip is recommended only for very experienced hikers.

Description

From Magee Roadend (0.0; 2940), follow the route of Trip 25 up Pima Canyon to the tributary (3.2; 3960) which comes down from Point 6628. As we continue up-canyon from this point, the trail grows progressively steeper, more overgrown with brush, and harder to follow. After crossing the creekbed in Pima Canyon near a small catchment dam built by the Arizona Game and Fish Commission, the narrow track rollercoasters steeply up and down (mostly up) the canyonsides on either side of the stream, passing occasional clumps of Mexican pinyon pine and one-seed juniper, signs of our rapidly increasing elevation. Presently we enter a narrow, cliff-bound defile, within which is Pima Canyon Spring (5.3; 5600), a reliable source of water except possibly during prolonged spells of dry weather. A poor campsite is nearby.

About 0.4 mile up-canyon from the spring is an unsigned junction marked with a cairn. The left-forking path climbs straight ahead a short distance to the head of Pima Canyon at Pima Saddle; a point just to the north of here commands a fabulous vista across the almost unbelievably rough-cut north slopes of Pusch Ridge. This is desert bighorn country, one of the few remaining sanctuaries for a race of wild, sure-footed mountaineers that once ranged widely over the Santa Catalinas and many of the other high mountains of the Southwest. The fact that these exceptionally man-shy animals have managed to hang on here, within a few miles of a major metropolitan center, testifies to the ruggedness and inaccessibility of this area.

Back at the cairn, the main trail sneaks out of Pima Canyon to the right, then switchbacks up to the lip of a small, pinyon-forested basin. The path is very difficult to follow in places as it strikes off southward up this basin; take your time through here, and look for ducks and cairns at confusing spots. After crossing a small drainage to its right (southwest) side we climb up a bit to a minor ridge, then climb steeply southeastward. Soon this ridge melts into a larger ridge at a broad saddle; here we swing to the left and climb the remaining distance to the comparatively level crown of Mount Kimball (7.1; 7255). Most of this mountaintop is forested with ponderosa pine; the clearest views are obtained by following a faint use-trail to a rocky promontory at the north edge of the flat summit area. From here there is an excellent vista across the chopped-up country drained by Montrose and Romero creeks. Cathedral Rock and Window Rock are both visible as well, rising beyond the head of Ventana Canyon. Those who are willing to carry food, water and bedding up this far will be rewarded with an opportunity to view the sunrise as it unleashes its splendors on the vast landscape sprawling below. At night the lights of Tucson put on a fine show, winking and shimmering between the black silhouettes of the pines. Caution: do not remain in the summit area if a thunderstorm seems imminent.

Return the way you came.

See Maps 9 and 10

Thimble Peak from near Mud Spring

Trip 27

Cactus Picnic Ground to Bridalveil Falls

11.0 miles round trip; 3000' elevation gain

Strenuous dayhike or backpack (2 hiking days)

Season November to April

Water available in Esperero Canyon (miles 4.1 to 5.5) during rainy periods only

Features

This trip, best done during the late-winter-early-spring wet season, ascends the front range of the Santa Catalinas to tiny, graceful Bridalveil Fall. This wispy cascade, a fine destination in its own right, makes a fine base for backpackers wishing to continue to The Window or Cathedral Rock.

Description

From the trailhead at Cactus Picnic Ground (0.0; 2840) follow the Esperero Trail as it heads gently uphill to the north. An unsigned spur trail soon branches left; we go right, climb up to a low saddle, and then cross a level section planted with prickly pear, ocotillo, paloverde, brittlebush and some impressive saguaros and mesquite trees. After swinging back down to the right we reach a signed junction, where we turn left. Shortly beyond here the trail climbs steeply up a ridgeline, then cuts left across a flat and drops into shallow Bird Canyon. At a fence here we temporarily leave Coronado National Forest (please do not camp in this privately owned area), then resume climbing steeply up another ridge. After gaining some 600 vertical feet the occasionally brushy path works its way left into an unnamed gulch and continues, a bit less relentlessly, uphill. Where this canyon forks, the trail follows the left branch, eventually reaching a saddle near its head (2.9; 4420). The last few hundred feet of this ascent are again quite steep. Here there is a nice view down into Esperero Canyon, and up to the cliff-bound heights of Window Rock and Cathedral Rock.

From this gap we ascend moderately up-canyon, staying high above Esperero Creek and passing a few mesquite trees, one-seed junipers, and clumps of shrub live oak. Soon the trail tops out at another small saddle, then drops down to the floor of Esperero

Canyon (4.1; 4640), where there are sycamores and some comparatively large oaks growing among the jumble of canyon-bottom
boulders. A few fair campsites can be found nearby, but do not expect to find any water except during and immediately following
rainy periods.

After crossing the creekbed, the trail meanders up-canyon,
rising and falling over short distances and crossing the watercourse
at frequent intervals. About a mile later the spur trail to Mormon
Spring branches right at a signed junction. (This spring apparently
no longer flows, but some potholes in the streambed above it often
provide water when the rest of Esperero Creek is dry.) Esperero
Canyon branches here; our route goes left, into the west fork, and
climbs 0.5 mile farther to Bridalveil Falls (5.5; 5360), off to the left
of the trail. This fall is hardly spectacular as waterfalls go, being
only about 30 feet high and rarely flowing with enough volume to
produce even a mild roar (in fact, it is likely to dry up completely
by early spring), yet is has a soothing, unpretentious beauty of its
own. Some impressive specimens of Arizona cypress grow just
across the creek, some of them leaning out slightly across the pool
at the base of the falls. There is an excellent campsite here, shaded
by an arching canopy of Emory oaks, within earshot of the quiet
cascade. A variety of wildlife frequents this area; Harris ground
squirrels scamper up and down the tree trunks, Coues deer and
desert mule deer occasionally come to drink out of the stream, and
ringtail cats, striped skunks and other nocturnal prowlers may pay
a visit to your camp if you elect to spend the night — drawn by
curiosity and, as often as not, by the alluring aroma of the food
stored in your pack.

Return the way you came, or continue on to The Window or
Cathedral Rock (see Trips 28 and 30).

See Maps 11 and 10

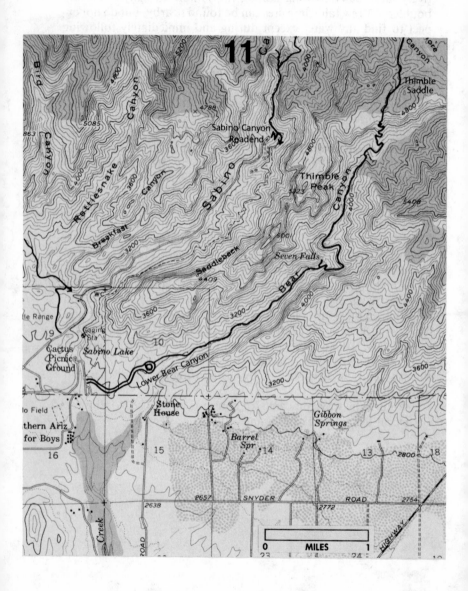

Trip 28 Cactus Picnic Ground to The Window

16.8 miles round trip; 5140′ elevation gain

Strenuous dayhike or backpack (3 hiking days)

Season all year, except after snowstorms

Water available in Esperero Canyon (miles 4.1 to 5.5) during rainy periods only

Features

After climbing up to Bridalveil Falls, this very strenuous route continues uphill to The Window, a small natural arch in a blade of rock perched nearly a vertical mile above Tucson. Even without this unusual feature for its destination, this trek would still be highly worthwhile, by simple virtue of the many fine vistas it affords along the way.

Description

From Cactus Picnic Ground (0.0; 2880), follow the route of Trip 27 to Bridalveil Falls (5.5; 5360). Here the trail veers right, proceeds a short distance up a tributary of Esperero Canyon, then commences climbing very steeply up a ridge to the left. This ascent continues unbroken for some 600 vertical feet, after which the trail temporarily levels off at a dry campsite on a flat atop the ridge. At a trail fork here we swing to the left and climb more moderately along the rather faint path, through a thickening forest cover of ponderosa pine, spiny Schott's yuccas and overarching white oaks to a signed junction with the Cathedral Rock Trail (6.4; 6120). The route now goes left, and continues ascending moderately to a saddle (7.2; 6680) at the head of Esperero Canyon. From this point one looks directly down into the rugged headwaters of Montrose Canyon, which fall away abruptly northward; to the southeast, the view stretches across the Catalina foothills to the graceful pyramid of Rincon Peak, rising above Tanque Verde Ridge in the Rincon Mountains.

From this gap the trail switchbacks steeply up the rocky northeast ridge of Window Rock. After gaining 600 feet of elevation we top out at a point just south of this peak's summit rocks (peakbaggers may wish to scramble up to the top from here). The trail next circles westward to a minor gap, then plunges downward, through much brush and past some spectacular cliffs and pinnacles, to The Window (8.4; 7000), a 15-foot-high, wind- and water-eroded perforation in a large fin of rock. There is a register here, of the type usually reserved for mountaintops, in which you may read the comments of others who have labored up to this lofty point, and in which you may record your own strenuous accomplishment. Be careful if you go scrambling around in the arch; it is a sheer, 100 foot drop out of the far side. When the sunlight strikes it at the proper angle, this natural "hole in the wall" is clearly visible from parts of Tucson; once you have been there, it is a pleasant sensation to view it from city level and mentally relive this excursion.

Return the way you came.

See Maps 11 and 10

horned owl

Trip 29   Cactus Picnic Ground to Magee Roadend via Bridalveil Falls, The Window, and Mount Kimball

19.0 miles one way (13-mile car shuttle required); 5240 ′ elevation gain

Strenuous backpack (3 hiking days)

Season all year, except after snowstorms

Water is almost always available at Pima Canyon Spring (mile 13.7) (check with Forest Service during dry weather spells); Esperero Canyon (miles 4.1 to 5.5) and Pima Canyon (miles 15.8 to 17.9) have water during rainy periods only

Features

After climbing up past Bridalveil Falls, this strenuous backpacking route stays high on the crest of the Santa Catalina front range, traversing across The Window and Mount Kimball before dropping back to the desert via Pima Canyon. With fine wet-season campsites located at Bridalveil Falls and near Pima Canyon Spring, this makes a good, albeit strenuous, 3-day outing.

Description

From Cactus Picnic Ground (0.0; 2880), follow the route of Trip 28 to The Window (8.4; 7000). After dropping steeply past The Window's base, the trail descends more gradually along a broad, open ridgetop. After a little over 0.5 mile we cut sharply to the left and switchback down into the head of Ventana Canyon. At a signed junction with the Ventana Canyon Trail we turn right, then climb gently past a pair of switchbacks to the saddle dividing Montrose and Ventana canyons. Several more switchbacks now bring us up onto a wide, gently sloping shelf just east of Mount Kimball, along which we climb very gradually, through an open forest cover of wind-tossed Mexican pinyon pines, sturdy alligator junipers and a variety of oaks. After 0.6 mile this gentle ascent suddenly ends, and the trail swings to the right and twists steeply uphill some 200 feet to a saddle with a good dry campsite and a nice view of Tucson (11.4; 6860).

At a signed junction in this gap, we turn right and follow a faint path that scrabbles steeply 0.5 mile up to the flat summit of

Mount Kimball (11.9; 7255). To complete your journey from here, reverse the steps of Trip 26 the remaining 7.1 miles to Magee Road-end (19.0; 2940).

See Maps 11, 10 and 9

Trip 30   Cactus Picnic Ground to Rancho Romero via Bridalveil Falls and Romero Pass

17.7 miles one-way (20-mile car shuttle required); 5260 ' elevation gain

Strenuous backpack (3 hiking days)

Season all year, except after snowstorms

Water available in Esperero Canyon (miles 4.1 to 5.5) and Romero Canyon (miles 11.5 to 12.6) during rainy periods only

Features

After climbing up to Bridalveil Falls in the Santa Catalina front range, this route crosses two high saddles and drops into Romero Canyon. Both Cathedral Rock and The Window are accessible via short sidetrips from the main route, and magnificent views alternate with shady forest closures almost the entire way. With delightful campsites located at convenient intervals in Esperero and Romero canyons, this makes a fine 3-day trek for the backpacker in good physical condition.

Description

From Cactus Picnic Ground (0.0; 2880), follow the route of Trip 27 to Bridalveil Falls (5.5; 5360). Here the trail veers right, proceeds a short distance up a tributary of Esperero Canyon, then commences climbing very steeply up a ridge to the left. This ascent continues unbroken for some 600 vertical feet, after which the trail temporarily levels off at a dry campsite on a flat atop the ridge. At a trail fork here we swing to the left and climb more moderately along the rather faint path, through a thickening forest cover of ponderosa pine, Schott's yucca and white oak, to a signed junction with the Cathedral Rock Trail (6.4; 6120). Turn left here if you wish to make the highly worthwhile, 4.0 mile round-trip detour to The Window (see Trip 28). To continue on the main route, we turn right and climb moderately along a rocky, brushy path, past good views of the distant Rincon Mountains, to a saddle (7.4; 6920) southeast of Cathedral Rock. Very experienced cross-country scramblers may wish to try for Cathedral's craggy, 7952-foot summit (the highest in the front range) from here. (This route is neither straightforward nor easy. Some technical rock-climbing experience is necessary to reach the highest point, and many climbers will want a rope.)

There is an obscure, unsigned junction in this saddle. Our route turns left and heads west a short distance, then drops north into a small basin forested with ponderosa pine, Douglas-fir and white fir. After passing a nice campsite (a creeklet nearby generally has water following heavy rains), we reach the lip of this basin, where we are treated to a nice view across the gap of Romero Pass to the Wilderness of Rocks and the heavily forested Mount Lemmon area. Red-tailed hawks can often be seen soaring and hunting above the brushy slopes below.

The trail now switchbacks steeply down a series of nearly shadeless, chaparral-covered slopes some 1000 vertical feet to a signed junction at the head of West Fork Sabino Canyon (9.1; 5500). The path which branches right from here is a variant of the West Fork Sabino Trail; our route goes left, across the bed of West Fork Sabino Creek (generally dry at this point), then proceeds uphill a short distance to the main West Fork Sabino Trail (signed). Here we take the left fork, and follow it a few hundred yards onto a ridge, whose crest is then followed the remaining 0.5 mile to often-windy Romero Pass (10.5; 6040), a major saddle separating the Santa Catalina front range from the main mountain mass. At a junction here we turn left, onto the signed Romero Canyon Trail, drop steeply down switchbacks into a tributary of Romero Canyon (usually dry), and then proceed more moderately down-canyon beneath a pleasantly shady forest overstory of tall ponderosa pines, lots of silverleaf and Arizona white oaks, and some velvet ash. About 1 mile beyond Romero Pass the trail reaches the main branch of Romero Canyon (11.5; 5320), where there is a good campsite and, during rainy periods, running water. To complete your journey from here, reverse the steps of Trip 24 the remaining 6.2 miles to Rancho Romero (17.7; 2720).

Trip 31   Cactus Picnic Ground to Sabino Canyon Roadend via Bridalveil Falls, and West Fork Sabino Canyon

16.7 mile near-loop trip (use Sabino Canyon shuttle to make a complete loop); 4280 ' elevation gain

Strenuous dayhike or backpack (3 hiking days)

Season all year, except after snowstorms

Water is available year-round at Hutch's Pool (near mile 12.7); Esperero Canyon (miles 4.1 to 5.5) has water during rainy periods only

Features

Beginning amid the cacti and shrubs of the Sonoran desert, this strenuous trek climbs past pretty, oak-and-cypress-shaded Bridalveil Falls to the pine-forested crest of the Santa Catalina front range. The West Fork of Sabino Canyon provides a convenient return route, one made all the more attractive by the easy access it provides to Hutch's Pool, a delightful, year-round swimming hole.

Description

From Cactus Picnic Ground (0.0; 2880), follow the Esperero and Cathedral Rock trails to the signed fork near the head of West Fork Sabino Canyon (9.1; 5500) (see Trip 30). Here we turn right, onto a variant of the West Fork Sabino Trail, and descend gradually 0.2 mile to the main West Fork Sabino Trail. The route now follows the latter down-canyon, crossing the rocky bed of West Fork Sabino Creek at frequent intervals (water during rainy periods only). This section of the trail is somewhat overgrown with mimosa and hikers in shorts will quickly learn to give these sharp-spined plants a wide berth. Occasional good campsites, partially shaded by overarching Emory oaks and sycamores, can be found near the stream. A lengthy lunch stop (or an overnight stay) in this pleasant area will allow you to become acquainted with the boldest, noisiest member of the local wildlife fraternity — the Mexican jay, a bird readily identifiable by its raucous call and impudent manners.

About 2 miles beyond the last junction, the trail crosses the creek from its left to its right side, climbs a bit, then traverses along the canyonside as the streambed gradually falls away below. The forest cover thins out as we leave the watercourse, with hardy one-seed junipers, shrub, live oaks and some beautiful Mexican blue oaks now forming its major components. Sharp-spined amole, sotol, and yucca begin to appear in the rocky, sunny spaces between trees. After winding in and out of a pair of minor side canyons we reach a saddle atop a low ridge, then drop down into and cross a small drainage. From here a few switchbacks bring us to an unsigned junction (12.7; 3920) near Sabino Creek. Hutch's Pool, with its good campsites, perennial water, and excellent warm-weather swimming, is a few hundred yards up the spur trail to the left (see Trip 32).

To complete your journey from here, reverse the steps of Trip 32 the remaining 4.0 miles to Sabino Canyon Roadend (16.7; 3330).

See Maps 11, 10 and 12

Sabino Creek below Hutch's Pool

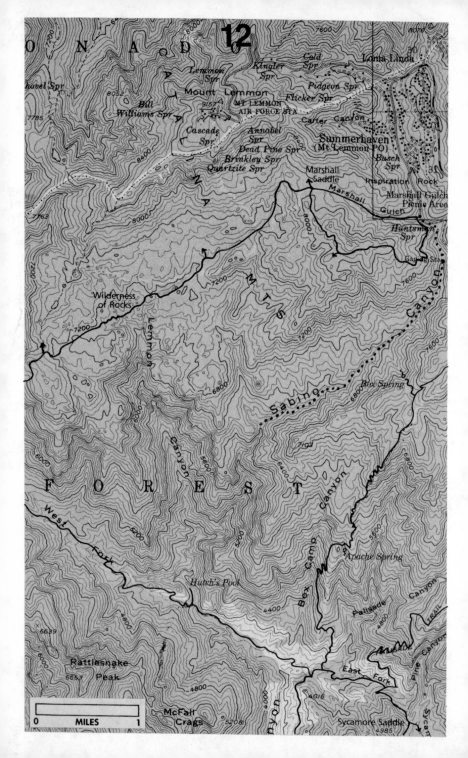

Trip 32   Sabino Canyon Roadend to Hutch's Pool

8.4 miles round trip; 950' elevation gain

Moderate dayhike or backpack (2 hiking days)

Season all year; hot in summer

Water available all year at Hutch's Pool (mile 4.2)

Features

Hutch's Pool, in the opinion of many, is by far the finest swimming hole in the Santa Catalinas. But it is not the only attraction of this route; along the way to the pool there are fine views down into rugged Sabino Canyon, and equally good vistas across the high, rough-cut ridges which drop abruptly from the high country to Sabino Basin.

This trip's season is given as all year, even though the route can be fiercely hot during the summer. Those wishing to enjoy the cool waters of Hutch's Pool during the hottest weather usually plan on being gone the entire day, leaving early in the morning and returning as the temperature drops in late afternoon. But be sure to get back to the trailhead in time to catch the last shuttle out of Sabino Canyon.

Description

From the trailhead at the end of Sabino Canyon Road (0.0; 3330) the signed Sabino Canyon Trail switchbacks moderately uphill through a sparse ground cover consisting mainly of saguaro, paloverde, amole, ocotillo and prickly pear. After climbing steadily for 0.5 mile we arrive at a signed junction with the Phoneline Trail, where we take the left fork and begin traversing the east wall of Sabino Canyon some 300–400 feet above the creek. About ¾ mile beyond here the trail climbs up to a notch (1.2; 3800) behind a large granite outcropping which stands like a sentinel above a narrow horseshoe bend in the canyon. Ever since the 1920's there have been sporadic proposals to build a dam at this point. Since the hydroelectric generating potential of Sabino Creek is rather inconsequential, and since the water which flows down the canyon is already stored quite efficiently in the subterranean aquifers beneath Tucson, it has never been made quite clear just what purpose such a dam would serve. The resulting reservoir would back up into Sabino Basin, and might provide "recreation opportunities" for boaters—but there are many who feel that this wild, beautiful area offers far better recreation opportunities in its present undrowned state.

A few hundred feet beyond this saddle a steep, rough trail of use drops down a ravine to some deep pools and good campsites along the creek. Our route continues traversing up-canyon, making a number of ups and downs as it winds in and out of a side drainage and passes behind some minor outcroppings. Presently we drop down a few switchbacks and step across Palisade Creek (water during rainy periods only) to a signed trail junction in Sabino Basin (2.5; 3680). Here the route turns left, then crosses the rocky wash of Box Camp Creek and a low ridge just beyond, and begins climbing gently up the sycamore-dotted floor of the basin. There are occasional good campsites in this area, off to the left by the stream. Watch out for the poison ivy which abounds here.

After proceeding a little over a mile upstream we cross Sabino Creek from its north to its south side. Shortly beyond here the trail prepares to switchback up the left-hand canyonside, but just before it begins this climb an unsigned spur trail branches right. We now turn onto the latter and follow it a few hundred yards to Hutch's Pool (4.2; 3860), a delightful, year-round swimming hole. There are several excellent campsites nearby, though this popular area has been picked clean of firewood. During the cooler months of the year, when there are not enough human swimmers here to keep the local brown and rainbow trout in a perpetual panic, the stream offers fair angling. Several more deep pools can be found upstream from Hutch's.

Return the way you came.

See Maps 11 and 12

Trip 33   Sabino Canyon Roadend to Lower Bear Canyon Picnic Ground

11.3 miles one-way (2-mile car shuttle and use of Sabino Canyon shuttle required); 1740' elevation gain

Moderate dayhike or backpack (2 hiking days)

Season November to April

Water available all year at Seven Falls (near mile 9.0); Palisade Creek (mile 2.5) and Sycamore Creek (near mile 4.6) have water during rainy periods only

Features

Hikers looking to stretch their legs during the winter months will appreciate this route, which features a very short car shuttle and samples a variety of pleasant country. The highlight of the trek is Seven Falls, a series of high cataracts which puts on an awesome spectacle following heavy rains.

Description

From Sabino Canyon Roadend (0.0; 3330), follow the route of Trip 32 to the signed trail junction at Palisade Creek in Sabino Basin (2.5; 3680). Turn right here, then proceed gently up-canyon beneath a pleasant riparian overstory of tall oaks and sycamores. Several excellent campsites can be found through here (and for the next mile or so up the trail), but water is available only during rainy periods. Soon we pass the signed, left-branching Box Camp Trail, where we turn right again and climb a single switchback onto a sunny slope planted with hardy one-seed junipers, low-growing mats of agave and sotol, and some small Mexican blue oaks and shrub live oaks. After gaining only a little elevation, we traverse eastward and presently find ourselves walking alongside the bed of Pine Creek, which has risen to our level. At the signed junction with the Palisade Trail (parts of which are visible descending from the high country to the north) the route turns right and climbs a moderate switchback up the canyonside, gaining some nice views back across Sabino Basin to the Romero Pass area.

From the top of this switchback the trail climbs southeast to Sycamore Saddle (4.6; 4600), where there is a fork. Backpackers looking for tentsites may wish to follow the left-branching pathway a short distance downhill to Sycamore Creek, which offers running water (during rainy periods only) and delightful camping beneath tall oaks, rustling sycamores, and some nice stands of Arizona cypress. Water is always available at Sycamore Spring Reservoir, about 1 mile down this trail from where it first meets the creek.

To continue on the main route, turn right at the junction in Sycamore Saddle and climb gently southward to nearby Thimble Saddle (5.2; 4840). From this, the high point of our trek, the trail proceeds very gradually downhill for 0.5 mile, then begins a long, switchbacking descent into Bear Canyon. A mile later (and some 700 feet lower) we cross Bear Creek (water during rainy periods only), then climb up the opposite canyonside a bit, and work our way down-canyon, staying about 50 feet above the streambed. Occasional fair campsites can be found among the jumble of flood debris in the watercourse below.

Soon a dropoff looms ahead in the canyon; now we climb slightly, and traverse around a rocky projection high above Seven Falls. The falls are not yet visible, but if Bear Creek is running high their roar will be easily audible from this area. After we descend moderately across the head of a large amphitheater, the falls come into view across the canyon, and we drop down a series of switchbacks to a signed junction near their base (9.0; 3320). The lowest fall is 0.2 mile down the right-branching trail. A string of deep potholes worn into the creekbed here offer water year-round and provide enjoyable swimming during warm weather. The continuation of our route goes left at the fork and descends gently the remaining 2.3 miles to Lower Bear Canyon Picnic Ground (11.3; 2800) (reverse the steps of Trip 34).

See Maps 11 and 12

Trip 34   Lower Bear Canyon Picnic Ground to Seven Falls

5.0 miles round trip; 480 ' elevation gain

Leisurely dayhike

Season all year; hot in summer

Water available all year at Seven Falls (mile 2.5)

Features

Right after a heavy rain, when the resurrected creeks of the Santa Catalinas are high and rolling — that is the ideal time to go see Seven Falls. At other times these steep cataracts are not so spectacular (or are even completely dry), but they may still be worth a visit to enjoy the fine swimming in the deep, perennially filled pools at their bases.

Description

From the end of the road at Lower Bear Picnic Ground (0.0; 2800), follow the wide, well-maintained trail as it drops gently toward Bear Creek, through a typical Lower Sonoran plant cover of honey mesquite, the omnipresent saguaro and prickly pear, low-growing pincushion cactus, yellow paloverde, ocotillo, teddy-bear and jumping cholla, and brittlebush. A few medium-sized sycamores and cottonwoods grow along the creek, which is soon crossed via the first of a series of low, rock-and-cement dams. The trail proceeds gently upstream for the next mile and a half, past several more crossings (the stream is generally dry or intermittent except during rainy periods), and then switchbacks moderately a short distance up the right-hand (south) canyon wall.

We now continue our way up-canyon, keeping 100 feet or so above the creek, until we arrive at a signed junction from where Seven Falls is visible in the deeply recessed, steep-walled amphitheater across the canyon. Here our route turns left and drops down slightly to Bear Creek, just below the lowest of the falls (2.5; 3280). It is possible to scramble up past several of the falls from here, although care should be taken when climbing the slippery, water-worn rocks. The potholes beneath the falls contain water all year long, and offer excellent swimming during warm weather.

Return the way you came.

See Map 11

Trip 35   Showers Point Campground to
                                          Mud Spring

5.4 miles round trip; 1420' elevation gain

Moderate dayhike or backpack (2 hiking days)

Season April to November

Water available all season at Mud Spring (mile 2.7)

Features

This route passes through tall forests of pine and fir on its way to an all-year spring perched high above the Catalina foothills and the city of Tucson. It is an excellent choice for dayhikers seeking an introduction to the middle reaches of the range, and for backpackers who appreciate a camp with a view.

Description

From the signed trailhead at Showers Point Campground (0.0; 7760) follow the well-maintained Palisade Trail as it drops along the slopes immediately above the head of Palisade Canyon. The trail works its way in and out of a few minor drainages as it passes well below the group campgrounds up on Organization Ridge. After passing through some majestic stands of ponderosa pine, Mexican white pine, Douglas-fir and Gambel oak, and perhaps seeing some of the Coues white-tailed deer that frequent these slopes during the summer, we swing out onto the crest of Organization Ridge, gaining some nice views to either side through the pines. After dropping a short distance along the gently descending ridgeline, the route veers off to the left, then drops more steeply down a brushy slope to a minor, oak-covered ridge. From here we switchback into a small ravine just west of Pine Canyon.

Shortly after crossing this ravine from east to west the trail passes an excellent campsite (2.5; 6600) just above the streamcourse to the left. This camp, in a pleasant mid-mountain forest of ponderosa pine, Schott's yucca, and silverleaf and Arizona white oak, is situated just above a rocky dropoff in the drainage, and it affords a grand view of spirelike Thimble Peak, lower Sabino Canyon, and much of metropolitan Tucson. This vista is even better at night, when a vast, sparkling sea of lights floats above the jagged, jet-black silhouette of the foothills — as though the stars had fallen from the sky and collected in a pool at your feet.

During the rainy season there is often water here, and sometimes a series of dashing falls below the dropoff. If not, water is always available at the cement tank of Mud Spring (2.7; 6440), about ¼ mile down the moderately descending, switchbacking trail. There are a couple of campsites near this spring, though they are not as nice as the one above.

Return the way you came.

See Map 13

Trip 36   Showers Point Campground to Sabino Canyon Roadend

10.0 miles one-way (35-mile car shuttle required); 4520´ elevation loss, negligible gain

Moderate dayhike or backpack (2–3 hiking days)

Season April to November

Water available all season at Mud Spring (mile 2.7); Palisade Creek (mile 7.5) has water during rainy periods only

Features

Beginning amid the pines and firs of the Catalina high country and ending among the shrubs and cacti of the foothills, this route transects four life zones — Canadian, Transition, and Upper and Lower Sonoran. Most of this long descent is made via open ridgelines, making for excellent vistas all the way down.

Description

From Showers Point Campground (0.0; 7760), follow the Palisade Trail to Mud Spring (2.7; 6440), continue moderately downhill past a few switchbacks, and then traverse to the right, onto the broad divide between Pine and Palisade creeks. There are excellent views from this ridge of Thimble Peak in the Catalina foothills, and across Sabino Canyon to the front range, dominated by craggy, 7952-foot Cathedral Rock. The plant cover here is thin-

Syke Knob
Butterfly Peak
Soldier Camp

Bill Williams Spr.

6000

Spencer Peak
Bear Wallow Spring
Picnic Area

Box Camp Trailhead
Microwave Tower

C   C   O

Mt Bigelow
VABM 8550
Lookout
Kellogg Mtn

Boy Scout Spr
8400
Palisade Rock

7560

Palisade Ranger Sta.

Palisade Spr.

Girl Scout Spr.

Showers Point Campground

Boy Scout Camp

Barnum Rock

HIGHWAY

San Pedro Vista

Girl Scout Camp

7600

Green Mtn
7890

7200

Picnic Area

Rose Canyon

Willow Canyon

Spencer Canyon

6800

7500

Lizard Rock
7328

Rose Peak
7299

6800

Mud Spring

6875

Horse Canyon Spr

Water Tank

General Picnic

7061

6800

6400 Canyon

6400

Bear Canyon Picnic Area

PALISADE

Pine Canyon

Sycamore

5600

Willow

Windy Point

6000

Canyon

N

5600

6107

6000

SPRING

TRAIL

6370

Seven Cataracts

Bear

4800

6/66

6264

Bug Spring

6090

5822

Prospects

Sycamore Canyon

Sycamore Spring Reservoir

5503

Reservoir

Reservoir

5200

5600

4800

Canyon

4800

Gibbon Mtn
580?

4800

FEDERAL HONOR CAMP

5153

Mercer Spring

Molino Basin

Picnic Area

4800

ner than above, with scrubby clumps of Mexican pinyon pine, one-seed juniper, shrub live oak, alligator juniper and manzanita growing in place of the ponderosa forests from which we have descended.

At a small rock shelf overlooking Palisade Canyon we resume switchbacking steeply downhill, passing many fine vistas. A surprising variety of wildflowers bloom in the spring on these dry, rocky slopes, including bright red Indian paintbrush, purple-tufted thistle, parry penstemon and aster. As you continue to lose elevation, look also for brittlebush, desert marigold, and low-growing mats of verbena. At length the trail makes a long traverse to the southeast, then drops down into lower Pine Canyon. Here we cross Pine Creek (water during rainy periods only) to a signed junction (6.4; 4080), where we turn right. There are several good campsites nearby (and for a mile or so downstream), shaded by a healthy riparian growth of large Mexican blue oaks and syca-mores. As we proceed gently down-canyon from the last fork, Pine Creek falls away gradually below, and the trail drops down a switchback or two to keep pace. After 1 mile the Box Camp Trail branches right, but we continue straight ahead a few hundred feet farther to the signed junction with the Sabino Canyon Trail (7.5; 3680). To complete your trek from here, turn right and reverse the steps of the first half of Trip 32 the remaining 2.5 miles to Sabino Canyon Roadend (10.0; 3330).

See Maps 13, 12 and 11

Trip 37   Mount Lemmon Highway to Sabino Canyon Roadend via the Box Camp Trail

9.3 miles one-way (37-mile car shuttle required); 4700′ elevation loss, negligible gain

Moderate dayhike or leisurely backpack (2 hiking days)

Season April to November

Water available all season at Box Spring (near mile 1.8); Palisade Creek (mile 6.7) has water during rainy periods only

Features

Before the construction of the Mount Lemmon Highway, the Box Camp Trail provided the quickest access to the Soldier Camp area in the high country. Today this historic track is a bit overgrown, though still easy to follow, and hikers will find it an interesting and highly scenic route through the heart of the wild Santa Catalinas.

Description

From the Box Camp Trailhead on Mount Lemmon Highway (0.0; 8040), climb steeply a short distance, pass beneath a power line, and then proceed gently up and down through a forest of magnificent ponderosa and Mexican white pines, intermixed with some white fir and Douglas-fir. After passing beneath the summit of Spencer Peak we follow a broad ridgeline southward, gaining occasional glimpses of the forested Santa Catalina high country through the trees to either side. During the autumn months, small stands of frost-yellowed aspens add flecks of color to the dark green slopes beneath Marshall Peak, across the deep gap of Sabino Canyon to the west. About a mile beyond the highway we drop steeply a short distance into a minor drainage, which we follow more gently downhill through a grassy, parklike area. Camping would be delightful here, but water is generally available only on the heels of the spring snowmelt and following very heavy rains. After crossing this drainage a few times the trail winds steeply downhill to a signed junction (1.8; 7440) with the right-branching spur to Box Spring. The spring, 0.3 miles down the sidetrail, apparently flows year-round. This area is the site of old Box Camp, a late 19th century military way-station of which very few traces remain.

Beyond here the trail passes through a minor saddle, then commences switchbacking moderately-to-steeply down a ridgeline. As we lose elevation the forest cover steadily thins out, and good views open up across the Catalina foothills to the Rincon and Santa Rita mountains. After descending some 1800 vertical feet, we drop into a rocky, oak-and-pinyon-forested drainage, which contains unreliable Apache Spring (4.5; 5560) (water only during very wet periods). The trail climbs out of this small watercourse via a saddle to the west, then descends the slopes above Box Camp Canyon, alternating long, downhill traverses with spates of very steep (and somewhat brushy) switchbacks. The ground cover continues to grow sparser as we drop, and by the time the trail levels off temporarily to cross a minor drainage basin, saguaro, prickly pear, mesquite and ocotillo have begun to appear.

Soon the trail resumes its very steep, switchbacking descent, bottoming out at Palisade Creek (6.6; 3760). There is delightful camping hereabouts, in a nice riparian forest of rustling sycamores and shady Mexican blue oaks. The creek flows only during rainy periods. After crossing the streambed, we proceed a short distance to a fork, turn left, and continue about 200 yards to a signed junction with the Sabino Canyon Trail. To complete your journey from here, turn left again and reverse the steps of the first half of Trip 32 the remaining 2.5 miles to Sabino Canyon Roadend (9.3; 3330).

See Maps 13, 12 and 11

Trip 38   Marshall Gulch Picnic Area to Sabino Canyon

6.4 miles round trip; 1420' elevation gain

Moderate dayhike or backpack (2 hiking days)

Season April to November

Water available all season along entire route

Features

Sabino Creek is one of only two perennial streams in the Pusch Ridge Wilderness, and this trip is included mainly for the benefit of anglers who wish to match wits with the trout that are stocked in it. Nonfishermen need not stay at home, however; they will find enjoyable camping at many spots, or can simply come and enjoy the quiet company of the stream for a few hours.

This route is cross-country all the way, and recommended for fairly experienced hikers only. Many sections of the creekbed are quite rough, and the going is often slow, so allow yourself plenty of time for this one.

Description

From Marshall Gulch Picnic Area (0.0; 7420) follow Sabino Creek directly down Sabino Canyon. The canyonsides above the stream are heavily forested with towering Douglas-firs, Gambel oaks and a few ponderosa pines, but the creekbanks themselves are too rocky and floodswept to support much more than water-loving willows and alders and an occasional stubborn bigtooth maple or two. It is possible to make reasonably rapid progress at first, but the canyon bottom soon becomes a maze of giant boulders which must be patiently scrambled over, around, and occasionally under. After the first mile or so the gorge widens out considerably and the going gets a bit easier. Scattered between here and the end of our route are occasional good campsites. (Because of the summer homes upstream, water from the creek should be purified before drinking.)

The Arizona Game and Fish Department stocks this part of Sabino Creek by helicopter with brown and rainbow trout, and fishermen will want to test their skills at the many pools here. Most of the fish are "pan-size" or smaller, though a few 16 and 18 inchers have reportedly been taken. Getting into and out of some stretches of the creek can be difficult because of boulders and brush.

At a point about 3 miles from the start — a distance that may seem twice as long because of the many brushy "boxes" and small falls which must be negotiated en route — a major tributary drainage drops down from the right (north) into Sabino Canyon (3.2; 6000). This point marks the end of our excursion. It is possible for skilled bushwackers to continue downstream from here to Hutch's Pool and the West Fork Sabino Trail, but the going is exceptionally difficult, even dangerous in places. Most hikers will probably have gotten enough of a taste of this rugged canyon by the time they get this far, anyway.

Return the way you came.

See Map 12

Trip 39   Aspen Loop (Marshall Gulch Picnic Area to Marshall Saddle and return)

3.7 mile loop trip; 780´ elevation gain

Leisurely dayhike

Season April to November

Water available all season in Marshall Gulch (miles 3.2 to 3.7)

Features

This trip, a fine, leisurely introduction to the varying moods of the Santa Catalina high country, has two chief attractions: a lovely grove of tall, straight-trunked aspens, and the lush, maple-lined defile of Marshall Gulch. Portions of the route are particularly beautiful during the fall, when sharp frosts nip at the yellowing, reddening leaves.

Description

From Marshall Gulch Picnic Area (0.0; 7420) follow the signed Aspen Trail as it climbs steeply across a hillside to the southeast. The severe gradient quickly eases, and we climb more moderately through a dense forest cover of Gambel oak, white fir and Douglas-fir, and some sun-loving Mexican white pine. Keep your eyes open for the Coues white-tailed deer that are occasionally seen through here. In a little less than half a mile the path drops slightly, then enters an open, parklike grove of mature aspens — an excellent spot to lay out a picnic spread, or simply to lie beneath the trees and enjoy the peace and quiet. Young aspens thrive in recently burned areas — this very opening may well have been cleared by a small blaze started by summer lightning — where they serve to enrich the blackened soil for the conifers that will eventually, in the course of natural succession, replace them. Beautiful in any season, aspen groves can be particularly striking during the fall, when the leaves turn, and in early spring, when the bone-white, leafless trunks stand in ghostly contrast to their dark-green coniferous surroundings.

A short distance beyond this grove the trail switchbacks very steeply up an oak- and ponderosa-forested ridgeline. After gaining several hundred feet of elevation the route levels off and traverses westward past a few minor ups and downs. At a signed junction with a spur trail to Lunch Ledge we stay right, and soon begin an occasionally steep descent that presently brings us to Marshall Saddle (2.5; 7960), a broad gap in a sunny, airy forest of ponderosa. At a signed, 4-way junction here our route turns right and drops into the head of Marshall Gulch. Soon we sidle up alongside a streamcourse, which usually contains at least intermittent pools of water. The canyonsides here are forested with pines and firs, and nice copses of Arizona alder and bigtooth maple line the banks of the tiny creek. A variety of wildflowers bloom in this lush area throughout the summer, including fleabane, aspen sunflower, and exuberant blue spikes of lupine.

Take your time in ambling through this serene, leafy canyon, for all too soon the trail leads us back to Marshall Gulch Picnic Area (3.7; 7420), just across the parking lot from where our trip began.

See Map 12

Trip 40   Marshall Gulch Picnic Area to Lemmon Creek and the Wilderness of Rocks

7.8 miles round trip; 1740' elevation gain

Moderate dayhike or leisurely backpack (2 hiking days)

Season April to November

Water available all season at Lemmon Creek (mile 3.6)

Features

This route climbs up lushly-forested Marshall Gulch to Marshall Saddle, then drops into the headwaters of Lemmon Creek, where backpackers will find perennial water and excellent camping. Just beyond is the Wilderness of Rocks, a fantasyland of wierdly eroded granite outcroppings that will whet the curiosity of the explorer.

Description

From Marshall Gulch Picnic Area (0.0; 7420), follow the signed Marshall Saddle/Wilderness of Rocks Trail up the shady defile of Marshall Gulch. The trail climbs gently-to-moderately through here, staying to the right of a small creek, which almost always flows at least intermittently. The slopes above the stream support some nice stands of ponderosa pine, Mexican white pine and white fir, while bigtooth maples and tangles of willow and alder flourish along the watercourse. Aspen sunflower, lupine and fleabane are among the wildflowers which dot the canyonsides during the summer.

The angle of ascent steepens as we approach the head of the gulch, and presently we top out at Marshall Saddle (1.2; 7960), where, in an open forest of ponderosa, there is a signed 4-way junction. Our route goes straight ahead at this crossroads, and then drops moderately to the west. After ¼ mile we pass a large rock outcropping—a precursor of many such formations to be met below. Beyond here we cross Lemmon Creek (which may be dry at this point) near its head, then continue descending more gently. As we gradually lose elevation, the forest cover of pines and firs is invaded by increasing numbers of silverleaf oak and Arizona white oak. A little over a mile after leaving Marshall Saddle the trail recrosses the creek and passes a good campsite by a copse of diminutive aspens. About 0.5 mile and several creek crossings later we reach a poorly signed, potentially confusing junction by the stream (2.9; 7280). Our route stays left here and continues down the creek a bit, then cuts to the left and meanders across the exposed tops of some low rock outcrops. The trail is often faint through here, but ducks and blazes generally show up to guide you at critical junctures.

Beyond this section we drop down and make one final crossing of Lemmon Creek. There is an excellent campsite here, and water is always available in pools along the streambed. After crossing the latter, the trail makes a short, steep climb up the far canyonside, then winds southwestward into the Wilderness of Rocks (3.9; 7100), an extensive maze of water-sculpted granitic domes, pinnacles and "balanced rocks" of every manner and shape. Several layover days could be spent exploring this delightful area. Cozy, secluded campsites can be found everywhere, but water generally has to be packed in from nearby Lemmon Creek.

Return the way you came.

See Map 12

Trip 41

Marshall Gulch Picnic Area to Sabino Canyon Roadend via the Wilderness of Rocks, Romero Pass and Hutch's Pool

15.8 miles one-way (40-mile car shuttle required); 5520′ elevation loss, 1440′ gain

Strenuous dayhike or moderate backpack (3 hiking days)

Season April to November

Water available all year at Lemmon Creek (mile 3.6) and Hutch's Pool (near mile 11.8)

Features

Roaming the mountains from top to bottom, this fine ramble gives the hiker a taste of everything the Santa Catalinas have to offer: hushed, cathedral-like forests of pine and fir; picturesquely eroded pinnacles and crags; wide-open vistas across rugged ridges and canyons; oak- and sycamore-shaded creeks; and rocky hillsides studded with saguaro cacti. The presence of perennial water and good campsites at Lemmon and Sabino creeks makes this an excellent choice for a 3-day backpack, even during spells of dry weather.

Parts of this route are rather hard to follow, and it is recommended only for reasonably experienced wilderness travelers.

Description

From Marshall Gulch Picnic Area (0.0; 7420), follow the route of Trip 40 to the Wilderness of Rocks (3.9; 7100). As we skirt the edge of this wonderfully sculpted area, most of the rock formations are off to the right, or north. Soon a pair of short, steep climbs bring us to an ill-defined saddle, where we exit the Wilderness of Rocks and proceed to meander up and down across the next basin. The trail is occasionally faint through here — look for ducks to guide you. After another short ascent we arrive at a signed junction with the Mount Lemmon Trail (5.4; 7280), atop a high ridge affording a nice view down the western Catalina slope. Our route goes left here and, after climbing for ¼ mile, passes just to the left of a huge, flat rock. Those who scramble out to the edge of this rock will be rewarded with a fabulous overview of the rugged bighorn-sheep country sprawling at the base of craggy Pusch Ridge.

Beyond here the rough trail drops, very steeply at times, toward Romero Pass, through a mixed forest cover of Arizona white oaks, silverleaf oaks, some thick-girthed alligator junipers, Mexican pinyon pines, ponderosa pines and, near the top of the descent, a few Douglas-firs. Views are excellent much of the way down: to the west lies the deep defile of Romero Canyon, and to the south and east, rising in the distance beyond the Catalina foothills, stand the Santa Rita and Rincon ranges.

At length we drop into Romero Pass (6.6; 6040). From a junction here our route goes left, descends moderately down a ridgeline for 0.5 mile, then cuts back right and reaches another junction near the head of West Fork Sabino Canyon. Here we turn left, proceed downhill 0.6 mile, and cross the usually dry bed of West Fork Sabino Creek to yet another junction (8.4; 5280). To complete your journey from here, turn left and follow the second half of Trip 31 past Hutch's Pool to Sabino Canyon Roadend (15.8; 3330).

See Maps 12, 10 and 9

in the Wilderness of Rocks

Trip 42

East Speedway Trailhead to Douglas Spring

12.2 miles round trip; 2250′ elevation gain

Moderate dayhike or backpack (2 hiking days)

Season November to April

Water available at Tina Larga Tank (near mile 3.0) and Douglas Spring (mile 6.1) during rainy periods only

Features

Beginning in a region which is a veritable showcase of Lower Sonoran vegetation, and part of Saguaro National Monument, this route soon climbs into the foothills of the Rincon Mountains and wanders through open forests of oak and juniper to Douglas Spring, where the Park Service maintains a trail camp. Along the way there are a number of pleasant vistas, both of the forested tops of the Rincons, swelling high above the hiker, and of metropolitan Tucson, sprawling across the flatlands so far below.

Description

From the trailhead at the end of East Speedway Road (0.0; 2750), walk a little south of east through a beautiful vegetative cover of exuberant, red-blossoming ocotillos, yellow paloverdes, creosote bushes, pale green prickly pears, staghorn, jumping and teddy-bear chollas, and some magnificent saguaros. During the spring months one can spend hours here identifying wildflowers; some of the more common ones you will likely see are brittlebush blossoms, delicate yellow paperflowers, narrowleaf asters and desert marigolds, not to mention the blossoms that appear on all the trees, shrubs and cacti mentioned above.

A few unsigned use trails come and go along this stretch as our route heads steadily eastward and, in ¾ mile, begins climbing moderately up a low ridge. Soon we work our way up a drainage to a minor saddle (2.2; 3720), where we pass through a fence that is part of the old Aguila Corral. From here the trail drops slightly, then winds back and forth across a wash that supports a few mesquite trees and some seepwillows. After exiting this wash we continue climbing moderately until we reach the crest of another low ridge, just beyond which is an unsigned trail junction (3.0; 4360).

The faint spur trail that branches south leads in about 300 yards to Tina Larga Tank, an artificially augmented catchment basin that holds water for a surprising length of time after heavy rains.

Staying left at this junction, we climb a short distance, then meander up and down across a rolling area, through a light forest cover of doughty alligator junipers, one-seed junipers and Mexican blue oaks. The rocky protuberance of Helens Dome is visible straight ahead, as is the high, pine-forested country around Mica Mountain. Off to the right stands Tanque Verde Peak, while far below to the left one can see Portoritas Tank, an artificial pond similar to Tina Larga Tank.

After topping a low, rather ill-defined ridgeline, the trail drops very gently down to Douglas Spring (6.1; 4680), where there are campsites equipped with tables, stoves and a toilet. A few velvet ash trees grow along the creekbed, along with the preponderant oaks and junipers, and the bright blossoms of thistle, parry penstemon, and desert marigold provide touches of color here and there during spring. The creek is the only source of water here, and it runs only during the rainy season. A camping permit is necessary for overnight stays.

Return the way you came.

See Maps 14 and 15

Manning Cabin

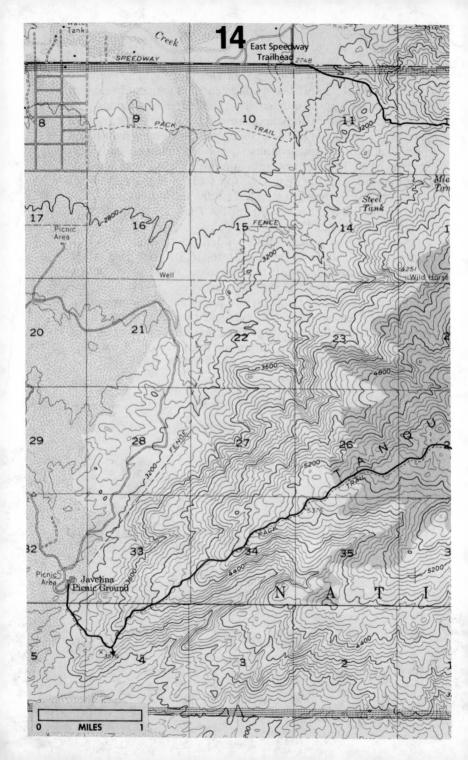

15

Trip 43

East Speedway Trailhead to
Manning Camp

24.8 miles round trip; 5800' elevation gain

Moderate to strenuous backpack (2–4 hiking days)

Season March to November

Water available all season at Manning Camp (mile 12.4); Tina Larga Tank (near mile 3.0) and Douglas Spring (mile 6.1) have water only during rainy periods

Features

This fine backpacking route, a good choice for a 3–5 day outing, climbs into the Rincon Mountains high country via Douglas Spring Campground and Cow Head Saddle. Along the way it passes through vegetation communities representing four distinct life zones — Lower Sonoran, Upper Sonoran, Transition and (if you elect to visit the north slope of Mica Mountain) Canadian. Manning Camp is a delightful campsite that offers hikers a choice of layover day activities — those with energy to burn can visit Mica Fire Tower, a lookout perched atop the highest point in the Rincons, while less energetic hikers can stretch out in the shade of a tall ponderosa pine, resting their bones, watching the sun track slowly across the deep blue sky, and listening to the wind as it sighs in the boughs.

Description

From East Speedway Trailhead (0.0; 2750), follow Trip 42 to Douglas Spring Campground (6.1; 4680). From here we continue along the Douglas Spring Trail, which swings southward and climbs — gently at first, then more steeply — through a scrubby vegetative cover of small Mexican pinyons, hardy alligator junipers, manzanita, cliff rose, Emory and shrub live oak, and Arizona rosewood. Shortly after working our way into a small canyon we pass through a fence, then climb steeply on a few switchbacks to Cow Head Saddle (8.5; 6120). The forest overstory is denser and shadier at this altitude, with silverleaf oak and ponderosa pine beginning to supplant the pinyons and junipers.

At a signed junction in the saddle we turn left and climb moderately-to-steeply in the direction of Helens Dome, the rocky crag which now and then can be seen ahead through the trees. After about 2.5 miles of continuous climbing the trail suddenly drops slightly, then crosses a minor drainage. There may be a trickle of water here in early spring; if so, you may see some Coues white-tailed deer stepping cautiously out of the surrounding forest for a drink. We next follow this watercourse gently uphill for a short distance, then climb more steeply to a signed junction with the North Slope Trail (11.8; 8040). Our route goes right at this fork, climbs a bit, and then drops steadily past the clearly signed, left-branching Fire Loop Trail to Manning Camp (12.4; 7940), where you will find perennial water, camp stoves and tables, a toilet, and a cabin and corral used by the Park Service, all shaded by a dense forest of mature ponderosa pines.

Manning Camp makes an excellent base for exploring the surrounding high country. A number of fine side trips are possible. Perhaps the best of these is the 5.3-mile loop hike up to Mica Mountain and Italian Spring (mileages given below indicate distances from Manning Camp, not from East Speedway Trail-head): At the signed junction just north of the Park Service cabin at Manning Camp, turn right and walk northeast up the floor of a minor drainage. At a succession of two signed forks we stay left; at a third, unsigned split, we veer right. As the trail climbs gradually up and around the east shoulder of Mica Mountain we catch occasional glimpses through the trees of Spud Rock and Mica Fire Tower. Just below Mica's rounded summit is a signed junction, where the trail to Italian Spring branches right; here we turn left and proceed 0.1 mile to the base of the lookout tower (1.4; 8666). To get a clear view from this, the highest summit in the Rincons, one must climb the tower to above treetop level. (Don't bother going all the way to the top, since the observation room is securely locked.) The vista from here is magnificent, with the green forests of the Rincons spreading in every direction below, melting by degrees into brownish foothills, gray valleys and plains, and a distant, encircling ring of blue mountains. Among the more obvious landmarks are Tanque Verde Peak (to the southwest), Rincon Peak (to the south), the Santa Catalina Mountains (to the northwest), Mount Wrightson (far to the south) and the Galiuro Mountains (to the northeast).

When ready to continue our sidetrip, we retrace our steps 0.1 mile to the preceding junction, turn left, and descend gently along a grassy ridgetop. At a fork about ¼ mile later the route goes left, then switchbacks down to Italian Spring (2.3; 8000), a dependable

year-round water source. At a junction here we turn left, onto the
North Slope Trail, and climb a few switchbacks to a saddle between small rock outcroppings. In early spring a few patches of
snow may linger in this area. For the next 2 miles the trail traverses
the northwest shoulder of Mica Mountain, gently rising and falling
over short distances and passing through some magnificent stands
of ponderosa pine, Mexican white pine, Douglas-fir and white fir.
The latter two species, generally associated with the Canadian life
zone, are not at all common elsewhere in the Rincons, but they
flourish on this high, north-facing slope.

At the end of this traverse we climb a few switchbacks,
detouring above a smooth, sloping slab of rock (the top of which
affords an excellent view of the distant Santa Catalina range).
After switchbacking back down the far side of the slab, the North
Slope Trail reaches a gap behind the monolith of Helens Dome,
just beyond which is the junction with the trail coming up from
Cow Head Saddle (4.7; 8040). Here we turn left and complete our
sidetrip by retracing the steps of our earlier route back to Manning
Camp (5.3; 7940).

Return the way you came.

See Maps 14, 15 and 16

ponderosa forest near Manning Camp

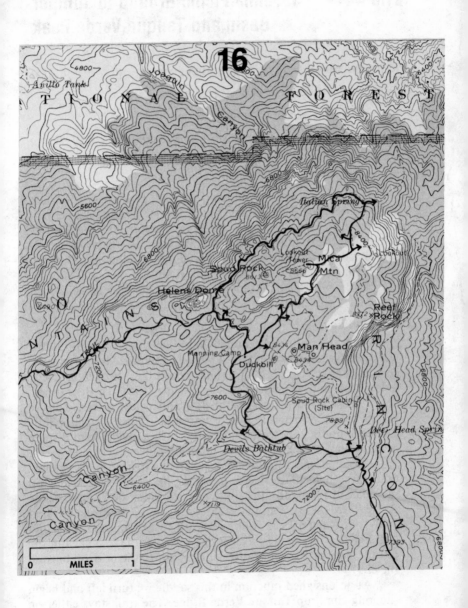

Trip 44 Javelina Picnic Ground to Juniper Basin and Tanque Verde Peak

17.6 miles round trip; 4080 ' elevation gain

Strenuous dayhike or backpack (2–3 hiking days)

Season all year, except after snowstorms

Water available at Juniper Basin Campground (mile 6.7) during rainy periods only (check with Park Service first)

Features

This strenuous route follows the broad, gradually rising back of Tanque Verde Ridge to 7049-foot Tanque Verde Peak, which affords a commanding view of both Tucson and the Rincon Mountains backcountry. Along the way the trail winds among tall saguaros, climbs wildflower-dotted slopes, and passes through delightful forests of oak, pinyon and juniper.

Strong hikers can make it to Tanque Verde Peak and back in a single day, but this trip is best done as a 2- or 3-day backpack.

Description

From the trailhead near Javelina Picnic Ground (0.0; 3120), walk gently downhill through a varied ground cover of magnificent saguaros, ocotillos, foothill paloverdes, hedgehog cacti, teddy-bear and staghorn chollas, prickly pear, brittlebushes, desert zinnias, purple-tufted thistles, narrowleaf asters, delicate yellow paperflowers, and desert marigolds. This rich panoply of Lower Sonoran zone vegetation puts forth a magnificent display of blossoms during the spring months, especially in wet years. After descending a short distance we cross a pair of small, shallow drainages, then climb, steeply in places, past a fence to a ridgetop saddle (1.0; 3480) atop the southwest extremity of Tanque Verde Ridge. Here there is a nice view eastward, across Madrona Basin to 8482-foot Rincon Peak, and westward to Tucson and the Santa Catalina Mountains. On a clear day it is possible to make out the distant spire of Picacho Butte, poking above the horizon beyond the city.

At an unsigned junction in this saddle we turn left and begin the long climb up Tanque Verde Ridge. The trail stays either on top of or just to the left of the top of the broad ridge, paralleling a fence much of the way. The grade along this ascent varies from level to steep, with very few switchbacks to even things out. As we gain elevation the saguaros and paloverdes of the Lower Sonoran life zone give way to sotol, amole and nolina, indicating that we have climbed into a grassland community of the Upper Sonoran zone. Shiny flecks of mica, a silicate mineral common in the Rincons, appear underfoot here and there.

After passing through a gate (3.3; 4800) we continue climbing, a bit less steeply now, then top out at a hump on the ridge and descend a short distance to a gap. Beyond here we climb again, soon entering a patchy forest cover of Emory oaks, hardy Mexican pinyons, spiny Schott's yuccas and stout-trunked alligator junipers that grows increasingly dense as we gain elevation. After rollercoastering over a few ups and downs the trail crosses a small, sandy wash (usually dry), then proceeds across a comparatively level section a mile or so to Juniper Basin Campground (6.7; 5960), where there are tables, camp stoves, toilets, and the ruin of an old cement cabin, all set in the dappled shade of an oak-juniper woodland. The only source of water here is a tiny creeklet that generally flows only during rainy periods (and sometimes not even then; check it out with the Park Service if you will be depending on it for water). A camping permit is needed for overnight stays.

To continue to Tanque Verde Peak from here, follow the trail as it climbs gently onto the ridge east of Juniper Basin. Once on this ridge we climb more steeply, gaining some nice views of Rincon Peak, looming closer now than before, and of the heavily forested crown of Mica Mountain, rising above the Manning Camp area. A smattering of ponderosa pines can be seen down in a basin to the right.

Presently we round a bend on the ridge, and the rocky cap of Tanque Verde Peak appears directly ahead. A few short, steep climbs now bring us to a signed junction (8.8; 7040), where we turn right and climb a short distance farther to a register at the base of the peak's summit monolith. A tricky 10 foot rock scramble is necessary to reach the highest point from here. Those who figure out how to get on top are rewarded with a spectacular 360-degree vista that fully compensates for the laborious hike up. Included in this panorama are the Santa Rita and Huachuca Mountains, the Little Rincons (peeking above Happy Valley Saddle, the wide gap between Mica Mountain and Rincon Peak), the Galiuro and the Santa Catalina Mountains, and the city of Tucson. Foregrounding these views are the broad, sweeping slopes of Tanque Verde Ridge, which fall away in gentle waves in every direction. This isolated aerie is an excellent place from which to observe red-tailed hawks and golden eagles, a few of which can almost always be seen soaring and hunting against the vast backdrop of desert and mountains sprawling below. Caution: do not remain in the summit area if a thunderstorm appears to be brewing.

Return the way you came.

See Maps 14 and 15

Trip 45   Javelina Picnic Ground to Manning Camp

30.4 miles round trip; 6960 ' elevation gain

Strenuous backpack (4 hiking days)

Season March to November

Water available year-round at Manning Camp (mile 15.4); Juniper Basin Campground (mile 6.7) has water following rainy periods only

Features

After making the long, stiff climb up to Tanque Verde Peak, this route drops into Cow Head Saddle and then climbs into the high country at Manning Camp, where, in a delightfully shady forest of ponderosa, hikers will find relief from the searing heat of lowland summers. Plan on spending at least one layover day exploring the cool, pine- and fir-forested highlands surrounding nearby 8666-foot Mica Mountain, the highest point in the Rincons.

Description

From the trailhead near Javelina Picnic Ground (0.0; 3120), follow the Tanque Verde Ridge Trail past Juniper Basin Campground to the trail junction just below Tanque Verde Peak (8.8; 7040) (see Trip 44). After making the short sidetrip up to Tanque Verde Peak's isolated, commanding summit, continue along the main trail, which descends moderately-to-steeply eastward through a semishady forest cover of ponderosa pine and silverleaf oak. After about a mile, the angle of this descent eases, and the trail makes a few ups and downs before dropping into Cow Head Saddle (11.3; 6120). At a signed junction here we go straight ahead and climb moderately-to-steeply in the direction of Helens Dome, the craggy monolith that can be glimpsed on occasion through the thickening forest cover. After about 2.5 miles of continuous climbing the trail drops slightly, then crosses a minor drainage which may contain a trickle of water during early spring. We next follow this watercourse gently uphill for a short distance, then climb more steeply to a signed junction with the North Slope Trail (14.6; 8040), coming over from Italian Spring. Our route goes right at this fork, climbs a bit, and then drops steadily (past the clearly signed, left-branching Fire Loop Trail) to Manning Camp (15.2; 7940), where there are year-round water, camp stoves and tables, and a toilet. Manning Cabin is used to house Park Service back-country personnel. Camping is delightful here, beneath a shady forest of Arizona white oak, silverleaf oak, and dense stands of mature ponderosa pine. A number of worthwhile side trips can be made from this centrally located spot; one of the finest of these, the 5.3-mile loop trip up to Mica Mountain and Italian Spring, is described in Trip 43.

Return the way you came, or via the Douglas Spring Trail to East Speedway Trailhead (9-mile car shuttle required; see Trip 43).

See Maps 14, 15 and 16

prickly pear cacti after spring storm

Trip 46   Miller Creek to Happy Valley Saddle Campground and Rincon Peak

16.2 miles round trip; 4280 ' elevation gain

Strenuous dayhike or backpack (2–3 hiking days)

Season April to November

Water available at Happy Valley Saddle Campground (mile 4.9) and at mile 6.7 during early spring and following periods of heavy rain

Features

This trip follows the shortest and least strenuous route to Rincon Peak, whose lofty, isolated crown affords one of the finest vistas in the entire state. It is still far from easy, however, entailing an elevation gain of over 4000 feet, and should be attempted only by those in good physical condition. Hikers who are both able and willing to invest the effort required to reach the top can be sure of reaping a commensurate dividend — the pride and satisfaction which are not earned with the attainment of easier summits.

Description

From the trailhead (0.0; 4200) follow the Miller Creek Trail up the imperceptibly sloping floor of Miller Canyon. After the first half mile or so, this canyon temporarily deepens and narrows; above this section, where the defile begins to open out again, we cross a succession of rocky side drainages, then veer to the left and climb steeply out of the main canyon. The route soon begins switchbacking uphill, through a scrubby forest cover of emory oak, Mexican blue oak and Mexican pinyon. As we gain elevation a nice view opens up across Happy Valley to the Little Rincon Mountains.

At length, after negotiating several short, steep climbs interspersed among lengthy sieges of switchbacks, we arrive at a saddle of sorts (3.6; 5800). Here the trail swings left onto the wall of a small ravine, which is then followed to its head at Happy Valley Saddle (4.3; 6160). After turning left at a signed junction in this broad, ponderosa-forested gap, we follow a gently descending, usually dry streambed to a junction with the signed Rincon Peak Trail (4.9; 6080). A hundred yards or so down the right-branching trail, in a serene forest of ponderosa pine, silverleaf and Arizona white oak, and Schott's yucca, is Happy Valley Saddle Campground. Here there are tables, stoves, a toilet and, in early spring, running water. Backpackers will need a permit from the Park Service to spend the night here.

To reach Rincon Peak from the campground, retrace your steps to the last junction. Turning right here (left, if coming directly from the Miller Creek Trail), we next follow the Rincon Peak Trail southward as it winds over a few ups and downs, then strikes off through a nice forest of oak and alligator juniper. Once beyond this rather flat area the trail begins climbing again, alternating long, uphill traverses with spates of steep switchbacks. At a small, rocky drainage (6.7; 7000) there may be a trickle of water.

As we continue to gain elevation we enter the partial shade of a moderate forest cover of Douglas-fir, white fir and, in the sunnier spots, Mexican white pine.

About 2.5 miles beyond Happy Valley Saddle the gradient suddenly grows exceptionally steep (so steep that the Park Service has closed this section of the trail to equestrian use). After grunting and straining up numerous dizzily canted switchbacks, we skirt a small copse of aspens (some of the very few aspens to be found in the Rincons), and then arrive at a trail register just below Rincon Peak. From here a rudimentary path wanders the remaining 200 yards up to the high point (8.1; 8482), where you will find a tall cairn, a summit register, and a world of mountains and valleys sprawling across the vast landscape at your feet. On a clear day, when a storm has cleansed the air of its dusty burden and a legion of broken clouds trail their deep blue shadows behind them across the refreshed earth, the view from this commanding summit can be unforgettable. With the aid of a detailed map it is possible to identify at least a dozen distinct mountain ranges, including the Baboquivaris, the Galiuros, the Santa Catalinas, and the Santa Ritas, to name just a few.

This peak is an obvious target for lightning bolts; should a thunderstorm appear to be brewing, vacate the summit immediately.

When thoroughly sated with vistas, return the way you came.

See Map 17

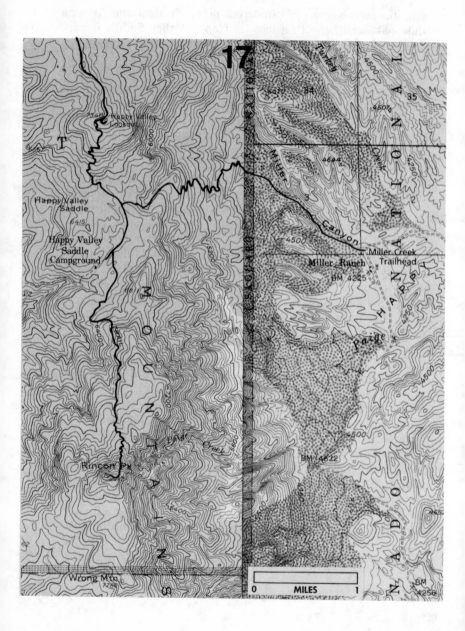

Trip 47   Miller Creek to East Speedway Trailhead via Happy Valley Saddle, Manning Camp and Douglas Spring Campground

23.0 miles one-way (50-mile car shuttle required); 4780 ' elevation gain

Strenuous backpack (3 hiking days)

Season March to November

Water available all season at Manning Camp (mile 10.6); Happy Valley Saddle Campground (near mile 4.4) and Douglas Spring Campground (mile 16.9) have water during rainy periods only

Features

This lengthy transmontane route can be rushed through in as few as two days, but ideally it should be stretched out over at least five, with layover days spent at Happy Valley Saddle and Manning Camp campgrounds. This pace allows one to make the highly scenic detours to Mica Mountain and Rincon Peak. Happy Valley and Tanque Verde peaks are also easily accessible from points along the route. This trek is thus a peakbagger's delight, passing within side-tripping distance of all of the Rincons' highest and most prominent summits.

Description

From Miller Creek Trailhead (0.0; 4200), follow the route of Trip 46 up to the signed trail junction in Happy Valley Saddle (4.3; 6160). Most backpackers will want to spend the first night of their trek at Happy Valley Saddle Campground, 0.6 mile down the trail to the left. A layover day here will allow you to make the strenuous but highly recommended side trip to 8482-foot Rincon Peak (6.4 miles round trip from the campground; see Trip 46).

When ready to continue our journey, we proceed northwest from Happy Valley Saddle and soon commence switchbacking steeply uphill, through a mixed forest cover of stunted ponderosa pine, Mexican pinyon, Emory oak, Arizona white oak, silverleaf oak, spiny Schott's yucca and alligator juniper. At length, after gaining 1000 feet of elevation, the trail swings left onto the west shoulder of Happy Valley Peak, levels off, and traverses across to a signed junction (6.3; 7200) just below Happy Valley Lookout. An 0.2-mile-long, switchbacking spur leads from here to the 7348 foot summit, which affords fine views of Rincon Peak, Tanque Verde Peak, Mica Mountain, the Galiuro Mountains and the Little Rincons.

From this junction the trail drops slightly onto Heartbreak Ridge, whose mostly shadeless crest is then followed northwest-ward, up and over three minor rises, to a fork (7.9; 7120), where the signed East Fork Trail veers right. We stay left here, on the Heartbreak Ridge Trail, and climb steeply up a brushy slope to a signed, 4-way junction (8.4; 7560). Our route now turns left, traverses a few hundred yards to a minor, ponderosa-forested ridgecrest, then drops slightly and crosses a tiny creeklet (9.1; 7440) (water during early spring and after heavy rains only). Just downstream from here is Devils Bathtub, where the creek (when it is running) spills down a 50-foot waterfall into a small pool at the bottom of a smooth, water-worn granite bowl. During warm weather, hikers may wish to scramble down into this bowl for an impromptu dip.

About 0.5 miles beyond the Bathtub we meet the signed Man-ning Camp Trail coming up from Grass Shack Spring; here we turn right and ascend a few switchbacks into a rockbound stream chan-nel. After paralleling a streamlet (water in early spring and follow-ing heavy rains) for a short distance, the trail crosses to the left and climbs steeply into a thickening forest of ponderosa pine. The angle of this ascent soon eases, and shortly we arrive at Manning Camp (10.6; 7920), where there are camp tables and stoves, a toilet and year-round water. Manning Cabin is used by Park Service backcountry personnel. Many fine side trips can be made from here; one of the best of these, the 5.3-mile loop trip up to lofty Mica Mountain and Italian Spring, is described in Trip 43.

To complete your trek across the Rincons, reverse the steps of Trip 43 to Douglas Spring Campground (16.9; 4680) and East Speedway Trailhead (23.0; 2750). Alternatively, follow the Tanque Verde Ridge Trail from Cow Head Saddle out to Javelina Picnic Ground (26.0 miles total; reverse the steps of Trip 45).

See Maps 17, 16, 15 and 14

Trip 48   Bog Springs Campground to Bog Springs, Kent Spring and Sylvester Spring

4.8 mile semiloop trip; 1600 ' elevation gain

Moderate dayhike or leisurely backpack (2 hiking days)

Season all year, except following snowstorms

Water is usually available at Bog, Kent and Sylvester springs (miles 1.4, 2.7 and 3.1); check with Forest Service during spells of very dry weather

Features

Easily completed in half a day, yet encompassing a variety of fine vistas, this pleasant ramble is a good introduction to the Santa Rita Mountains. Included on the itinerary are four near-perennial watering holes, making this an especially good route for observing wildlife.

Description

From the trailhead at Bog Springs Campground (0.0; 5080) follow a rocky jeep track (now closed to motor vehicles) as it crosses a small drainage, then ascends moderately through a forest cover of emory oak, Arizona white oak, alligator juniper and silverleaf oak. The road steepens a bit as it climbs up to a saddle (0.7; 5340). A cairn here marks the beginning of a narrow trail which can be seen sneaking off to the left; we turn onto it and work our way up onto a hillside that affords a pleasant view across Madera Canyon to the tawny grasslands beyond. About 0.6 mile after leaving the road we cross a small drainage, then climb a short distance to Bog Springs (1.4; 5880). Here there are a few fair campsites, beneath a shady overstory of Arizona walnuts, rustling sycamores, silverleaf oaks, some tall Apache pines, and a few Douglas-firs. This is a good spot to observe wildlife; Mexican jays are common (as are a variety of other birds — see Trip 49 for a partial listing of species that might be seen in this area), and wild turkeys and Coues white-tailed deer are frequent visitors during the cooler months of the year. The spring almost always has water, but check it out with the Forest Service if you will be depending on it during dry weather.

From here the trail proceeds up a ravine a short distance, then climbs out steeply to the right. After gaining a ridge, we switch-back more moderately uphill, and an impressive view opens up across the densely forested headwaters of Madera Canyon to the rugged, cliffbound summit of 9453-foot Mount Wrightson. Presently the switchbacks cease, and we traverse across a sunny, south-facing slope planted with Chihuahua pine and Mexican pinyon pine to signed Kent Spring (2.7; 6640), about as reliable as Bog Springs. There are campsites here, but they are not as attractive as the ones at Bog Springs.

Here our route rejoins the abandoned jeep road, which leads very steeply downhill, following the pleasantly forested ravine draining Kent Spring. In about 0.5 mile we pass Sylvester Spring, climb out of the ravine to the left, and drop into a tributary of Madera Creek. This tributary often has running water, but it of-fers only poor campsites. At an unsigned fork in the road we go right, and proceed a short distance back to the same saddle we crossed earlier in the day (4.1; 5340). To complete your trek, retrace your steps 0.7 miles to Bog Springs Campground (4.8; 5040).

See Map 18

oaks in Madera Canyon

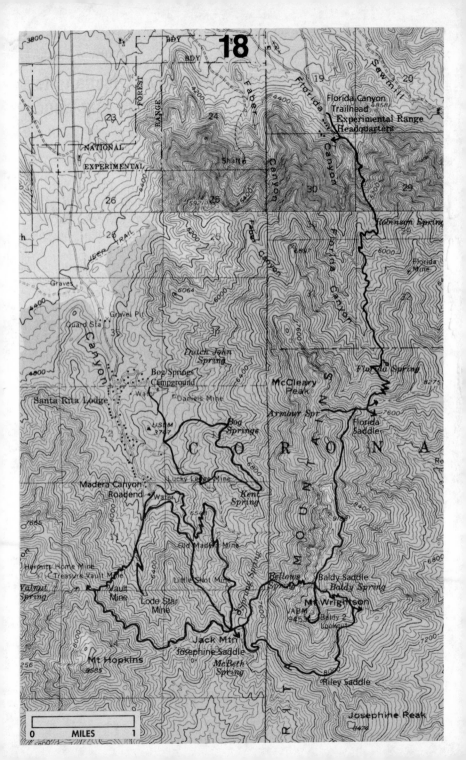

Trip 49
Madera Canyon Roadend to Lode Star Mine

3.2 miles round trip; 960 ' elevation gain

Leisurely dayhike or backpack (2 hiking days)

Season all year, except after snowstorms

Water available intermittently along Madera Creek, except possibly during very dry periods

Features

Nominally, this trip's destination is Lode Star Mine, an abandoned working near the head of leafy Madera Canyon. But far more attractive than the mine is the canyon itself — threaded by a near-perennial creek, shaded by a mixed forest of hardwoods and conifers, and famous across the nation for the variety of its birdlife. This short hike can be rushed through in just two hours, but its lush, sylvan setting warrants a more relaxed pace. Bird-watchers — and others — will find enough here to occupy them all day — and may even wish to spend the night.

Description

From the parking area at the end of Madera Canyon Road (0.0; 5440), walk gently uphill, south, along an old road, now closed to motorized traffic, through a varied vegetative cover of prickly pears, saw-edged agaves, Emory oaks, sycamores, Arizona madrones and some Apache pines. In 0.3 mile the signed Old Baldy Trail branches off to the left; our route continues straight ahead here, on the Very Steep Trail (which is not steep at all at this point). Nearby Madera Creek, shown as a perennial stream on the topo, generally dries up into a series of disconnected pools during spells of dry weather, but a single heavy thunderstorm can turn it into a torrent in less than an hour. The creek is perhaps at its best in early spring, when it gurgles softly with the last of the high country snowmelt, and when its banks are graced here and there with showy yellow columbine blossoms.

The forest overstory grows lusher as we proceed up-canyon, and during the spring and summer the air comes alive with the songs and calls of the many birds that nest hereabouts. Among the many species you might spot (bring along binoculars and a field guide) are the solitary vireo, acorn woodpecker, Mexican jay, black-headed grosbeak, red-shafted flicker, western tanager, sulfur-bellied flycatcher, Mexican junco and coppery-tailed trogon. The last three birds on this list are essentially Mexican species, and are rarely seen in the U.S. outside of the southeastern Arizona mountains. A sighting of the rare coppery-tailed trogon, an iridescently plumed relative of the fabulous quetzal of Mexico and Central America, is especially prized among birdwatchers.

Presently we reach an unsigned junction marked with a cairn (0.9; 5880), where we leave the Very Steep Trail and continue straight ahead, up Madera Canyon. In a few hundred yards the route cuts to the right, climbs steeply a short distance up a wooded ridge, then traverses to the left, back toward the creek. There are some pleasing vistas along this section, down the length of Madera Canyon to the grassy flatlands beyond. A few Gambel oaks grow on this north-facing hillside, along with Apache pines, Arizona pines and, down in the streambed, some velvet ash. Shortly after swinging into near-contact with the creek we arrive at Lode Star Mine (1.6; 6400). Molybdenum, along with traces of gold and silver, were taken from this mine during its active years, but it is no longer being worked. A rusting boiler and lots of other relics remain in the area. Fair campsites can be found nearby, and water is almost always available in the stream (check with the Forest Service during dry periods, or pack up your own supply).

Return the way you came.

See Map 18

Trip 50   Madera Canyon Roadend to Vault Mine and Josephine Saddle

6.3 mile loop trip; 1840' elevation gain

Moderate dayhike or backpack (2 hiking days)

Season April through November

Water almost always available at Sprung Spring (near mile 4.1) (check with Forest Service during dry weather spells)

Features

After sampling a portion of leafy Madera Canyon, this trip climbs steeply past Vault Mine to a pretty aspen grove high on the slopes of Mount Hopkins. Returning via Josephine Saddle and the Old Baldy Trail makes for a varied, scenic loop route.

Description

From the parking area at the end of Madera Canyon Road (0.0; 5440), follow the route of Trip 49 to the unsigned trail fork (marked with a cairn) in Madera Canyon (0.9; 5880). Turn right here, proceed a short distance up a ravine, then swing to the left and switchback exceptionally steeply uphill (one can now see why the Forest Service calls this the "Very Steep Trail"). As we gain elevation, occasional nice views open up across a densely forested basin draining into Madera Canyon.

Some ¾ mile after leaving the floor of the canyon, the trail passes the mouth of Vault Mine (1.6; 7000), which produced gold and silver before its short vein "pinched out." The shaft is not deep at all, and may be safely entered. From here the route continues steeply uphill, along a minor ridgeline, about ¼ mile to an unsigned junction marked with a cairn. We now turn left, onto the Agua Caliente Trail, and traverse across the shady northeast face of 8585-foot Mount Hopkins. This section offers several good views down the length of Madera Canyon to the distant Rincon and Santa Catalina ranges. Mount Wrightson's rocky, 9453-foot summit is also visible. Soon after leaving the Very Steep Trail we arrive at the edge of a beautiful grove of tall aspens — perhaps the finest such grove in the Santa Rita Mountains. This spot makes a fine lunch stop for dayhikers.

Beyond here the trail proceeds past a number of minor ups and downs, touching but not crossing two saddles on the ridge between Hopkins and Wrightson. Each of these gaps has a fair campsite (no water), and affords a grand vista to the south, across Sonoita Valley and on into Mexico. Presently we drop a short distance into often-windy Josephine Saddle (4.1; 7080), where there are several good campsites, beneath a shady forest cover of silverleaf oak, Arizona pine and Apache pine. Water is usually available at Sprung Spring, ¼ mile down the signed Super Trail from the saddle. (During spells of dry weather, this spring should be checked out with the Forest Service.) A pair of plaques here memorialize three Boy Scouts who, on November 15, 1958, "passed this way on their way to the Better Place" (the trio perished in an uncommonly fierce, early-season snowstorm).

Several trails come together in this saddle. Our route turns left, onto the signed Old Baldy Trail, and switchbacks moderately down the wall of a ravine. Stay on the recently reworked trail where it tangles with an older, steeper pathway. Presently we traverse to the left, across several minor ridges and drainages, then drop past a treeless area affording an open view of Mount Wrightson. Shortly after passing a covered water tank we reach the signed junction with the Very Steep Trail back in Madera Canyon; to complete your trek from here, turn right and retrace the morning's route the remaining 0.3 mile to the trailhead (6.3; 5440).

See Map 18

Trip 51   Madera Canyon Roadend to Mount Wrightson

12.8 miles loop trip; 4020´ elevation gain

Strenuous dayhike or backpack (2–4 hiking days)

Season May through October

Water almost always available at Sprung Spring (miles 3.5 and 10.6), Bellows Spring (mile 4.9), and Baldy Spring (mile 7.5) (check with Forest Service during spells of dry weather)

Features

9453-foot Mount Wrightson, the goal of this fine trip, is the highest and by far the most prominent summit in the Santa Rita Mountains. The route is fairly strenuous, but the trails used are well maintained and moderately graded all the way, and the great view from the top fully justifies the effort required to reach it.

Description

From the north end of the parking area at Madera Canyon Roadend (0.0; 5440), follow the signed Super Trail as it climbs moderately a short distance, then swings right to a tributary of Madera Creek, where the gradient eases. This creeklet often has running water, and supports a nice riparian growth of sycamore, walnut, and velvet ash. In spring, showy yellow columbine blossoms grace the moist streambanks here and there. Soon we cross the creek to its left side, then climb through a forest cover of silverleaf oak, emory oak, Arizona white oak and alligator juniper onto the dry slope above. After a single switchback the trail cuts up-canyon, staying at about the level of the tops of the broadleaf trees lining the watercourse. About 1 mile from the trailhead we temporarily return to creekside, then begin switchbacking moderately uphill. At length, after gaining an excellent view down the length of Madera Canyon, we reach an unnamed saddle (2.2; 6440). There is a good view of the long, rocky crest of Mount Wrightson from this gap.

Apache pines, Mexican white pines and Chihuahua pines gradually integrate themselves into the forest cover as we climb gently southward from the saddle. In 1.2 miles we arrive at Sprung Spring, which almost always has potable water (check with the

Forest Service if you will be depending on this spring during very
dry spells). About ¼ mile farther along is Josephine Saddle (3.6;
7080), where there is a memorial to three Boy Scouts who lost their
lives in a fierce November snowstorm back in 1958. Several good
campsites can be found in this forested, sometimes windy gap. The
nearest water is at Sprung Spring.

At a signed junction in this saddle we turn left, onto the combined Super Trail/Old Baldy Trail. In 0.2 mile, where these two
paths part ways, we turn left again, and follow the Old Baldy Trail
as it switchbacks onto the west slope of Mount Wrightson. After
we round a ridge containing a good but dry campsite, the steep
cliffs of Wrightson's rugged northwest face loom directly ahead. A
short traverse and a few more switchbacks now bring us to Bellows
Spring, about as reliable as Sprung Spring. From here we traverse
northward a bit, past some avalanche-harried aspens and Gambel
oaks, then ascend many tight switchbacks through a break in the
spectacular cliffs. This climb tops out at Baldy Saddle (5.5; 8880).
At a signed junction here we turn right and walk a short distance
south to a second junction, where the Super Trail comes in from
the left. Backpackers will find a number of windy, exposed campsites in this area; more sheltered ones are available at Baldy Spring,
just down the Super Trail (see below).

To continue on to Mount Wrightson, go straight ahead here,
and climb gently along a shady slope forested with Mexican white
pine and a smattering of Douglas-fir. The trail soon steepens, then
twists up several short, rocky switchbacks to the treeless summit
(6.4; 9453). Views from this lofty, isolated mountaintop are as
beautiful as they are extensive. The distinctive spire of Babo-
quivari Peak pokes above the desert flats to the west, while the
Santa Catalina, Rincon and Galiuro Mountains rear up in the
north. The dark, forested cap of Chiricahua Peak is clearly dis-
cernible on the eastern horizon. To the south, long chains of ridges
and peaks recede to the vanishing point, deep in Mexico. The view
to the southwest is spoiled somewhat by a raw road scar that cuts
across the face of nearby Mount Hopkins. The cement foundation
here is all that remains of old Baldy Lookout, which was removed
in 1958. Remember that this peak is a prime target for lightning
strikes; be sure to head back down the trail if you see a
thunderstorm building up nearby.

After taking in the view (and signing the summit register),
retrace your steps for 0.9 mile, turn right onto the signed Super
Trail and proceed a short distance downhill to Baldy Spring (7.5;

8760). This spring does not produce much water during the summer months, and sometimes dries up completely; check it out with the Forest Service if you plan to camp in this sheltered area. A lookout cabin stood here until 1974, when it was burned down by an arson.

From Baldy Spring we drop down a pair of switchbacks, then descend moderately through a forest of tall pines and firs to a signed junction with the Gardner Canyon Trail, where we stay right. Just beyond here we are treated to a good view of Mount Wrightson's "back" side — as rocky and cliffbound as its "front" — and of the swelling waves of bluish mountains receding southward, nicely framed by Riley Saddle, the forested gap to the right of 8474-foot Josephine Peak. After traversing beneath the east face of Wrightson, the trail crosses Riley Saddle, then drops very gently across a sunny, south-facing slope densely planted with netleaf, silverleaf and white oak. About a mile beyond the saddle, we drop down a few switchbacks, rejoin the Old Baldy Trail, and continue a short distance farther to Josephine Saddle (10.6; 7080). To complete your journey from here, follow the signed Old Baldy Trail the remaining 2.2 miles back to Madera Canyon Roadend (12.8; 5440), just across the parking lot from where the hike began (see Trip 50).

See Map 18

author in Lanphier Canyon, in the Blue Range

Trip 52

Florida Canyon Trailhead to Florida Spring

7.4 miles round trip; 2760' elevation gain

Strenuous dayhike or backpack (2 hiking days)

Season all year, except following snowstorms

Water available at Robinson Spring (mile 1.7) and Florida Spring (mile 3.7) during rainy periods only

Features

Beginning at the edge of an Upper Sonoran grassland region, this route climbs quickly up the north slope of the Santa Rita Mountains to a dense, shady grove of Douglas fir near the head of Florida Canyon. Here, in a hushed, cathedral-like atmosphere, the hot, sun-drenched lowlands seem light-years away. Florida Spring makes an excellent base for backpackers on their way to Mount Wrightson.

Description

From the Florida Canyon Trailhead (0.0; 4240), follow an abandoned road as it crosses the usually dry bed of Florida Creek and proceeds gently uphill along the east bank. The watercourse supports a lush riparian growth of Mexican blue oak, sycamore and hackberry, while on the parched slopes just a few yards away, little can survive besides ocotillo, prickly pear, and a few other drought-tolerant shrubs and cacti. After climbing over a small rise we drop to a signed junction near the Florida Canyon Experimental Range Headquarters. Here we turn left, and work our way, on a trail now, into a tributary drainage. The forest cover is sparser in this smaller, apparently drier canyon, and consists mostly of mesquite, Emory oak and some diminutive Mexican blue oaks. Among the many wildflowers that bloom here in the spring are pinkish-red parry penstemon, verbena, filaree, white-blossomed sacred datura, brittlebush and prickly poppy. During the summer-thunderstorm season, water sometimes pools up behind the many small catchment dams along the streambed.

After crossing the wash a few times, the trail climbs steeply up a series of ridgelines to the left. As we gain elevation a nice vista opens up across the tawny, oak-dotted Santa Rita foothills to the

north. About 1 mile after leaving the Florida Creek tributary, the
trail threads a minor saddle, then drops a short distance back into
the same drainage and climbs a bit to Robinson Spring (1.7; 5320),
an unsigned, unreliable seep down in the canyon bottom (water
during rainy periods only). Sycamore, velvet ash, Arizona walnut,
hanging tendrils of canyon grape, silverleaf oak and alligator
juniper all grow in this area. Camping is poor.

At the canyon forks just above the spring, the trail heads up
the left branch a short distance, then crosses over to the right-hand
prong and switchbacks steeply up to a small saddle. From here we
swing left, continue climbing steeply along a ridgeline, then
traverse southward across a shallow ravine and ascend to a larger
saddle with a dry campsite and a good view across the rugged amphitheater drained by Florida Creek. As we continue south from
this saddle, Apache pine, Mexican pinyon pine, Arizona pine and
Chihuahua pine become predominant in the forest cover. But not
for long — soon a few Douglas firs appear, and by the time we approach the head of Florida Canyon these trees form a dense, nearly
pure stand. There is a fine campsite in this shady, soothingly quiet
grove. Just beyond is a ravine, in which is found Florida Spring
(3.7; 7000) about 50 feet above the trail (water during rainy periods
only). Coues white-tailed deer and wild turkeys are frequent
visitors to this area, and camping is delightful.

Return the way you came.

See Map 18

Trip 53   Florida Canyon Trailhead to
                                          Mount Wrightson

15.2 miles round trip; 5540' elevation gain

Strenuous dayhike or backpack (2–4 hiking days)

Season May through October

*Water almost always available at Baldy Spring (near mile 6.7)
(check with Forest Service during dry weather periods); Robinson
Spring (mile 1.7) and Florida Spring (mile 3.7) have water during
rainy periods only*

Features

This trek reaches lofty Mount Wrightson via Florida Saddle and the Crest Trail — a route that is more strenuous, more scenic, and less-travelled than the more popular trails beginning in Madera Canyon. With delightful camping available at Florida Spring, this trip makes an excellent choice for the summit-bound backpacker.

Description

From the Florida Canyon Trailhead (0.0; 4240), follow the route of Trip 52 to Florida Spring (3.7; 7000). After crossing the ravine below the spring, the trail switchbacks, very steeply at first, through more Douglas firs to Florida Saddle (4.7; 7880). At a signed intersection here we go right (west) and follow the Crest Trail a bit less steeply 0.3 mile to the signed, right-branching spur to Armour Spring (0.4 mile down the spur; water during rainy periods only). There is a good campsite here.

From this junction the trail climbs moderately along the east side of the long ridge that drops northward from Mount Wrightson. It is instructive to note how the forest cover varies along this crest — Arizona pine and Mexican white pine are predominant in windy, exposed areas and on south-facing slopes, while Douglas-fir prefers sheltered pockets on north-facing slopes, where one would expect deep drifts of snow to accumulate in winter. Views are excellent from several points, across the eastern Santa Rita foothills to the wrinkled landscape drained by Cienega Wash, with the Whetstone and Huachuca mountains rising in the distance. About 1.7 miles beyond Florida Saddle, the trail tops out near a rocky ridgelet, then descends to Baldy Saddle (6.7; 8880) where, at a quick succession of signed forks, the Old Baldy Trail branches right and then the Super Trail goes left. To reach the bald summit of Mount Wrightson we proceed straight ahead at each junction, and follow the rocky, switchbacking trail the remaining 0.9 mile to the top (7.6; 9453). For a description of the summit area, see Trip 51.

Return the way you came, or via either the Super Trail or Old Baldy Trail to Madera Canyon Roadend (9-mile car shuttle required; see Trip 51).

See Map 18

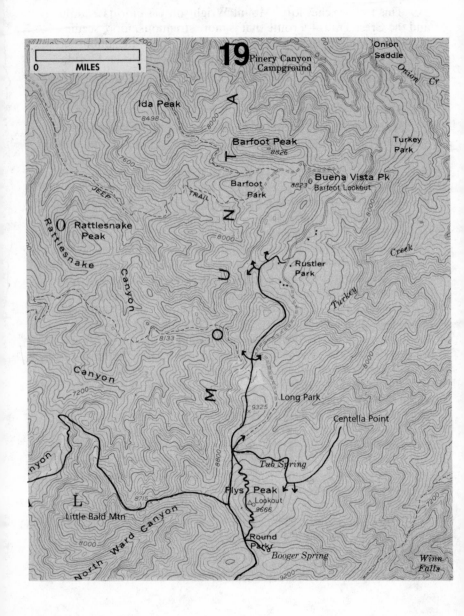

19

Pinery Canyon
Campground

Onion
Saddle

Onion Cr

Ida Peak
8498

Barfoot Peak
8826

Turkey
Park

Buena Vista Pk
8823
Barfoot Lookout

Barfoot
Park

Creek

Rattlesnake
Peak

Rustler
Park

Turkey

Rattlesnake

Canyon

8133

Canyon

7200

Long Park
9325

Centella Point

Tub Spring

8800

Little Bald Mtn
8715

Flys Peak
Lookout
9666

North Ward Canyon

8000

Round
Park

Booger Spring

9200

Winn
Falls

7200

Trip 54   Rustler Park to Fly Peak

6.4 miles round trip; 1420 ' elevation gain

Moderate dayhike

Season May to October

No water available along route

Features

Rustler Park is the highest trailhead in the Chiricahua Mountains, and provides the most convenient access to the range's loftiest peaks. This trip, an excellent introduction to the Chiricahua high country, passes through dense stands of spruce and fir before climbing up to 9666-foot Fly Peak, where gaps in the forest cover provide glimpses across the vast expanse of mountains and desert sprawling below. An added bonus is the opportunity of detouring to highly scenic Centella Point.

Description

From the trailhead (0.0; 8410) our route heads west and almost immediately begins climbing gently. In less than 0.5 mile, after staying left at a junction with the trail leading to Buena Vista Peak, we top the forested backbone of the Chiricahuas and turn left (south) onto the signed Crest Trail (0.4; 8640). As the path ascends gently onto a shady, north-facing slope, the gradual change that has been taking place in the forest cover reaches its climax, and the hiker will notice that the sun-loving Chihuahua and Apache pines, which were so dominant on the drive up to Rustler Park, have been almost wholly supplanted by Douglas-fir, Engelmann spruce and quaking aspen — snow-tolerant trees of the Canadian life zone.

Almost immediately we meet the Rock Creek Trail coming up from the west (1.5; 8880), where we stay left. About 0.9 mile beyond is a junction where five trails come together (2.4; 9080). If you are low on water at this point, you may wish to detour to usually reliable Tub Spring, 0.3 mile east down the left-branching trail. To reach Fly Peak, take the signed fork leading southeast and follow a series of broad switchbacks to the top (3.2; 9666). On the summit you will find a cement foundation and some rusting metal posts set in the ground, remnants of the cabin and lookout tower that once stood here. Off to the side stands a crude iron plaque, which reads: *In memory of Fly Peak Lookout, July 1911–July 1971. U.S.F.S.* (The lookout became outmoded with the advent of airplanes and helicopters as firefighting aids, and the abandoned tower was dismantled to preserve the surrounding area's wilderness character.)

Fly's gently rounded summit is forested, and the only clear vista it offers is through a break in the trees to the southwest. Those who hanker for a better view should make the side trip to strategically perched Centella Point (1.9 miles one way): Retrace your steps 0.8 mile to the last junction and turn right (east) onto the path to Tub Spring. About 0.5 mile beyond the spring you will come to two junctions in quick succession; stay left at each, and continue for 1 mile to the airy overlook of 9320-foot Centella Point. Here you will find excellent views across the deep, beautifully sculptured canyon of Cave Creek, with its broad, forested basins and needle-sharp ridges and pinnacles.

Return the way you came.

See Map 19

near the head of Rucker Canyon

Trip 55   Rustler Park to Fly Peak, Anita Park and Chiricahua Peak

11.8 miles round trip; 2020' elevation gain

Moderate dayhike or backpack (2 hiking days)

Season May to October

Water available all season (except possibly during very dry years) at Booger Spring (near mile 3.7) and Anita Spring (near mile 5.3)

Features

Picking up where the preceding trip left off, this fine route continues on to bright green Anita Park, a good base from which to explore the forested tops of the Chiricahuas, and culminates at 9796-foot Chiricahua Peak, the highest point in the range. The cool, shady forests which dominate the entire route provide welcome relief from the heat and glare of lowland summers; the most difficult part of this excursion may well come at the very end, when you must convince yourself to return to the hot desert below.

Description

Follow the directions for Trip 54 to the summit of Fly Peak (3.2; 9666). To continue to Chiricahua Peak, look for a faint trail heading south from the clearing at the top. This path becomes more distinct as it winds downhill, occasionally steeply, and we quickly arrive at Round Park, a small meadow studded with aspen sunflowers and the nodding yellow heads of cutleaf coneflower. Coues white-tailed deer are often spotted here during the summer months. When the trail you have been following begins to fade out in the grass, move a few steps to the right onto the obvious Crest Trail. (If you wish, you may bypass Fly Peak by following the well-signed Crest Trail from the preceding junction directly to this point.)

We now proceed south, reentering the trees and continuing past a signed junction with the spur trail to Booger Spring (a short distance east; water except in extremely dry years). About ¼ mile later we pass another path to this spring, then continue across a broad saddle to the signed junction with the Greenhouse Trail (4.4; 9240). Cima Park is just to the left. Our route continues south along the Crest Trail, past the right-branching Mormon Ridge

Trail, and then arrives at the signed spur to Anita Park and Anita Spring (5.3; 9520). Anita Park, with its delightful camping, lies a short distance up this trail to the north-northeast; the almost always reliable spring is a few hundred yards beyond the park, down the hillside to the east. This is a good area in which to observe wildlife — deer frequent the meadow, and the surrounding forest is often alive with darting, singing Mexican chickadees, a species rarely seen elsewhere in the U.S. Black bears have also been known to visit occasionally, and campers may wish to safeguard their food supply by suspending it out of harm's reach from a high tree limb.

Just south of the Anita Park spur trail is Junction Saddle. To reach Chiricahua Peak we turn first left, then right, at a succession of forks here, passing a dry campsite and a sign informing us that we have reached the southernmost limit of the Engelmann spruce's range. About 0.4 mile more of moderate climbing brings us to the forested summit of Chiricahua Peak (5.9; 9796), where there is a good campsite for those who wish to spend the night at the loftiest point in the Chiricahuas (and who pack up enough water from Anita Spring). Trees limit the view in every direction, and a USGS benchmark next to the campsite is about the only evidence we have that we are indeed on top of this corner of the world.

To return to Rustler Park, retrace your steps to Round Park, staying left at the junction with the faint path used to descend Fly Peak, and follow the Crest Trail back to the trailhead (11.8; 8400).

See Maps 19 and 20

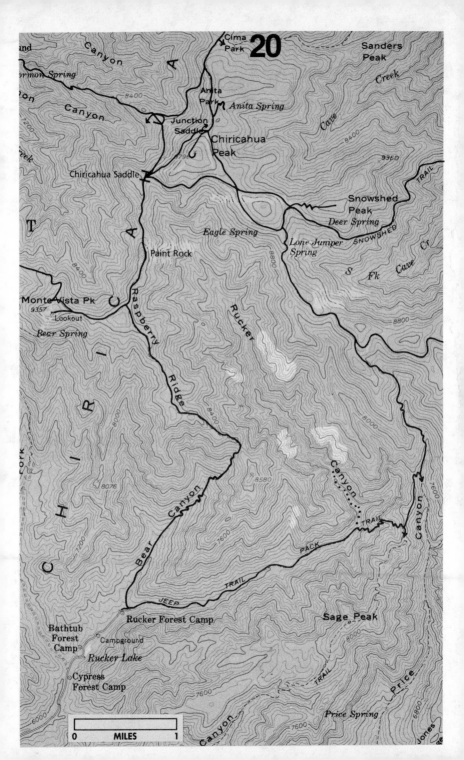

Trip 56   Turkey Creek to Anita Park and
Chiricahua Peak via the Saulsbury Trail

13.1 mile near-loop; 3640´ elevation gain

Strenuous dayhike or backpack (2 hiking days)

Season May to October

Water available all season (except possibly during extremely dry years) at Anita Spring (near mile 6.3)

Features

An abundance of airy, exposed ridges over closed-in drainages makes this one of the most scenic routes in the Chiricahuas. Covering a much greater altitudinal sweep than the preceding two trips, this trek gives the hiker a more balanced feel for the range as a whole — from the oaks and cypresses of the midaltitude canyons to the aspen and spruce of the high country. If some of that "feel" tends to lodge in one's knees and ankles during the bone-jarring descent of steep Mormon Ridge, well, that too is an integral part of the Chiricahua experience.

Description

From the Saulsbury Canyon trailhead at Turkey Creek (0.0; 6320) we walk gently uphill along an abandoned dirt road through a forest cover of silverleaf and emory oak, Apache and Chihuahua pine, Schott's yucca and a few Arizona cypresses. After the first half mile or so, the track assumes the more congenial dimensions of a trail and begins crossing and recrossing the usually dry bed of Saulsbury Creek. A mile from the start we pass a drift fence, then begin climbing steeply up the right-hand canyon wall. Several hundred feet higher, after making a few token switchbacks, the trail finally snakes up into wooded Saulsbury Saddle (1.9; 7480). At a sign here we turn right to another sign visible nearby, then move to the right again onto the southwest slope of the rocky ridge east of the saddle. The ensuing steep climb offers good views across the deep canyon of Turkey Creek. Soon we cross a minor saddle to the ridge's Gambel-oak-shaded north side, trading the preceding vista for an equally rewarding overlook of Rock Canyon and distant Sulphur Spring Valley.

As we approach the rocky crown of Little Bald Mountain the trail levels out a bit, allowing us to catch our breath for the first time since leaving the floor of Saulsbury Canyon some 1500 feet below. Here we come to the wilderness area boundary, then to a sunny notch from which we can see the rounded, invitingly forested tops of Fly and Chiricahua Peaks, still 1300 feet above us. After traversing beneath Little Bald Mountain the trail suddenly leaves the oaks, pinyons and agaves of the foothills behind and enters the welcome shade of a dense copse of Douglas-fir, New Mexican locust and Engelmann spruce. As we begin climbing again, we pass our first quaking aspen — a sure sign that we have made it to the high country at last — and presently we arrive at a signed junction with the Crest Trail (4.4; 9280). (Hikers should make it a point to get here well before noon, as the trail to this point can get quite hot by midday.)

Here we turn right and then walk south along the Crest Trail to the forested saddle that contains Round Park. Those who wish to make the sidetrip to Fly Peak should search for a faint, unmarked junction at the south end of this wildflower-studded meadow, then follow the indistinct path that leads north 0.5 mile to the summit (see Trip 55). To reach Chiricahua Peak we stay on the Crest Trail, continuing south past several well-signed turnoffs until we arrive at a signed junction with the Anita Park/Anita Spring spur trail. Backpackers will find good camping at Anita Park, a few hundred yards north. Anita Spring, down on the hillside east of the park, has potable water except in the driest of times.

To continue to Chiricahua Peak, walk south a short distance to Junction Saddle (6.4; 9540). Stay left here, then go right at an unsigned turnoff just beyond and ascend moderately the remaining distance to the top (6.9; 9796). Here, at the highest point in the Chiricahuas, there is a good dry campsite. Views are unfortunately blocked by the heavy forest cover.

To return to Turkey Creek, we retrace our steps to the last junction, where we turn right and begin a traverse of Chiricahua Peak's east slope. In 0.7 mile we reach another fork, turn right again, and continue along the peak's south face. After dropping moderately a short distance, the trail brings us to Chiricahua Saddle (9.0; 9200), where we turn right onto the signed Mormon Ridge Trail, a rough but scenic route that plunges down some 3000 feet in less than 4 miles. From the saddle this unmaintained but easy to

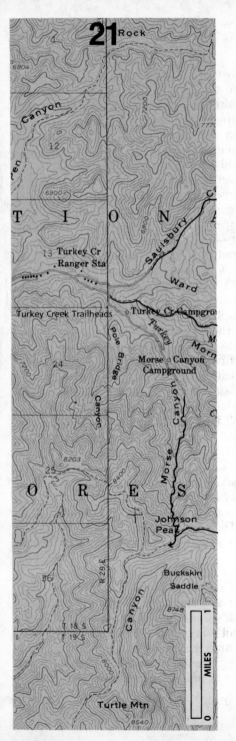

follow track descends slightly, crossing a talus-chocked ravine and obliging us to step over numerous fallen firs. About 0.7 mile later we meet the Mormon *Canyon* Trail on our left, and another branch of the Mormon *Ridge* Trail on our right; we go straight ahead, and soon begin dropping steeply. Most of this descent is made on the ridge's south side, keeping below the crest, and with only an occasional switchback to ease the gradient. While descending, the hiker will doubtless be struck by the sharp contrast between Mormon Canyon's densely forested south wall and the hot, brushy north wall upon which, unfortunately, our trail happens to have been built.

A small expanse of burned pines marks the halfway point of the descent. About a mile beyond this burn area the ridge begins to level out, large oaks and junipers appear on the parklike flats, and the walking gets easier and easier until we at last cross tiny Turkey Creek and climb up to the road just beyond (13.1; 6160).

See Maps 21, 19 and 20

Trip 57 Turkey Creek to Monte Vista Lookout via the Morse Canyon Trail

7.8–13.4 miles, round trip or shuttle trip; 2720–3760´ elevation gain

Strenuous dayhike or backpack (2 hiking days)

Season May to October

Water available all season (except possibly during very dry years) at Anita Spring (near mile 6.9) and Booger Spring (near mile 8.7). No reliable water along Morse Canyon and Mormon Ridge return routes.

Features

Monte Vista Peak is not the highest point in the Chiricahua Mountains, but it is strategically located, and the views from its summit are among the best in the range. This route makes a stiff climb up to the peak, then traverses across the spine of rocky, sunny Raspberry Ridge into the heart of the spruce- and fir-forested high country, where hikers who linger are presented with a wide variety of side-trip possibilities.

Description

From the end of the Turkey Creek Road (0.0; 6640) the trail enters a moderately dense forest cover of Chihuahua pine, Apache pine and Douglas-fir as it curves into Morse Canyon. Almost immediately an unidentified spur trail branches off to the right; we stay left and continue up-canyon. After crossing the rocky and usually dry streambed a few times, the path begins switchbacking moderately up the left-hand canyonside. This ascent continues unbroken for 1900 vertical feet, until we suddenly top out at lofty Johnson Saddle (2.3; 8560). At a signed junction here we turn left and continue climbing, more gently now, along the ridgecrest leading to the lookout tower visible in the southeast. About ¼ mile farther is the wilderness-area boundary sign, and a mile after that is a junction just below Monte Vista Peak, where we stay right, as we do at a second fork just beyond. The trail now doubles back and continues uphill a few hundred yards to the summit (3.9; 9357).

On top you will find the lookout tower, a cabin and some small outbuildings, and fine vistas to the west and south across Sulphur Spring Valley and the rugged chain of peaks and ridges that recedes southward into Mexico. Views to the north and east are obscured by trees; one could obtain a 360-degree panorama from atop the lookout, but a sign at its base requests that you not climb the tower.

After soaking up the view, retrace your steps ¼ mile to the signed junction with the Crest Trail. If you cannot manage the very short car shuttle between the beginning of this route and either the Saulsbury Canyon or the Mormon Ridge Trailhead, turn left here and retrace your steps back to the Morse Canyon Trailhead (7.8 miles total). Otherwise, follow the Crest Trail as it veers to the right, then doubles back and continues gently downhill to a junction with the Raspberry Ridge Trail coming up from the south (4.7; 9240). Turning left, our route now eases onto Raspberry Ridge, the high divide between Rucker Canyon Creek, in the deep canyon to the right, and Turkey Creek. With a pair of binoculars it is usually possible to spot several golden eagles soaring in the vast airspace on either side of this ridge, especially now that excessive trapping of coyotes has reduced the eagles' chief competition for the small rodents on which they feed.

Soon we pass the thumblike projection of Paint Rock (mistakenly labeled "Raspberry Peak" on the topo) on its east side, then make a few rough ups and downs as the ridge temporarily grows jagged and narrow. A short, moderate ascent brings us to Chiricahua Saddle (6.0; 9200), where we have a choice of routes. Backpackers will wish to continue northeast along the Crest Trail and a spur trail 1 mile to Anita Park and Spring, where there is good camping, and then return to Turkey Creek via the Saulsbury Trail (walk the first 6.4 miles of Trip 56 in reverse; 13.3 miles total). Dayhikers will probably prefer to return via the shorter Mormon Ridge route, in which case they should turn left at Chiricahua Saddle and follow the directions for the last leg of Trip 56 back to the road (10.1 miles total). In either case the "shuttle" involved is short enough to be walked, if necessary; if you elect to do this, you may want to park your car at your destination, rather than at Morse Canyon, thus saving your tired legs the trouble of walking back up the dusty, dreary road in the heat of the afternoon.

See Maps 21 and 20

Trip 58   Rucker Forest Camp to
Rucker Canyon Creek

5.2 miles round trip; 440' elevation gain

Leisurely dayhike or backpack (2 hiking days)

Season all year; best in spring and fall

Water available intermittently along entire route

Features

Only two perennial streams reach back significantly into the Chiricahua backcountry. One of them, Rucker Creek, graces the entire length of this fine, leisurely outing. The creek's reliable water supports a variety of wildlife and a dense, diversified forest of conifers and hardwoods. The mood here is tranquil, relaxed; the murmuring creek and rustling leaves foster an air of carefree repose not to be found in the harsher realms of desert and mountaintop. This trip is a good choice for the hiker seeking to "warm up" for the coming season — or for one who has wearied of the strenuous exploits of seasons past.

Description

From the trailhead above Rucker Forest Camp (0.0; 6160) walk up-canyon along the continuation of the Rucker Road. In a few minutes you will pass the signed Bear Canyon Trail branching left, then a small storage shed, beyond which the road begins to deteriorate. Soon the track begins crossing and recrossing bouldery Rucker Creek — whose flow may be intermittent at this point, particularly in the fall. A wide variety of trees flourish along the alternately sunny and shady stretches of the canyon bottom, with species representing three distinct life zones (Upper Sonoran, Transition and Canadian) growing side by side with the riparian species one would expect to find here — silverleaf oak and Schott's yucca with Douglas-fir, cypress with maple, Apache pine with velvet ash, all in a mix that may disappoint the hiker who prefers that nature adhere strictly to the rigid divisions of textbook biology. Among the animals which make their homes here are the night-prowling ringtail cat and coatimundi, the bold Mexican jay, and a few rare Chiricahua fox squirrels. The iridescently plumed, coppery-tailed trogon, a relative of the renowned Mexican quetzal, occasionally nests here in the spring, though it is more commonly seen in South Fork Cave Creek Canyon. A few rainbow and black speckled trout, remnants of plants made in years past by sportsmen, somehow manage to eke out an existence in the tiny creek. (Fishing is legally allowed here, but between the droughts and floods that occur locally almost annually the fish probably have enough survival problems without being further harried by fishermen.)

After 1½ miles all traces of the old road are behind us. The canyon grows narrower as we proceed upstream, and just before it makes a pronounced swing to the left, the trail doubles back and begins switchbacking up the south wall (2.6; 6600). This point marks the end of today's excursion; there are fair campsites here, but better ones may be found a short distance either up or downstream. Explorations up the remainder of Rucker Creek's rugged, cliffbound canyon can be rewarding, but just how far you will be able to go depends on your cross-country scrambling ability.

Return the way you came.

See Map 20

Trip 59   Rucker Forest Camp to Rucker Creek, Chiricahua Peak and Junction Saddle

17.1-mile loop trip; 4200 ′ elevation gain

Strenuous dayhike or backpack (2–3 hiking days)

Season May to October

Water available all season along Rucker Creek (to mile 2.6; creek may be intermittent); at Lone Juniper Spring (mile 7.7) until late summer; and at Anita Spring (near mile 10.1) (except possibly during very dry years)

Features

This long, strenuous loop trip samples all the varied aspects of the Chiricahuas: deep, thickly wooded canyons; exposed, scenic ridges; oddly sculptured cliffs and pinnacles; and the crisp air of the conifer-topped peaks. Grand vistas alternate with intimate forest closures the entire way.

Dayhikers will have to move right along — all day — on this lengthy route, but backpackers may wish to take the time to explore the numerous side-trip possibilities available. Peakbaggers especially should take advantage of the ready access this trip provides to Sentinel, Snowshed, Chiricahua, Fly and Monte Vista Peaks — the highest summits in the range.

Description

Follow the directions for Trip 58 to the point where the Rucker Canyon Trail begins switchbacking away from Rucker Creek (2.6; 6600), then continue along the trail as it climbs steeply up the right-hand canyon wall. Near the middle of this 1000-foot ascent the path winds back and forth across a rocky ravine, and is occasionally brushy and hard to follow. At the top of the climb we meet the Red Rock Canyon Trail (3.9; 7640) at a signed junction beneath an overhanging, curiously eroded rock outcropping. The route now turns left and follows a brushy, shadeless ridgetop past a slight rise, and then descends a few hundred feet into Price Canyon, the invitingly shaded gorge on the right. Here we join the Price Canyon Trail (4.6; 7480), turn left, and climb (steeply at times) up the rocky canyon bottom. You might spot some wild turkeys or Coues deer in this area, particularly early in the season, when there is generally a trickle of water down in the streambed.

After a mile or so Price Canyon widens a bit, stately pines and firs begin to replace the oaks, and the hiker begins to sense that he has reached the high country at last. After surmounting a series of broad switchbacks at the head of the canyon we meet the signed trail to Sentinel Peak (6.5; 8960), where our route goes left, on the eastern branch of the Crest Trail. A little over a mile of easy walking through a sunny forest of Apache, Chihuahua and Mexican white pines brings us to a junction at Lone Juniper Spring (water until late season), where we turn left again and continue to a second junction ¾ mile beyond (8.5; 9480). Stay on the clearly signed Crest Trail here, and follow it for 0.7 mile northwest to the point where the Chiricahua Peak Trail branches off to the left (southwest). This trail then climbs moderately 0.4 mile to the forested summit of Chiricahua Peak (9.6; 9796). Here, at the highest point in the Chiricahua Mountains, there is a good campsite (but no water and no open views).

To return to Rucker Forest Camp, retrace your steps to the Crest Trail, then turn left and walk a short distance north to Junction Saddle (10.1; 9540). Backpackers looking for campsites —

and dayhikers who are low on water — will want to continue north
along the Crest Trail a few hundred yards to the signed Anita
Park/Anita Spring spur trail (see Trip 55). Otherwise we turn left
and proceed gently downhill to Chiricahua Saddle (10.9; 9200),
where we turn neither left nor right, but follow the Crest Trail as it
descends straight ahead onto the spine of rocky, sunny Raspberry
Ridge. The monolithic crown of Paint Rock (mislabeled
"Raspberry Peak" on the topo) is soon passed on its left flank,
and 1.4 miles later we reach the signed turnoff to Monte Vista
Lookout (12.2; 9240). If you have sufficient time and energy remaining, you can make the 1.6-mile round trip to the lookout,
which offers unexcelled views across the southern Chiricahuas (see
Trip 57). If not, turn left here and continue along the crest of
Raspberry Ridge, dropping steeply at times, until reaching a wooded saddle at the head of precipitous Bear Canyon (14.3; 8280).
Here the trail abruptly plunges downward, switchbacking irregularly and passing several steep, tricky sections where washouts
have occurred. As we lose elevation, agaves and Schott's yuccas
begin to appear in the sunny patches between the pines and firs — a
sign that we have left the Canadian life zone far behind and
reentered the Transition zone. After 2 miles the switchbacking
ceases and we descend a short distance directly down a dry, brushy
creekbed, from which we emerge onto a gently sloping, wide-
bottomed canyon which is heavily forested with silverleaf, Emory
and Arizona white oak. From here the walking grows easier and
easier as we march the final ¼ mile to the Rucker Road. Rucker
Forest Camp (17.1; 6160) is just down-canyon to the right.

See Map 20

Trip 60
South Fork Forest Camp to Maple Camp

3.2 miles round trip; 280 ' elevation gain

Leisurely dayhike or backpack (2 hiking days)

Season all year; best in spring and fall

Water available intermittently along entire route

Features

The South Fork of Cave Creek is one of only two perennial streams that penetrate significantly into the roadless Chiricahuas. It is thus something of an oasis, both for the solitude-seeking human visitor and for the wide variety of man-shy wildlife that has been driven here by the steady encroachment of roads, fences, and predator traps into the surrounding country. It is also a haven for migrating birds — over 200 distinct species have been spotted in the area, including the rare, spectacularly colored eared trogon and the coppery-tailed trogon. This trip is a must for birdwatchers, but the beautiful and serene South Fork Canyon contains enough nonavian attractions to recommend itself to all other hikers as well.

Description

From the end of the road at South Fork Forest Camp (0.0; 5300) our route follows a wide, well-maintained but unobtrusive trail up the imperceptibly sloping floor of South Fork Canyon. The forest cover in this sheltered, well-watered area is a fabulous montage of disparate species — rustling sycamores, walnuts, towering Apache and Chihuahua pines, Douglas-firs, silverleaf and emory oaks, velvet ash trees, madrones, bigtooth maples, and some magnificent, thick-trunked specimens of Arizona cypress.

Just beyond the trailhead you may encounter a sign asking that birdwatchers register their names and addresses and take a card on which to report any unusual sightings — particularly of the eared trogon or the coppery-tailed trogon, two richly plumed relatives of the legendary Mexican quetzal bird that fly northward each spring to nest in this verdant canyon. Birders come from all over the nation to catch a glimpse of these exotic species, which do not generally appear elsewhere in the country. The trogon may be easily identified by its raucous call and its iridescent green and red plumage. Should you see one, please obey the posted request and do not approach too closely or otherwise disturb it.

After crossing South Fork Cave Creek a few times we pass through a drift fence via a "revolving door" gate. Soon the canyon bottom grows rougher, though no less beautiful, and the trail makes a few gentle ups and downs as it weaves along the line of least resistance. By late summer/early fall the creek may be dry up to this point, but there is always enough of a surface flow beyond here to support a few water ouzels, or dippers — small, semi-aquatic birds that forage the bottoms of flowing streams for insects and crustaceans. The ouzel is readily identified by its habit of flying just inches above the surface of the water, and tracing every twist and turn of the streamcourse in its flight.

Presently we reach the signed junction of the South Fork Trail with the Burro Trail (1.6; 5600), the return route of Trip 61. Maple Camp, a good campsite, is just off to the right. Other fine campsites can be found ¼ mile or so upstream. A worthwhile side trip can be made from here: walk up the Burro Trail about 0.5 mile to a rocky saddle between two branches of the South Fork, then leave the trail and scramble northeast 0.3 miles to an airy peaklet, where you will be treated to a spectacular overlook of the canyon and a high cliff looming beyond it. Visible behind the cliff is the long, forested skyline of Snowshed Ridge, which culminates in 9640-foot Snowshed Peak, at the head of the South Fork.

Return the way you came. Or, if you have an abundance of energy, make the long, rewarding loop trip up to Sentinel Peak and Horseshoe Pass (see Trip 61).

See Map 22

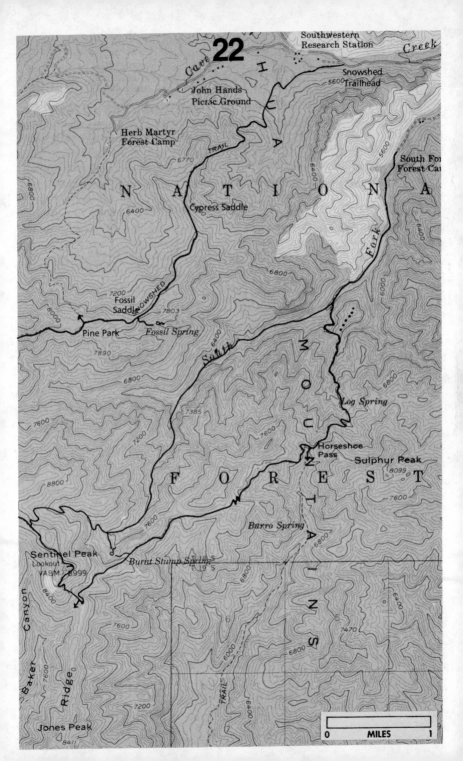

Trip 61   South Fork Forest Camp to Maple Camp and Sentinel Peak; return via Horseshoe Ridge

16.7-mile semiloop trip; 3920′ elevation gain

Strenuous dayhike or backpack (3 hiking days)

Season May to October

Water available all season along South Fork Cave Creek (miles 0.0 to 3.4 and 15.1 to 16.7), and during early season at Burnt Stump Spring (near mile 5.2) and Log Spring (mile 12.9)

Features

This lengthy excursion is a study in contrasts — between the antipodal worlds of canyon and crest, streambank and mountaintop. After tracing insular, sylvan South Fork Cave Creek to its headwaters, the route climbs skyward to pine-topped Sentinel Peak, a high, isolated summit standing apart from the central mountain-mass of the Chiricahuas and commanding an excellent view. But the climax of this trip may well be the long, ridge-hugging descent to Horseshoe Pass and back to Maple Camp — a kaleidoscope of far-reaching, ever-changing vistas.

Description

Follow the directions for Trip 60 to Maple Camp (1.6; 5600). At the junction with the Burro Trail we stay right and work our way up-canyon, passing occasional good campsites off to the left. As the trail approaches the base of the huge cliff that looms on our right, it crosses the stream, climbs steeply up a short distance and back down again, and makes several more creek crossings before climbing a short distance up the right-hand canyonside to an obscure junction. Here we ignore the faint track leading off to the right, and continue winding up-canyon under a forest cover of oak, juniper and Schott's yucca a hundred feet or so above the stream. After gaining some good views up and down the canyon we drop back down, pass an excellent campsite just beyond a sign indicating the wilderness boundary, and make one final trip across the rocky streambed to a poorly signed junction (3.4; 6160), where we turn left up a tributary of the South Fork.

The first mile up this side canyon is steep and rough, and the trail frequently disappears in the boulders of the creekbed. The track is not hard to follow, however, and its brusque, demanding character serves well to heighten the sense of wildness and seclusion the hiker feels in this isolated, infrequently visited area.

As we gain elevation, clumps of quaking aspen begin to appear, giving rise to the hope that we are finally "getting up there" to the high country. Sure enough, the narrow confines of the canyon soon fall behind us, pine duff appears underfoot, and we find ourselves switchbacking moderately up a conifer-shaded slope. Presently a sign indicates a spur trail (5.2; 7640) branching left to Burnt Stump Spring (reliable water in early season only). Our route takes the right fork here and continues upward, passing through a grassy area where the trail temporarily grows faint, and finally reaches the top of the pine-clad ridge northwest of Sentinel Peak. Here we turn left onto the Crest Trail and traverse along the ridgetop for 0.5 mile, then climb a short distance to a junction just below the peak. Turn right here; the high point (7.3; 8999) is just beyond.

On the summit you will find the remains of old Sentinel Lookout, and an iron memorial similar to the one on Fly Peak, erected by Forest Service lookouts with fond memories of the long hours spent in the "cage" atop the tower that once stood here. Without a tower on which to climb above the level of the surrounding trees, it is hard to get a clear view; a point about 100 yards down the trail provides a more open vista than the very summit.

For the return to Maple Camp, retrace your steps a short distance to the last trail junction, then turn right and begin switchbacking (occasionally quite steeply) down Sentinel Peak's brushy southeast slope. After dropping about 400 feet we reach a poorly signed junction with the Baker Canyon Trail, where we stay left. A short distance beyond is another junction. The right branch is apparently just a variant of the Baker Canyon Trail, and we go left, easing onto the long, sinuous crest of Horseshoe Ridge. About 1 mile after passing a path coming up from Burnt Stump Spring, the route crosses a minor saddle and switchbacks moderately down a forested slope, which offers the only substantial shade along this leg of the journey. After a mile-long traverse of the ridge's south side, with good views over the wide gap of Horseshoe Canyon and across the southern Chiricahuas, we arrive at Horseshoe Pass (11.9; 7240), a deep notch at the foot of hulking, 8099-foot Sulphur Peak. Here we turn left onto the signed Burro Trail, gaining breathtaking vistas across Cave Creek Canyon as we swing out onto the slopes high above the South Fork. The trail is temporarily thin and tricky at a washout here — watch your footing.

Soon the inevitable switchbacking begins again, and we descend moderately past the signed spur trail to Log Spring (water in early season only). After crossing the usually dry bed of a tributary of the South Fork, the path climbs a short distance to a saddle, where we are treated to another fine view, this time of Snowshed Ridge and the spectacular cliffs across South Fork Canyon. A final spate of switchbacks then lands us at Maple Camp (15.1; 5600), from where we retrace our steps the remaining 1.6 miles to South Fork Forest Camp (16.7; 5320).

See Map 22

Trip 62   Cave Creek to Snowshed Peak and Anita Park via the Snowshed Trail

17.4–19.2 miles round trip; 4300 ′ elevation gain

Strenuous dayhike or backpack (2 hiking days)

Season May to October

Water available all season (except possibly during extremely dry years) at Deer Spring (mile 7.6) and Anita Spring (near mile 19.2)

Features

Scenic Snowshed Ridge offers a lengthy, strenuous and rewarding route up to the Chiricahua highlands. For well-conditioned dayhikers, this trip reaches its climax at lofty Snowshed Peak, which overlooks the ruggedly eroded drainage basin of Cave Creek. Backpackers, on the other hand, will find that the Snowshed Trail has brought them only to the threshold of the high country, where a wealth of enticing trails wait to be explored.

Description

From the trailhead on the Cave Creek road (0.0; 5300) climb up a few yards to a sign, then turn right and strike off west through a moderate forest cover of Mexican blue oak, Chihuahua pine and alligator juniper. Early risers are shielded from the sun's rays along this often warm, scantily shaded stretch by some high bluffs that loom up in the east. After 0.5 mile we cross a dry wash, whose mud-colored walls are brightened by the fresh green leaves of a few Arizona walnuts and madrones that somehow extract a livable ration of water out of the gravelly ravine. The trail is occasionally obscure as it winds through a rocky area just beyond here — watch for ducks.

Soon the path grows more distinct and begins switchbacking onto the toe of Snowshed Ridge. Two miles of moderate climbing now bring us to Cypress Saddle (2.9; 7080), where we gain an excellent view across the jumbled cliffs and crags of Cave Creek Canyon which made the region such an effective wartime citadel for the Chiricahua Apache. After passing to the north side of the ridge we continue ascending, and soon Gambel oaks and Douglas-firs begin to appear among the junipers and Mexican pinyons — welcome evidence of our increasing elevation. Because of Snowshed Ridge's varying steepness and exposure, the various life zones of the Chiricahuas are locally compressed into an unusually narrow altitude range, and by the time we amble up to Fossil Saddle (and the steep spur trail down to unreliable Fossil Springs) a few Engelmann spruce have appeared.

About 0.5 mile beyond Fossil Saddle we meet the Basin Trail (4.9; 7920) coming up from Herb Martyr Dam to the north. Just above this signed junction we climb steeply and pass through a narrow, rocky defile to Pine Park, a pleasantly shaded flat astride the ridge. About 0.5 mile farther the trail rounds a steep, rocky spur ridge which offers a good view across the deep gash of South Fork Canyon to the aspen-dotted ramparts of Sentinel Peak.

Until this point we have remained on or near the crest of Snowshed Ridge, but now the crest rises high above us as our gentle climbing-traversing is unable to keep pace. The route is well shaded through here, except at a steep, barren talus slope which we cross in one mile, and aspen and spruce soon become integral parts of the forest cover. About 2 miles beyond Pine Park the trail finally begins switchbacking in a belated effort to catch up with the runaway ridge; 0.5 mile later, after crossing a dizzying, talus-choked dropoff, we arrive at the cement tank of Deer Spring (may be stagnant in fall). 0.4 mile beyond is a signed, 4-way trail junction in a saddle (8.1; 9320), where we are presented with a wide range of options. Backpackers may wish to continue 1.5 miles to the good campsites and almost always reliable water at Anita Park and Spring, from where the summits of Fly and Chiricahua peaks are readily accessible. (To reach Anita Park proceed straight ahead 0.5 mile, then turn right onto the Crest Trail and follow it 0.7 mile farther to Junction Saddle, just beyond which is the signed spur trail to Anita Park.) 9640-foot Snowshed Peak is 0.6 mile up the rough path which branches right from here; this is a good destination for dayhikers.

Return the way you came, or via the Crest Trail and the South Fork Trail to South Fork Forest Camp (3-mile car shuttle required for this option; see Trips 60 and 61.)

See Map 22

coppery-tailed trogon (m.)

Area 3:
The Eastern
Highlands

The eastern highlands region takes in the high, heavily forested, mostly rolling country of the White Mountains and the Blue Range, in east-central Arizona near the New Mexico border. Two separate areas, encompassing much of the region's best hiking, have been officially set aside for nonmotorized use — the Blue Range Primitive Area and the Mount Baldy Wilderness.

Elevations in the 173,000-acre Blue Range Primitive Area range from above 9000 feet, near Hannagan Meadow, to well below 5000 feet along the Lower Blue River. Dense Canadian-zone forests of Engelmann spruce, white fir and Douglas-fir, and some quaking aspen blanket the very highest areas. Below this, a transition-zone mixture of ponderosa pine, Gambel oak, alligator juniper and silverleaf oak prevails, giving way to a sparse, Upper-Sonoran-zone cover of one-seed juniper and pinyon pine below about 6000 feet. A number of small but perennial streams within the wilderness are lined with magnificent forests of riparian hardwoods such as sycamore, walnut, bigtooth maple, box elder and velvet ash. The canyon of the Blue River, swept frequently by flash floods, is considerably more barren than its tributaries; its bouldery banks support only isolated stands of mesquite, cottonwood and sycamore.

The two greatest determinants of the Blue Range's topography are the Blue River, which flows from north to south and whose deep canyon divides the primitive area neatly in two, and the Mogollon Rim, which bisects the area from west to east. Elevations are therefore greater along the eastern and western fringes than in the center, and greater in the north than in the south. The zones of discontinuity between high and low areas — known locally as the Blue River "breaks" — tend to be heavily eroded, with numerous small cliffs and outcroppings cut out of the red conglomerates and lighter volcanic rocks that cover the area.

With its wide elevation range, the primitive area includes habitats amenable to a variety of wildlife. Javelina, bobcat and mountain lion inhabit its lower reaches, while Rocky Mountain elk, Coues white-tailed deer and mule deer are fairly common in the higher forests. A number of rare and endangered species find sanctuary here, including the spotted owl, peregrine falcon, Arizona woodpecker, kit fox and southern bald eagle. The Blue River and its perennial tributaries are home to a limited number of brook, brown and rainbow trout.

As of 1980 a proposal to reclassify the Blue Range Primitive Area as the Blue Range Wilderness had been sent to Congress. It has not yet been acted upon, but eventual approval is expected. Some small-scale cattle grazing is unfortunately currently allowed within the primitive area boundaries, and will likely continue for some time following a wilderness designation.

The 6975-acre Mount Baldy Wilderness, in the White Mountains, is one of the smallest but most pristine areas included in the federal wilderness system. Elevations range from 9200 feet, at Sheep Crossing, to 11,403 feet atop Mount Baldy. It is one of the few places in Arizona where one can hike in the Hudsonian (or subalpine) life zone. Except for a few wildflower-sprinkled meadows and the Baldy summit area, the entire region is heavily forested with Colorado blue spruce, white fir, corkbar fir, ponderosa pine, white pine and quaking aspen. Several major streams have their headwaters on Baldy's gently rising slopes, including the East Fork White River, the West Fork Black River, and the East and West Forks of the Little Colorado River.

Mount Baldy itself is an extinct volcano, a remnant of a broad lava dome formed by a series of eruptions that ceased some 8 or 9 million years ago. Most of this ancient dome has since been eroded away, both by water and by the glaciers that, during the so-called ice ages of the Pleistocene era, bulldozed their way down the slopes of the mountain. Erosion by glaciers tends to widen the valleys that contain them, forming broad-bottomed, U-shaped troughs rather than the narrow-bottomed, V-shaped canyons formed by stream erosion. This is one reason why the drainages in the Mount Baldy Wilderness are so much more open and parklike than those at lower elevations. (Compare, for example, the stretch of the West Fork Little Colorado River Canyon above Sheep Crossing to the stretch below.) Rocks picked up by these rivers of ice were carried slowly downhill; at the end of a glacier, where the ice constantly melted, the rocks were deposited loosely in wide arcs called terminal moraines. With the advent of the warmer weather of the modern era the glaciers receded and disappeared, spreading morainal material irregularly along the length of the occupied canyons. Stream water later pooled up behind some of the moraines, creating small ponds; these gradually filled with silt, eventually forming the beautiful meadowed flats which now grace the area.

A variety of animal species prosper in the lower reaches of the wilderness, including Rocky Mountain elk, black bear, mule deer, porcupine, wild turkey and blue grouse. A few beaver colonies are active along the forks of the Little Colorado.

Severe thunderstorms are common over the White Mountains during July and August, and hikers are advised to vacate exposed areas by early afternoon during those months.

The actual summit of Mount Baldy is on the Fort Apache Indian Reservation. Reservation regulations require that persons entering Indian land purchase beforehand a Special Use Permit, available for a small fee from the Recreation Enterprise Office in Whiteriver (see address below).

Clifton Ranger District
P.O. Box 698   southern Blue Range Primitive Area
Clifton, AZ 85533
    (602) 865-2432

Alpine Ranger District
P.O. Box 469   northern Blue Range Primitive Area
Alpine, AZ 85920
    (602) 339-4384

Springerville Ranger District
P.O. Box 640   Mount Baldy Wilderness
Springerville, AZ 85938
    (602) 333-4372

White Mountain Apache Enterprise
Fort Apache Indian Reservation
P.O. Box 218   Mount Baldy summit area
Whiteriver, AZ 85941
    (602) 338-4385

Approaches/Trailheads

Blue Range Primitive Area:

Blue Lookout Roadend   From Clifton, drive north approximately 65 miles along U.S. 666 to the signed Blue Lookout Road.
(Alternately, proceed 35 miles south along U.S. 666 from Alpine
to this point.) Then turn right (east) and follow the semi-improved
dirt road (O.K. for ordinary passenger cars) 5 miles to its terminus
at a sign indicating the primitive area boundary.

Lower Blue River   From Clifton, proceed north along U.S.
666 approximately 30 miles, then turn right onto Forest Road 475.
Drive down this dirt road past the Juan Miller Campgrounds to the
junction with Forest Road 475, about 11 miles. Turn left here and
continue 2.9 miles further to the Blue River at Fritz Ranch.
Beyond here the road grows rougher, and crosses the Blue River
several times. Approximately 3.5 miles beyond Fritz Ranch you
will encounter a locked gate; park here, but do not block the road,
which is still used occasionally by the owners of HU Bar Ranch.
(The road beyond the primitive area boundary is closed to public
vehicle use, and is designated as Forest Trail 101.)
    Ordinary passenger cars will have trouble with this approach.
The last portion is impassable during high water periods.

Blue Camp   From Clifton, drive north along U.S. 666 to
Beaverhead Lodge (about 85 miles). Turn east onto Forest Road
567 (Red Hill Road) and follow it 12 miles to the Blue River at
Forest Road 281. Turn right here, and follow Forest Road 281 3
miles south to a sign reading "Blue Administrative Site," a.k.a.
Blue Camp. The start of the *Foote Creek Trail* is indicated by a
sign on the west side of the main road a short distance beyond here.
To reach the trail to *Lanphier Creek*, *Largo Canyon*, and *Bear
Mountain Lookout*, park your car off the main road and walk
down the spur road which branches left. Stay right at the junction
with the road to the Forest Service buildings, continue a short
distance past the I.M. Swapp place, then pass through a gate

(please remember to close the gate). Follow the road across the Blue River to another gate, just beyond which is a sign indicating the start of the trail.

Forest Roads 567 and 281 are readily negotiable by ordinary passenger cars. F.R. 567 is normally snowed in from January 1 to March 15; F.R. 281 is normally open year-round.

Hannagan Meadow   Approximately 75 miles north of Clifton on U.S. 666 is Hannagan Meadow Lodge. Just south of the lodge turn east onto a good dirt road; follow this a short distance past Hannagan Administrative Site to a sign indicating the trailhead. (The old, overgrown road branching left here is the start of the Steeple Mesa Trail).

Blue River at the *Steeple Mesa Trail*   To reach the bottom of the Steeple Mesa Trail (at the end of Trip 71) drive south along Forest Road 281 8 miles past Blue Camp. The trailhead is signed, but it is difficult to locate the trail from below.

KP Cienega   At a point 1.5 miles north of the Blue Lookout Road (approximately 65 miles north of Clifton), U.S. 666 meets Forest Road 25 coming in from the northwest. Just north of this junction a well-graded dirt road branches off the highway to the southeast. Follow this for 1 mile to the signed trailhead just above KP Cienega Campground.

Blue River at *Grant Creek*   From Blue Camp continue south along Forest Road 281 for 4.0 miles. (The road is still quite close to the river at this point, but veers away just beyond.) Park here, cross the Blue River, and follow it a short distance downstream to the confluence of Grant Creek. A sign indicating the bottom of the Grant Creek Trail (at the end of Trip 74) is just north of the creek.

Upper Blue River   From Blue Camp, continue south along Forest Road 281 to its terminus, about 12 miles. Forest Trail 101 (which soon turns into a cross-country route) begins just beyond the primitive-area boundary sign.

Mount Baldy Wilderness:

Sheep Crossing   From Show Low drive southeast along Highway 260 past Pinetop and McNary, then turn right onto Highway 273. 25 miles beyond McNary the road turns sharply to the west and dips into the canyon of the West Fork Little Colorado River (not a river but a stream at this point). Just before crossing the West Fork, turn right onto a spur road and proceed 0.5 mile to the trailhead.

Phelps Cabin   Follow the preceding approach to the West Fork Little Colorado River crossing, then continue 2.7 miles on Highway 273 to a signed junction. Turn right here; the trailhead is 0.2 mile beyond.

Highway 273 is not paved beyond the Fort Apache Reservation boundary, and the last 5 miles or so of these approaches is over a wide, well-graded dirt road. Ordinary passenger cars should find it readily passable, except possibly immediately after a heavy rain.

Trip 63   Blue Lookout Roadend to Blue Lookout

2.2 miles round trip; 500′ elevation gain

Leisurely dayhike

Season June to October

No water available along route

Features

Offering a maximum of view for a minimum of effort, this trip to Blue Lookout is an excellent introduction to the Blue Range high country. Hikers seeking refuge from the sweltering midsummer lowlands will find this to be delightfully cool sweater country, even in August, while those willing to brave the midautumn chill will find the slopes aflame with frost-yellowed aspen leaves.

Description

From the end of the Blue Lookout Road (0.0; 8840) we follow the trail east as it traverses the north side of the ridge leading to the lookout. The forest cover of spruce, fir and aspen is so dense along the way that we will not be treated to an open view until reaching the very top, but the immediate feeling of wildness and isolation which that density fosters more than makes up for the lack. During the summer these woods are home to small herds of Rocky Mountain mule deer and Coues white-tailed deer. Blue grouse and wild turkeys are also fairly common in the area, and with luck you might hear some of these large, ground-dwelling fowl clucking and gobbling off in the trees, or even come upon them strutting unconcernedly along the trail.

Climbing gently, we soon reach a signed junction with a branch of the KP Creek trail (0.6; 8920), where we stay right. A short distance later the path begins climbing more steeply, and makes one long switchback before arriving at the base of Blue Lookout. Because of the trees that crowd the mountaintop, the clearest views are obtained from the top of the lookout tower. Those who wish to ascend the steep stairway to the "cage" may do so, but please honor the request posted at its base, and go up in groups of no more than four at a time. If you arrive before or after the lookout's manned season (normally May 1 to August 1) you will find the trapdoor leading into the observation room locked, but you may still climb to the top of the stairs for a better view.

This summit offers a more extensive vista than perhaps any other point in the Blue Range. This is so because it is perched on the edge of the Mogollon Rim, the 300-mile-long escarpment that separates the Sonoran Lowlands from the Colorado Plateau. To the north we look out across the high, spruce- and aspen-forested tops of the Blues; to the south the mountains fall away abruptly to the oak-and-ponderosa country beyond Strayhorse Divide, making a final resurgence at 8786-foot Rose Peak. Beyond that the view is likely to be obscured by the horrifying sulfurous pall that emanates from the Morenci copper smelters, but on a rare clear day one can barely make out the faint blue outline of the Chiricahua Mountains, just north of the Mexican border some 120 miles distant. To the west and east it is instructive to trace the irregular scarp of the Mogollon Rim as it winds out of central Arizona, breaks down at the deep gap cut by the Blue River to the east, and then rises again to continue into New Mexico.

Return the way you came.

See Map 23

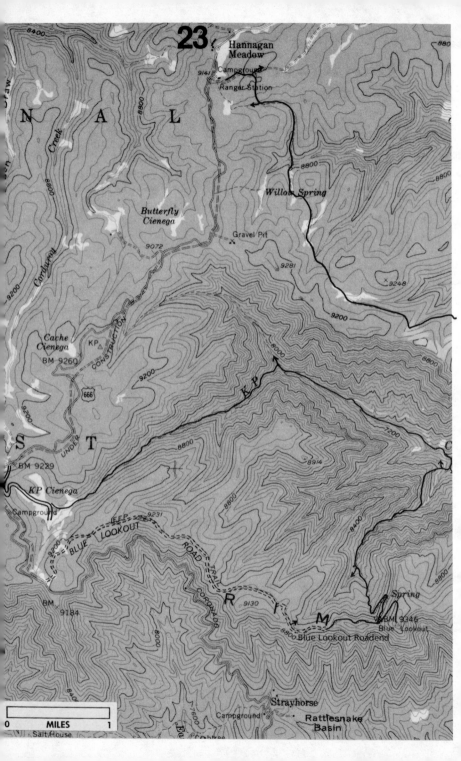

Trip 64   Lower Blue River Trailhead to HU Bar Box and Upper Blue River Trailhead

4.6–11.0 miles one-way (90-mile car shuttle if you go all the way); 270′–600′ elevation gain

Leisurely to moderate dayhike or backpack (2 hiking days)

Season all year; hot in summer

Water available all year along entire route

Features

The Blue River is dogged by roads for its entire length, with the exception of the 7-mile segment above HU Bar Ranch, which is protected against motorized intrusion by its inclusion within the Blue Range Primitive Area. Even this unroaded stretch is not completely "primitive," for you are likely to see some quite domesticated cattle grazing along its banks at all-too-frequent intervals. But it is peaceful country, sycamore-forested and automobile-free, well worth a visit by anyone who would know all the varied facets of the Blue Range.

Description

From the gate at the "end" of Forest Road 475 (0.0; 4480), walk northeast along the bulldozed track that parallels the Blue River. Though designated "Forest Trail 101" beyond the trailhead/primitive area boundary, this track is still very much a road for its first 4 miles (from here to HU Bar Ranch). You may see fresh tire tracks along this stretch, because the road is still used on occasion (under a Forest Service Special Use Permit) by the owners of the HU Bar property.

Vegetation along the Blue River's alternately sandy and gravelly floodplain is sparse, though there are some tall cottonwoods and sycamores scattered about. Mesquite trees grow along the dry margins of the canyon, and pinyon pines and scrub oaks dot the surrounding hillsides. Fishermen may wish to stop and cast for some of the skittish brown and rainbow trout (mostly small) that inhabit the river.

After crossing the river twice in quick succession (these fords can be difficult when the water is high), the road veers well to the right of the watercourse. After a half mile or so we reach Little Blue Creek (0.6; 4500), at a nice grove of sycamores. After crossing the Little Blue (which is sometimes dry at this point), the road continues gently up-canyon, passing beneath small cliffs and crossing and recrossing the main river at frequent intervals. Beyond the confluence of perennial Thomas Creek (2.0; 4560) the canyon grows narrower and, for a while, somewhat shadier. About a mile after the country begins to open up again we arrive at HU Bar Ranch (4.1; 4660), where there are a few corrals and small outbuildings.

From here we walk a short distance to a pull gate, where the road ends. Beyond the gate, our route follows a cattle track northward until it fades out in the rocky, jumbled debris of the Blue River's floodplain, and for the remainder of our trip we alternate boulder-hopping with slogging through soft sand. At a second fence, 0.5 mile beyond the ranch area, the canyon sides close in abruptly, and we enter the deep, vertical-walled slot known as HU Bar Box (4.6; 4670). To get through this narrows, we must cross and recross the river as it winds from cliff to cliff. After heavy rains and during the spring runoff this part of the route may be impassable. Backpackers will find excellent campsites on grassy, cottonwood- and sycamore-shaded flats both immediately above and immediately below the Box. Those with enough time to linger can sample the limited fishing in the river, go exploring up a side canyon, or simply relax and meditate beneath the rustling leaves of a sycamore. You can also continue upstream; it is about 5.4 miles (cross country all the way) to the confluence of perennial Strayhorse Creek (10.0; 4940), from where it is a mile farther (along a faint trail) to the southern terminus of Forest Road 281 at Upper Blue River Trailhead. But HU Bar Box is by far the most interesting feature of this roadless stretch of river, and most parties will want to turn around here.

Often during high-water periods the river is not blue, but muddy and brown. This is a perfectly natural occurrence, the result of heavy erosion of the myriad thinly vegetated slopes which drain into the Blue River.

See Maps 24 and 25

Trip 65   Lower Blue River to Hannah Hot Spring, Little Blue Box and Dutch Blue Creek via Little Blue Creek

10.2 miles round trip; 780′ elevation gain

Strenuous dayhike or moderate backpack (2 hiking days)

Season all year; hot in summer

Water available intermittently along entire route

Features

Crystalline Hannah Springs Creek and its narrow, rock-ribbed gorge are the highlights of this fascinating trip. Those who venture farther, beyond Little Blue Box, will also want to explore the wild, exceedingly remote country along Dutch Blue Creek and the upper Little Blue, with its abundant wildlife and strangely eroded canyons.

Most of the route along Little Blue Creek is cross-country, and the one short section of trail is tricky in spots, making this a trip for skilled hikers only.

Description

From the gate at the end of Forest Road 475 (0.0; 4480), follow the route of Trip 64 to the point where Forest Trail 101 crosses Little Blue Creek (0.6; 4500). From here, walk cross-country east through a sycamore grove, then pass a drift fence and continue up the trailless canyon of the Little Blue, alternately rock-hopping and bushwacking up the creek banks. The stream is sometimes dry through here, but soon it should begin to show at least intermittent signs of life. After the first 0.5 mile the brush thins out considerably, and the generally barren aspect of the watercourse is relieved by a riparian growth of walnut, sycamore and alder. Mesquite trees grow in the drier parts of the canyon floor, while a heavy pinyon-juniper forest dominates the sun-baked hillsides.

Some 3 miles upstream Hannah Springs Creek (3.7; 4700) branches off to the right and disappears up its narrow canyon. To reach Hannah Hot Spring, scramble up the slotlike gorge for about 0.4 mile, circumventing a troublesome pool of water by

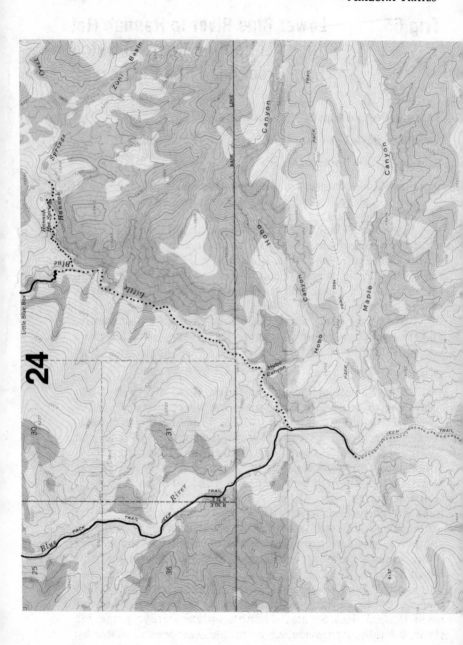

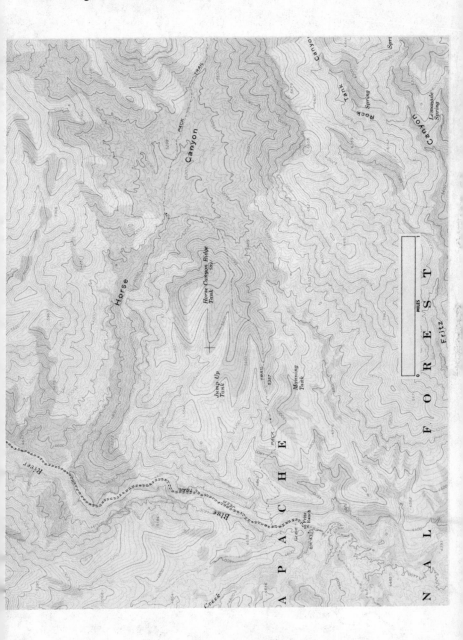

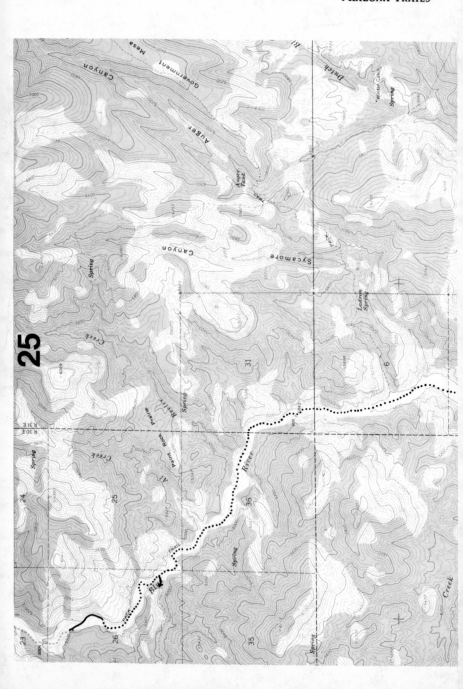

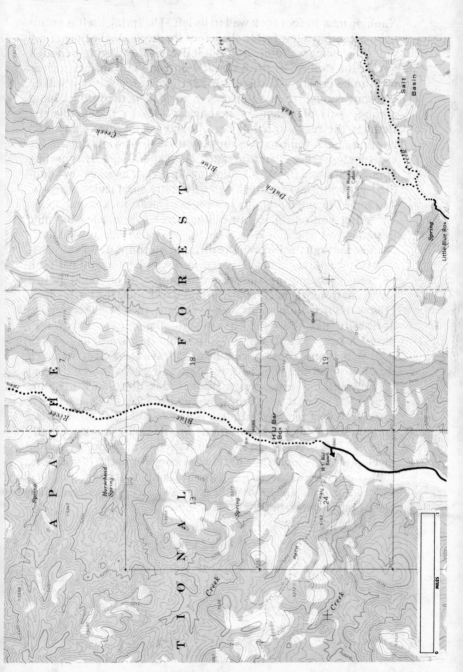

climbing up a 10 foot rock wall to its left. The spring itself is an anticlimactic seep a few feet to the left of the creek. At the time of my visit, this spring was quite hot, but it did not flow strongly enough to take the chill off of the water downstream. Hot springs such as this can be notoriously capricious; perhaps in the future it will be vigorous enough to allow hikers to soak their tired bones amid curling wisps of steam, or perhaps it will dry up completely. Perhaps the real attraction here is Hannah Springs Canyon — twisting, steep-walled, overhung with trees growing out of the cliffs high overhead, and threaded from end to end by sparkling Hannah Springs Creek. Continuing upstream another few hundred yards will reward the hiker with more spectacular narrows, and some bracing swimming in a series of clear, rockbound pools.

After you return to Little Blue Creek it is another 0.4 mile upstream to Little Blue Box, a cliffy, "boxed in" narrows. Direct passage through the Box is quite difficult; to continue up-canyon it is best to backtrack a few hundred yards to where a faint path can be seen scrabbling up the west canyonside. (This point is just upstream from where Hannah Springs Creek joins the Little Blue.) Follow this track as it winds steeply upward, then begins traversing northward high above the Box. In about 0.6 mile the narrow trail passes a steep section where a slip could be hazardous — watch your step. Approximately ¾ mile after leaving the creek we reach the crest of a ridge which forms the south wall of a well-defined ravine; here our route drops steeply back down to Little Blue Creek. We are now upstream from the Box, and it is a short, easy walk the rest of the way to Dutch Blue Creek (5.1; 4820). This is a good base for further explorations up the oddly sculptured canyons of Little Blue, Dutch Blue and Ash creeks. You may see some javelinas in this area and, during the cooler months of the year, some Coues white-tailed deer as well. Camping is where you find it; look for flat spots among the trees away from the water (flash floods occur here), but don't be too picky.

Return the way you came.

See Maps 24 and 25

Trip 66   Blue Camp to Lanphier Creek and Indian Canyon

5.8 miles round trip; 800' elevation gain

Leisurely dayhike or backpack (2 hiking days)

Season all year; best spring and fall

Water available all year from mile 0.7 to end of route

Features

Tiny, murmuring Lanphier Creek and its pleasantly shaded canyon are both the means and the end of this short trip, which offers a maximum of seclusion and wilderness "feel" for a minimum of effort. You will likely find nothing spectacular or awe-inspiring along this quiet route — just the gurgling creek, the grapevine-laced trees, and plenty of peace and contentment.

Description

Immediately after passing the primitive-area boundary sign behind Blue Camp (0.0; 5640) the trail begins climbing away from briefly glimpsed Lanphier Creek. Fortunately, before we can quite get out of breath, the route levels off and begins a rocky, winding, shadeless traverse in and out of ravines a hundred feet or so above the stream. 0.5 mile later we stay right at an unsigned junction and descend back toward the creek. A short distance farther is a signed fork (0.7; 5720), where we go left and then climb gently up-canyon through a riparian forest of box elder, Arizona walnut, New Mexican locust, maple, and an occasional Douglas-fir or ponderosa pine. The route crosses and recrosses Lanphier Creek, and it is rather easy to lose the trail in the boulders near the water. If lost, however, it can easily be picked up again by scouting around on the other side of the stream. An impressive variety of birdlife congregates in this leafy canyon, particularly in the spring, and bird-watchers may be able to spot and identify such rare species as the olive warbler and the Arizona woodpecker. A host of mammals inhabit this area as well; squirrels frolic in the trees, deer are common, and cougars and bears are at least occasional visitors. Hikers who are abroad in the predawn hours may come upon a family of skunks parading along the trail, or surprise a raccoon in the process of washing up in the creek — or divesting a carelessly unguarded backpack of its food stores.

After two miles of alternate trail-walking and boulder-hopping, the creek turns to the south and enters Indian Canyon (2.9; 6300). Backpackers will find good campsites in the vicinity, especially on the benches above the stream. This is the end of our route, though you may wish to scramble up trailless Indian Canyon a short distance. The path we have been following continues up Lanphier Canyon into the ponderosa country (see Trip 68), but beyond here it is steep, ill maintained, and difficult to follow.

Return the way you came.

See Map 26

Trip 67   Blue Camp to Largo Canyon and Bear Mountain Lookout; return via Telephone Ridge

12.8 mile semiloop trip; 3150 ' elevation gain

Strenuous dayhike

Season May to October

Water available all season at Lanphier Creek (miles 0.7 and 12.1) and Maple Spring (miles 3.2 and 9.6)

Features

After crossing leafy Lanphier Creek, this route takes the hiker through stately forests of oak and ponderosa to broad-backed Bear Mountain, whose strategically located summit affords unsurpassed vistas across the rugged canyon of the Blue River.

Description

Immediately after passing the primitive-area boundary sign behind Blue Camp (0.0; 5640) the trail begins climbing away from briefly glimpsed Lanphier Creek. Fortunately, before we can quite get out of breath, the route levels off and begins a rocky, winding, shadeless traverse in and out of ravines a hundred feet or so above the stream. About 0.5 mile later we stay right at an unsigned junction and descend back toward the creek. A short distance farther is a signed fork (0.7; 5720), where we continue straight ahead, cross

the stream, and climb steeply up to the crest of a low divide (1.5; 6120) separating Largo and Lamphier canyons. Beyond here we pass through a ponderosa-forested flat, then descend into Largo Canyon. The route now turns up-canyon, weaving back and forth across the bouldery creekbed (often dry) and occasionally rising and dipping steeply. This section is moderately shaded by a mixture of Gambel oak, bigtooth maple and ponderosa pine.

One mile after entering Largo Canyon we come to Maple Spring (3.2; 6600), at a round cement tank surrounded with watercress. This is the highest reliable water on our route, so be sure to replenish your supply here.

At the spring is an unsigned junction, where we stay left, continuing up-canyon to a signed fork a few hundred yards beyond. The path coming down from the right here is part of our return route, the Telephone Ridge Trail. Again we continue straight up-canyon, ignoring the occasional faint spur trails that branch off to the left. After 1.5 miles of moderate climbing we arrive at an unsigned junction (5.1; 7480) with the trail to Bear Valley and Campbell Flat (see Trip 68). This time we go right, wind our way up a low ridgelet between two branches of Largo Canyon, and enter a burned-over ponderosa forest. The hulking back of Bear Mountain is now visible through the blackened trees to our right. Shortly after exiting the burn area the path suddenly grows steeper, and soon we make the first of many switchbacks that climb the brushy, scantily shaded east shoulder of the peak. At the top of this occasionally steep ascent we meet the signed Telephone Ridge Trail coming up from the north; here we turn left and complete the final ¼-mile climb to Bear Mountain (6.5; 8550).

Atop the peak you will find a cabin, shed and corral — all ancillary to the maintenance of the lookout. Since Bear Mountain's entire crown is heavily forested with ponderosa pine, it is necessary to climb the series of steep ladders to the cage atop the tower to obtain an unobstructed view. Visitors are advised by a sign at the bottom that, though welcome, they climb at their own risk. Before and after the lookout's manned season (normally May 15 to July 15), the observation room will be locked, but you can still get a good view from the platform immediately below.

Among the landmarks visible from the tower are Sawed Off Mountain, Blue Peak and Rose Peak, rising above the rough-cut Blue River "breaks" to the west. The high point to the east is 8827-foot Whiterocks Mountain, situated just across the border in New Mexico. Since Bear Mountain stands on the Mogollon Rim, it is interesting to note the difference between the views to the north and to the south: to the north, rising and swelling in waves above the deep gap cut by the Blue River, is the densely forested high country surrounding Alpine, while to the southwest the mountains fall away steadily toward the sere lowlands beyond Clifton and Morenci.

When saturated with vistas, retrace your steps ¼ mile to the top of the Telephone Ridge Trail, turn left, and begin descending Telephone Ridge, passing occasional good views to the left and right as the initially gradual descent steepens. About 2 miles later we reach an unsigned junction, where we double back to the right and plunge down steep switchbacks to the Largo Canyon Trail just above Maple Spring (9.6; 6600). From here, retrace the morning's route the remaining distance to Blue Camp (12.8; 5640).

See Maps 26 and 27

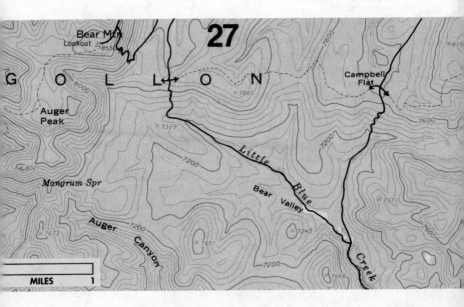

Trip 68   Blue Camp to Largo Canyon, Bear Valley and Lanphier Canyon

18.1-mile semiloop trip; 3440' elevation gain

Moderate to strenuous backpack (2–4 hiking days)

Season May to October

Water available all season at Lanphier Creek (mile 0.7), Maple Spring (mile 3.2) and Lanphier Canyon (miles 15.2 to 17.4); Little Blue Creek (mile 8.8) may be dry

Features

Ater passing within side-tripping distance of lofty Bear Mountain, this lengthy loop route descends into remote, infrequently visited Bear Valley, which sees as much of its namesake the black bear as it does of man. An added highlight is the return trip through Lanphier Canyon, with its spectacular hardwood forests and tiny, burbling creek.

Much of this route is along trails that are unmaintained and difficult to follow, and it is recommended only for experienced wilderness hikers.

Description

Follow the directions for Trip 67 to the unsigned trail junction at the head of Largo Canyon (5.1; 7480). Those who wish to make the side trip to Bear Mountain (highly recommended) should turn right here and follow the route of Trip 67 to the summit (1.4 miles one way). Others will stay left and continue climbing gently through ponderosa to a poorly signed junction in a saddle (6.0; 7720). The trail is rather indistinct in this area — look for blazes and sawn-through logs to stay on the right track. At the saddle we turn neither right nor left, but descend straight ahead down a hot, brushy slope to the head of Little Blue Creek in Bear Valley. The creek is often dry at this point, but as we veer left and walk gently down-canyon it should begin showing signs of life. By the time we arrive at a corral and a signed trail junction (8.8; 6840) there is generally enough surface flow to support a tiny green meadow and good camping. (During dry years, and late in the season, it is advisable to check with the Alpine Ranger District about the water supply here.)

On the hillsides south and west of Bear Valley you may see signs of a recent wildfire — the legacy of the 1979 Horse Fire, which was allowed by the Forest Service to burn for several weeks before being suppressed. This action, or nonaction, was part of a new fire policy adopted in light of a greater understanding of wildfire's vitalizing role in certain natural ecosystems. Close inspection of the burned hillsides above the trail will reveal that not all of the adult trees were killed by the flames; the net effect of the fire was simply to clear away the dense, brushy understory which was competing with ponderosa seedlings, thus clearing the way for the germination and growth of a whole new generation of pines.

To complete the loop back to Blue Camp, proceed north from the trail junction, following a faint path that climbs gently along a streamcourse. After a mile this trail veers left and switchbacks up a brushy, shadeless slope to a saddle, just beyond which is a poorly signed junction in wooded Campbell Flat (10.6; 7560). We go straight ahead at this 4-way crossroads, rising and falling gently as the trail traverses an area devoid of landmarks. At length, when we appear to be approaching a dropoff of sorts, the trail swings right, cuts across a low, oak-forested ridge, and then descends into a minor, northward-trending drainage. Our route stays left at an unsigned fork here, then continues gently downhill to a signed junction (13.0; 7320). Here we go left again, past the remnants of an old cattle camp, and then drop steeply down to Cashier Spring, a muddy, unreliable seep in the hillside next to a solitary carved aspen.

Below Cashier Spring the route is confused by a plethora of use trails; the correct path crosses to the right of Lanphier Canyon Creek (often dry here), heads straight down-canyon for 0.5 mile, then ascends to a bench on the right-hand canyonside. After traversing a dry, rocky slope high above the creekbed, we drop steeply back down and rejoin the creek just upstream from Indian Canyon (15.2; 6280). Here there is excellent camping and perennial water.

To complete this semiloop trip, retrace the steps of Trip 66 the remaining 2.9 miles to Blue Camp (18.1; 5640).

See Maps 26 and 27

Trip 69 Blue Camp to Lower Blue River via Largo Canyon, Bear Valley and Little Blue Creek

27.9 miles one way (85-mile car shuttle required); 2440' elevation gain

Strenuous backpack (allow at least 3 hiking days)

Season April to October; hot in midsummer

Water available all season at Lanphier Creek (mile 0.7) and Maple Spring (mile 3.2), and intermittently along Little Blue Creek and Lower Blue River (miles 8.8 to 27.9)

Features

This long, demanding trek pierces the wild heart of the eastern Blue Range. Along the way it passes through magnificent stands of oak and ponderosa, threads its way through narrow, steep-walled canyons, skirts the mammoth pedestals of towering rock pinnacles, and traces the length of Little Blue Creek from its pine-forested headwaters to its dissolution in the lower Blue River. Rewarding side trips are possible to Bear Mountain, with its extensive vistas, and up Dutch Blue and Hannah Springs creeks.

Over half of this route is cross country, making it a trip for the experienced, well-seasoned backpacker only. And remember — this is exceptionally remote, rarely visited country. You'll be on your own all the way.

Description

Follow the directions for Trip 68 to the signed trail junction in Bear Valley (8.8; 6840). Here we turn right and drop moderately down the quickly deepening canyon of Little Blue Creek. After winding through a miniature narrows, we reach a generally reliable spring situated just across the creek from a cluster of high, spectacularly eroded reddish pinnacles. Shortly beyond the last of these rock towers the trail passes through an elaborate gate, then meets a spur trail coming down from a side canyon to the west. Our route stays left here, and continues down the now well-defined canyon of Little Blue Creek, past several inviting campsites beneath an airy overstory of tall oaks and ponderosas, until it

arrives at the confluence of Yam Canyon (11.5; 6250). Wildlife is
plentiful in this area — you may surpise a herd of Coues deer and
send them bounding noisily away through the underbrush, or
come upon the track of a bobcat or cougar in the mud by the
stream. With luck you might even glimpse a rare kit fox or spotted
owl, two members of the rare-or-endangered species list which still
cling to existence in the remote backcountry of the Blues.

At this point the trail we have been following turns left (east)
and begins climbing up to the grazing lands atop Alma Mesa. We
continue downstream, however, and embark on a virtually trailless, 15-mile trek out to the Blue River. Passing beneath more high
cliffs to the right, we wind our way along the pleasantly shaded,
deep defile between Alma and Horse mesas. Where the canyon
walls begin to break down some 4 miles later is an old corral (15.9;
5580). Here you may pick up a rudimentary trail that parallels the
creek for a short distance, but do not expect your cross-country
labors to cease just yet; the path is apparently used only to move
livestock back and forth between the two mesas, and it soon veers
away from our route. About 3 miles further down-canyon we encounter a barbed-wire fence and another corral, and the traveler
may well begin to resent these domestic intrusions into this hard-
to-reach, otherwise primitive area.

Between here and its confluence with Dutch Blue Creek (22.8;
4820) Little Blue Creek passes through a series of shallow, steep-
walled gorges, occasionally slipping beneath its overhanging banks
or pooling up in an eerie grotto beneath huge boulders that have
fallen from above. The forest cover continues to change as we lose
elevation, and in place of ponderosa and Douglas-fir we find
sycamore, pinyon, walnut, juniper, a wide variety of oaks and,
along the streambanks, refreshingly green copses of ash and alder.

A short distance beyond Dutch Blue Creek the Little Blue
makes a sharp bend to the south and enters Little Blue Box — a
deep, vertical-sided narrows, which is often filled with water from
wall to wall and virtually impassable. To continue our journey we
must bypass the Box; ¼ mile below Dutch Blue Creek, at a point
where a prominent ravine comes down from the west, look for a
cairn on a rock shelf a few feet above Little Blue Creek. This marks
the start of an obscure trail which can be seen switchbacking up the
ridge that forms the ravine's south wall. Follow this path as it
climbs steeply some 150 feet up the ridge, then turns left (south)
and begins paralleling the stream high above the gorge. About ¾
mile later we drop abruptly down a rocky slope back to the creek.

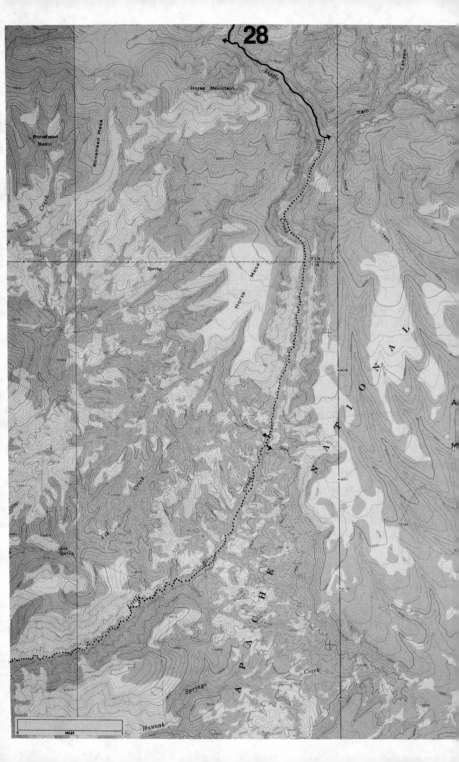

sacred datura blossom

During warm weather a short swim may seem in order by this time, and a pool suitable for this purpose can be found a short distance upstream, at the lower end of the Box.

Just downstream from the Box we encounter Hannah Springs Creek (24.2; 4700), flowing out of a side canyon to the left. The 15-minute scramble up to Hannah Hot Spring is well worth the trouble; the spring itself is not particularly impressive, but the canyon above it is a delightful pastiche of singing cascades, deep "boxes" and clear, sparkling swimming holes — definitely worth an exploratory visit. The only major difficulty along this detour occurs a few hundred yards up the canyon, where the narrow cleft is blocked by a pool; either wade across the pool, or bypass it by scrambling up a 10 foot rock wall to the left. A short distance beyond is the hot spring, a weak seep a few feet to the left of the main creek. This geothermal "leak" was hot enough at the time of my visit, but its flow was unfortunately not strong enough to noticeably improve the temperature of the pool into which it emptied.

When ready to complete your journey, return to Little Blue Creek and resume rockhopping down-canyon. In 3 miles you will encounter a drift fence, just beyond which is Forest Trail 101 (a jeep track at this point, closed to public vehicle travel) and the Blue River. Turn left here, and walk down the trail/road the remaining 0.6 mile to Lower Blue River Trailhead (27.9; 4480) (reverse the steps of the first half of Trip 64).

See Maps 26, 27, 28, 25 and 24

Trip 70   Blue Camp to Foote Creek

5.8 miles round trip; 1040 ' elevation gain

Moderate dayhike or leisurely backpack (2 hiking days)

Season all year; best spring and fall

Water available all year at Cedar Springs (mile 1.2) and Foote Creek (mile 2.9)

Features

Enroute to delightful Foote Creek, this trip passes through two distinctive ecological communities — a dry, sunny, Upper Sonoran woodland, where pinyons and junipers grow against a backdrop of distant mountains, and a lush, shady riparian forest, where the sunlight is more congenial, the views more intimate. Hikers who are new to the lower Blue Range will find this route a good introduction to the contrasting moods of this little known, infrequently visited country.

Description

The most strenuous part of this trip comes at the very beginning, in the form of a steep, switchbacking ascent up the shadeless, cactus-studded canyonside opposite the trailhead at Blue Camp (0.0; 5640). After gaining some 500 feet in the first 0.5 mile we suddenly break out onto a rolling, savannahlike mesa, and the winded hiker can relax with the knowledge that the worst is behind him. The trail is occasionally faint through here, but it maintains a straight course as it descends gently westward, and is not hard to follow. Views to the south are pleasant, reaching out across pinyons, junipers and waving grasses to distant ridges receding into the haze that hangs above the San Francisco River country. Mule deer, Coues white-tailed deer and Rocky Mountain elk are occasionally seen in this area, particularly in winter and early spring, when the high-country meadows are still buried in snow.

Presently the trail drops into a shallow ravine that contains the trickling runoff from Cedar Springs (1.2; 5920). After crossing this tiny freshet and climbing back out of its channel, we pass through a pull gate, then descend into another branch of the springs' effluence. Beyond here the trail rises and falls over short distances as it begins the long traverse toward Foote Creek, which is slowly rising to meet us on the left. Soon we round a bend, where we get our first glimpse of Foote Creek canyon heading north toward the high mountains. Here the trail runs up alongside a barbed-wire fence, an unwelcome intrusion from civilization which continues to dog us as we drop into a ravine, climb out again, and resume our traverse. Finally we leave the fence behind us at another gate, then descend moderately to shaded Foote Creek (2.9; 5840). Several fair to good campsites can be found nearby, in sylvan groves of sycamore, walnut, Arizona cypress and maple. Fishing in the creek is fair for rainbow, brown and brook trout.

Down-canyon the stream quickly dries up into a series of disconnected pools (except during the spring runoff), but those who wish to camp further up-canyon will find reliable water at all seasons for the next two miles or so; beyond that the creek is often intermittent.

Return the way you came.

See Map 26

Trip 71   Hannagan Meadow to the Blue River via Mud Spring and Steeple Mesa

13.3 miles one way (45-mile car shuttle required); 4100' elevation loss, 500' gain

Moderate dayhike or backpack (2 hiking days)

Season June to October

Water available all season at Willow Spring (mile 2.1); Mud Spring (mile 7.5) generally reliable throughout the summer rainy season

Features

The "breaks" of the Blue River country — the broken, choppy ridges that drop abruptly from the alpine high country to the riverine lowlands — transect three major life zones. The descending Steeple Mesa Trail takes the hiker through each in orderly succession, starting with the Canadian zone, where thick forests of aspen, spruce and fir enclose bright green meadows; then through the oaks and ponderosa pines of the Transition zone; and finally through the cactus-studded, wildflower-carpeted, pinyon-and-juniper country that touches on the Upper Sonoran zone. The trail also provides backpackers with access to the delightful camping along KP and Grant creeks.

Infrequently maintained and often difficult to follow, this route is recommended only for experienced hikers.

Description

From the trailhead (0.0; 9120) walk east ¼ mile along an old dirt road to a signed junction, then turn right onto the Steeple Mesa Trail. The path is rather faint at first beneath the dense, ferny undergrowth, but it soon grows more distinct as it proceeds through a thick forest of Engelmann spruce and Douglas-fir. After walking another ¼ mile due south we meet an unsigned trail branching right; ignore this fork and go left (east). For the next mile we follow a shallow, gently descending valley as it leads us east, then south, to a meadow at the head of Grant Creek (water in early season). After crossing this leafy, grassy swale, we re-enter the trees and continue south, topping a gentle rise and then dropping to a second meadow, which contains perennial Willow Spring (2.1; 8840). (Another spring to the northwest is erroneously labeled "Willow Spring" on the topo.) Rocky Mountain elk can occasionally be seen grazing in this meadow.

Beyond the spring, the trail is temporarily obscure, but it quickly becomes clearer as it proceeds south into the forest. After a short, steep climb we reach the top of a wooded ridge, then drop down into another cienega, where the trail again grows faint. This time the track can be found again where it re-enters the trees a short distance to the east. Now we rise and fall gently for the next mile or so, passing through a lovely grove of tall aspens before beginning the steep descent into Steeple Creek canyon. Here the forest cover changes rapidly. Before, the prevailing trees were the spruce and fir of the Canadian life zone, with only an occasional ponderosa pine growing in some particularly dry and sunny spot; now the ponderosas become dominant, and it is the spruces and firs that look out of place. Gambel oak and bigtooth maple soon appear along the banks of the mostly dry creek, and some three miles after beginning this descent we arrive at Mud Spring (7.5; 6840) (may be dry before August 1). There are a few poor campsites here, but they are not particularly inviting; backpackers may wish to detour to either KP or Grant Creek (see Trip 74).

At a poorly signed trail junction by the spring, the Grant Creek/Paradise Park trail branches left. Hikers who are impatient for a clear view can walk out on it a few hundred yards to an overlook of the Blue River country to the east. Otherwise, stay right and continue down-canyon 0.2 mile to an old corral, at which point we cross to the right side of the creekbed and begin climbing the south canyon wall. After gaining about 300 feet we encounter a barbed-wire fence. Walk along the fence 50 yards to the left, then pass through a pull gate (8.0; 7000). Here the KP Creek Trail comes in from the right; we continue the other way, paralleling the fence on its south side, rising and falling along the ridge that leads out to KP and Steeple mesas, and gaining good views across the canyon of KP Creek toward aptly named Sawed Off Mountain. About 1.5 miles beyond the gate, the country levels off and we begin the trek across the two mesas. Steeple comes first; then, marked only by a subtle dip and rise in the trail a mile later, comes the transition to KP Mesa. The forest cover on these dry plateaus becomes increasingly dominated by alligator juniper, a tree whose coarse, scaly bark leaves no doubt as to the origin of its name. There are no open views along this stretch, but during late summer and early fall spectacular displays of bright yellow snakeweed blossoms blanket the interstices between the trees, making up for the lack of broad vistas.

At length, just when it may begin to seem that the flat, viewless expanse of mesa must go on forever, we pass through a gate and ease off the edge of the plateau. A few broad switchbacks bring us to a small saddle, where we have a good view across KP Canyon. As we continue steeply down a ravine and onto the backbone of a ridge the forest cover metamorphoses once again: cholla, prickly pear and pincushion cacti appear, and Colorado pinyons begin to supplant the long-reigning alligator junipers. After passing through yet another gate, the trail (faint again) switchbacks down to a sign announcing a junction with the MM Ranch Trail (12.9; 5480), where we veer left toward a duck indicating the continuation of our route to the Blue River. One more gate, one more set of indistinct switchbacks, and one more sign appear in quick succession, after which the trail finally makes good its continuing threats by vanishing completely. But it is too late for us to get lost now — to complete our journey, we simply walk 100 yards straight down the hill to Forest Road 281 (13.3; 5320).

See Maps 23, 31 and 29

29

Paradise Park

White Oak
Spring

×7764

Grant

×7010

N   A

6800

Mud Spr

Steeple

×6911

×7010

Panther

Creek

Creek

Creek

×6761

7200

6400

6800

6400

×7112

Steeple
Mesa

KP

×5539

30

R 30 E
R 31 E

KP Mesa

Horse

6400

5756

Blue

×6865

6354

36

5600

31

Canyon

5600

Sweetie

T 3 N
T 2 N

BM ×5354

McKittrick

The
Box

Moonshine

Thomas
Lake

6000

Grapevine

Creek

5662

5992

Red Bluff

0   MILES   1

Trip 72   KP Cienega to KP Creek

5.8–10.0 miles round trip; 1280´–2120´ elevation gain

Moderate dayhike or backpack (2 hiking days)

Season May to October

Water available all season along entire route

Features

KP Creek has its headwaters in the coniferous high country, but for most of its length it drops steadily through leafy midmountain hardwood forests on its way to the sun-drenched lowlands along the Blue River. It is an in-between country, tucked away in a hidden fold between desert and sierra, cactus thorn and pine needle. Here leaves rustle softly in the wind, rather than moan or sigh, and their shadows dance in soothing patterns on the ground. A profound sense of remoteness and intimacy prevails throughout this trip, out of all proportion to the modest distances involved, and even the most city-weary pilgrim will quickly find the sort of refreshment and rejuvenation that only the wilderness can provide.

Description

From the trailhead (0.0; 8920) we set off east, paralleling a wooden fence at first, and gradually descend into the nascent canyon of KP Creek. The trail, though easy to follow, is occasionally overgrown with New Mexican locust — a plant which looks innocuous enough from a distance, but which in reality harbors a wicked armory of thorns beneath its tender green leaves. As the canyon grows deeper and narrower, we cross and recross the fledgling creek, and the progress of our descent may be gauged by the gradual disappearance of the spruces and firs and their replacement by increasing numbers of riparian, deciduous trees such as Arizona walnut and bigtooth maple. Peace and quiet reign in these groves, though the silence may be interrupted now and then by the exuberant cackling of a Steller's jay or the obstinate hammering of an Arizona woodpecker, a rare species that has found a refuge from possible extinction in the wild country of the Blue Range. Both the long-eared Rocky Mountain mule deer and the smaller, more graceful Coues white-tailed deer frequent this area, particularly early and late in the season. Blue lupine and yellow columbine are among the flowers that bloom in isolated pockets of the bouldery canyon floor.

After dropping nearly 1300 feet we meet a tributary of KP Creek (2.9; 7640) spilling down from a small waterfall on the left. The creek has by now grown to respectable proportions, and skilled anglers may be tempted to try deceiving some of the extremely skittish brook, brown and rainbow trout that inhabit its deeper pools. There are occasional good campsites here, but most are small, just happenstance flats here and there amid the jumble of roots and boulders which covers the canyon floor; large parties will not be able to bed down all their members in one spot.

Those whose legs are not yet fully stretched out, and who wish to continue down-canyon from the waterfall, should cross the creek and scramble steeply a short distance up its north bank to an unsigned trail junction. Here a left-branching trail climbs back up to U.S. 666; we turn right and resume our rock-hopping, creek-crossing descent, passing through more delightful groves of maple, walnut, Douglas-fir and Gambel oak. Two miles later, where a small but perennial tributary flows in from the right, we arrive at a signed junction (5.0; 6800) which marks the extremity of our excursion. Backpackers will find several small tentsites at this quietly soothing, delightfully isolated spot, and fishermen will find challenging fishing for small trout along the sun-dappled creek.

Return the way you came.

See Map 23

Trip 73   KP Cienega to KP Creek and Blue Lookout Roadend

9.7 miles one way (7 mile car shuttle required); 2540 ′ elevation gain

Strenuous dayhike or backpack (2–3 hiking days)

Season June to October

Water available all season along first 6.8 miles of route only

Features

This trip partakes of the best of two worlds. After traveling down the lovely, forested canyon of KP Creek, we explore an infrequently visited, densely wooded tributary stream, where the sun is just a remote twinkling somewhere far above the filtering treetops. After a stiff climb the trip suddenly reaches its climax at lofty Blue Lookout; there we burst into the light, a vast panorama falls away at our feet, and the intimacy and closeness of the canyon world are traded for the expansive vistas of the mountaintop.

Description

Follow the directions for Trip 72 to the signed trail junction beside KP Creek (5.0; 6800). Here we turn right, hop across a tributary stream to its east side, and begin climbing. Almost immediately the trail forks; ignore the left branch and head for a duck and a blaze visible ahead. Soon we veer right, cross the tributary again, and come to another unsigned junction. This time the route goes left, and then begins climbing very steeply up the crest of a low ridge. After a few hundred yards of strenuous scrambling the angle of ascent eases somewhat, and we soon find ourselves cloistered in a delightful canyon that shelters an incredibly rich and varied forest of maple, walnut, box elder, towering Douglas-fir, New Mexican locust, Gambel oak and quaking aspen. At times the sky is lost entirely behind the leafy, overarching canopy, and the hiker may get the feeling of passing through an immense, steeply canted tunnel. But even while marveling at the lush forest cover, one is tempted to curse the poorly maintained trail, which is steep and rough all the way, and frequently blocked by fallen trees.

After working our way up-canyon for a little less than 2 miles we reach a ramshackle cabin (6.8; 8160) which dates back at least to 1925 and was once used to quarter the firefighters who manned Blue Lookout. Here there is an unsigned junction offering a choice of routes. The right-hand trail leads in 1 mile to a grassy flat on the Blue Lookout road, 4.5 miles east of U.S. 666 and 0.5 mile west of the roadend. Those who wish to continue directly to Blue Lookout, without intercepting the road, should follow the left branch as it crosses the creekbed and winds up the hillside east of the waning stream. After a mile of moderate climbing along the latter path we meet the Blue Lookout Trail at a signed junction (8.1; 8920). Here we turn left and continue up a single long switchback to the base of the lookout tower (8.6; 9346).

For a description of the view from the top, see Trip 63. To reach Blue Lookout Roadend, retrace your steps 0.5 mile to the KP Creek trail junction, turn left, and walk gently downhill another 0.5 mile to the trailhead (9.7; 8840).

See Map 23

Trip 74   KP Cienega to the Blue River via KP Creek, Mud Spring and Grant Creek

19.1 miles one way (45-mile car shuttle required); 1620′ elevation gain

Moderate backpack (3 hiking days)

Season May to October

Water available all season along first 5.8 miles of route, and at two points on Grant Creek (miles 11.4 and 16.0); Mud Spring (mile 9.2) generally reliable throughout the summer rainy season

Features

Shady canyons alternate with open, sunny forests of oak and ponderosa along this lengthy route. Inviting campsites can be found 5, 11, and 16 miles from the trailhead, providing the backpacker with a good opportunity to make a long trip at an enjoyable, leisurely pace. Anglers can sample the fishing in two separate drainages, and all hikers will enjoy the pleasant vistas across the muted contours of the Blue River bottomlands.

The trails along this trek are occasionally difficult to follow, and the route is recommended only for experienced wilderness travelers.

Description

Follow the directions for Trip 72 to the signed trail junction on KP Creek (5.0; 6800). At the junction we turn left and continue down-canyon, passing occasional fair campsites, until we reach a huge, overhanging wall of mud, where the creek has severely undercut its banks and left large boulders suspended above the trail, seemingly ready to drop at any moment. Passing rather hurriedly through here, we soon come to a corral (5.7; 6560). At this point we are on the right-hand side of the stream, but approximately ¼ mile down-canyon we cross to the left and begin winding up a gentle, ponderosa-covered slope, gradually leaving the creek behind. (It is rather easy to miss this crucial crossing, as the trail is faint through here; if you come to a series of 50-foot-high clifflets rising directly above the south side of the creek, you've gone 0.3 mile too far.)

As we meander along the slopes north of KP Creek, we gain some fine views of Sawed Off Mountain — an abruptly terminating ridgeline whose continuation was "sawed off" by the tremendous erosive action of the Blue River. The dry, sunny spaces between the pines along this stretch are occasionally brightened by the yellow blossoms of bladderpod and snakeweed. After two miles of rising and falling, the occasionally obscure path sidles up against a barbed-wire fence atop the divide between KP and Steeple creeks. A short distance east is a pull gate (8.7; 7000), where we meet the Steeple Mesa Trail. Continuing east would take us to Steeple Mesa; our route, however, passes through the gate, doubles back west a short distance along the north side of the fence, and then begins descending into the canyon of normally dry Steeple Creek. After "hitting bottom" at a corral 0.4 mile later, we cross the creekbed and begin climbing up-canyon. Soon a few wet spots may appear in the watercourse, presaging our arrival at Mud Spring (9.2; 6840) (may be dry before August 1). The spring is down in the streambed just left of a poorly signed trail junction; a few poor campsites are located just up-canyon, but backpackers should plan on spending the night at far more congenial Grant Creek, 2.5 miles further along.

At the trail fork here, the left branch is the continuation of the Steeple Mesa Trail, which climbs up to the high country at Hannagan Meadow. We take the right fork, cutting back above Steeple Creek, and begin another long, winding traverse, this time around the ridge that divides Steeple and Grant creeks. Route finding through here is made difficult at times by the presence of numerous intertwining cowpaths, which are often indistinguishable from the infrequently maintained Forest Service trail. The exasperated backpacker will likely form his own opinion at this point of the Forest Service Multiple Use policy, which allows cattle grazing within designated wilderness areas. Perhaps someday this policy will be altered to reflect the new wilderness ethic, but until then travelers in the Blue Range will have to put up with bellowing cows, needlessly spooked wildlife, and ruined trails — all of which *do* "conflict unduly with wilderness values and recreation," despite Forest Service representations to the contrary. Anyway, look for ducks and old sawn-through logs to stay on the right track here.

A mile beyond Mud Spring, after gaining some nice views across the Blue River lowlands, we reach the top of the Steeple Creek-Grant Creek divide (10.4; 6880). The forest cover here consists mainly of silverleaf oak and some robust alligator junipers, but as the trail doubles back left (west) and begins descending gently toward Grant Creek, ponderosa pine and Douglas-fir become dominant. At Grant Creek (11.4; 6740) there is delightful camping in a riparian forest of box elder, bigtooth maple and Arizona walnut, and fair fishing for small brook, brown and rainbow trout.

To continue to the Blue River we cross Grant Creek, turn right where a faint side trail branches upstream, and wind our way uphill northward 1.5 miles to Paradise Park, a gently rolling, nearly pure expanse of ponderosa pine. Many of the young trees here can be seen to be of almost exactly the same age, a sign that they all germinated at the same time — most likely after a wildfire had cleared away the underbrush that normally chokes off aspiring ponderosa seedlings.

Cattle graze in and around the Park, and again we must rely on log cuts and blazes to locate a signed junction (13.0; 7640) in the midst of the pines, where we turn right. As we proceed, Gambel oaks begin to appear, breaking up the uniformity of the forest cover, and presently we emerge from the forest onto an ill-defined ridgetop offering a good vista across the gaping canyon of the Blue River. Hikers armed with a pair of binoculars should be able to pick out a few golden eagles from this point, and watch them as they wheel and soar against the vast backdrop of mountains and canyons beyond. A few specimens of that shamefully rare and endangered species, the southern bald eagle, make their nests along the Blue, but they are rarely sighted; count yourself lucky to see one.

From here the trail switchbacks steeply down barren, rocky slopes some 1400 feet back to Grant Creek (16.0; 6040). On the way down, a glance at the precipitous "breaks" through which the creek flows will explain why the trail did not proceed directly down-canyon from the last crossing. For those who wish to spend one last night within the healing sway of the wilderness, there is an excellent campsite where the trail first rejoins the stream, at the confluence of an intermittently flowing tributary. The remainder of the trip is an easy, if occasionally brushy, 3-mile walk out to the Blue River. A wide variety of trees flourish along this stretch, including sycamore, walnut, maple, alligator juniper, ponderosa pine and Arizona cypress. Many of the trunks and branches are gaily festooned with wild grapevines, whose seedy but tasty fruits ripen in the fall and compensate the late-season traveler for the imminent loss of wildness at the trailhead.

After a mile or two Grant Creek may grow intermittent. All too soon we reach a barbed-wire fence and a sign indicating the primitive area boundary; the Blue River is just beyond. To reach Forest Road 281 we turn left and walk a short distance upstream to the point where the road swings into near contact with the river (19.1; 5440).

See Maps 23, 31 and 29

Trip 75   Sheep Crossing to Baldy Peak

13.8 miles round trip; 2180 ' elevation gain

Moderate dayhike or backpack (2–3 hiking days)

Season June to September

Water available all season along first 3.2 miles of trail only

Features

Lush meadows, magnificent forests of spruce and fir, and a sparkling stream all lend their charms to this delightful alpine route. Views from the summit of 11,403-foot Baldy Peak are superlative, and the West Fork Little Colorado River offers good fishing for rainbow, brook and cutthroat trout.

Description

From the trailhead at the Mount Baldy Wilderness boundary (0.0; 9220), our trail climbs gently beside the right bank of the West Fork Little Colorado. Fishermen will find this as good a place as any to unpack their rods and reels, for the trail soon moves off to the right and maintains a rather inconvenient distance from the water. Along the fringes of this meadowed stretch the dominant tree is Colorado blue spruce, a lovely "frosted" conifer whose Arizona range is restricted to the White Mountains region and the area north of the main Colorado River near the Utah border. (A spruce may be distinguished from other evergreens by the square cross section of its needles, which makes them difficult to roll between one's thumb and forefinger. The Colorado blue may be told from the more common Engelmann spruce by squeezing a sprig of needles: if you say "Ouch!" you are holding a blue.)

The trail continues to climb gently away from the stream, but several small creeklets (water until early fall) provide refreshment along the mostly sunny, grassy canyonside. You may see some mule deer or elk grazing in the verdant greensward below, though you are more likely to see just a few head of cattle, members of the Greer Allotment herd, which is unfortunately still allowed to graze within the wilderness. The large boulders strewn about the canyon floor are glacial "erratics" — chunks of mountain debris that rode the ancient glaciers down from the Baldy summit area and were subsequently left stranded here when the icefields receded. Among the many wildflowers that flourish along this stretch are scarlet penstemon, meadow cinquefoil, leafybract aster and aspen fleabane.

About 2.5 miles from the trailhead, after gaining some fine views of Baldy Peak's densely forested flanks, we curve to the right and begin a wide, 180-degree circuit of a lush, inviting meadow. Immediately following the last glaciation of this area, this meadow was probably a small pond, its waters dammed up behind a "moraine," or wall of boulders which accumulated during a temporary halt in the glacier's retreat. (What is left of this moraine is now visible as the low, forested ridge adjoining the southeast edge of the meadow.) Over the millennia the pond filled with streamborne silt, becoming the meadow it is today; several centuries hence this natural succession may well culminate with the grasses being wholly replaced by the trees which are already invading the fringes of the meadow.

Soon the trail crosses a tributary of the West Fork (3.2; 9820), along whose banks camping is excellent. The forest cover here is less homogeneous than below; mixed in with the spruce you will find corkbark fir (an aptly named local variant of subalpine fir) and an occasional southwestern white pine. Here and there your eye may be caught by a showy yellow columbine blossoming in some moist, shady nook.

Beyond the meadow our route rounds a hillside, climbing

steeply at times, until it once again parallels the West Fork Little
Colorado southwestward. The canyon walls steepen as we enter a
stand of Engelmann spruce, and the trail is soon forced to make a
few switchbacks beneath some rocky bluffs. A short climb from
here brings us to a notch atop a ridge (5.3; 10,860), where we are
presented with a pleasant vista toward White Mountain Reservoir
and the rolling country to the north. From this point on, the trail
stays on top of or just below the crest of the ridge leading to the
Baldy summit area, and it is not advisable to proceed farther if a
thunderstorm seems imminent.

Continuing our moderate ascent, we soon meet the signed
East Fork Little Colorado River Trail coming up from the east
(6.1; 11,180). A few poor, exposed campsites can be found here,
but the nearest water is 0.4 mile away, at a tiny spring down on the
East Fork Trail. From the junction we continue south across a gentle rise, then drop slightly into a shallow saddle before finally
scrambling onto the rocky summit of Baldy Peak (6.9; 11,403).
(Just beneath the top a faint trail branches off to the left. This is
the old East Fork Trail, which is no longer maintained and not
recommended for travel.)

On the summit you will find a register to sign, and extensive
views in every direction. A mile to the northwest is 11,036-foot
Mount Warren, easily recognizable by the light green "hanging
meadow" which contrasts so sharply with the dark forests on its
southeast flank. Due west is 11,150-foot Paradise Butte, rising
abruptly above the deep gash of the East Fork White River canyon. Beyond the Butte, ridge after forested ridge falls away toward
the horizon; on a clear day one can see nearly halfway across the
state in this direction.

Sadly, not all of the summit views are so pleasing. Particularly
odious is the sight of a road which has been bulldozed up the canyon of Reservation Creek to the southeast, ending at a raw clearing
strewn with cut timber. Although technically this scar is outside
the wilderness area, its impact on the viewer is nonetheless
substantial. One can only hope that no more such cutting will take
place nearby.

After taking in the view, return the way you came, or via the
East Fork Trail (4 mile car shuttle required; reverse the steps of
Trip 76.)

See Map 30

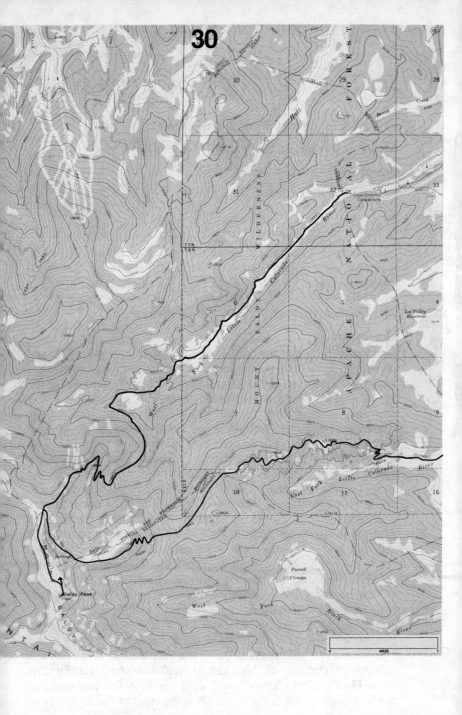

Trip 76   Phelps Cabin to Baldy Peak

13.4 miles round trip; 2000′ elevation gain

Moderate dayhike or backpack (2–3 hiking days)

Season June to September

Water available all season along first 0.8 mile and at mile 5.5

Features

Spectacular cliffs and pinnacles contrast with bright green meadows along the lower part of this varied excursion, while far-reaching vistas await the hiker who continues on to the wind-whipped summit of Baldy Peak. The sparkling East Fork Colorado River provides Arizona fishermen with a rare opportunity to sharpen their skills in a pristine alpine environment.

Description

From the end of the road at Phelps Cabin (0.0; 9400) you pass through a gate, then walk west a few hundred yards through a fenced pasture to a second gate. Still heading west, paralleling the East Fork Little Colorado River, we soon come to what apparently was once a small earth-fill dam, then to a sign announcing the wilderness boundary. Fishing in the small stream is fair-to-good for brook, rainbow, and an occasional native cutthroat trout. One mile from the trailhead, after passing through a spacious meadow sprinkled with aster and fleabane (and often a few cattle of the Voigt grazing allotment), the trail veers right, away from the creek, and begins a moderate, switchbacking ascent up the north canyon wall. Almost immediately we reach the base of the first of a series of dramatically shaped basalt pinnacles which stand like tirelessly attentive sentinels along the next 1.5 miles of our route. These out-croppings are the exposed remnants of lava flows that oozed out of the Baldy volcano between 8 and 15 million years ago. After this volcanic activity ended, a series of glaciers moved down the East Fork canyon, undercutting the base of the basalt canyonside and rendering it particularly vulnerable to the frost wedging and water erosion which have since sculpted the rock into its present form.

About 0.5 mile beyond the first of the outcrops, we attain a ridgetop, where the switchbacks cease and we resume traveling due west. The East Fork is now out of sight some 500 feet below us, but the loss of that delightful stream is compensated for by the good views we have gained of the dense aspen and fir forests across the canyon — views picturesquely framed by the craggy tops of the rock towers, which are *also* below us now. This stretch of trail is only lightly shaded, but soon after passing the last of the pinnacles we cross an indistinct saddle to the north side of the ridge, which is generously wooded with a mixture of ponderosa pine, southwestern white pine, Douglas-fir and a few aspen. Just beyond the saddle is a sign informing us that we are entering the Fort Apache Indian Reservation (3.5; 10,460). After another mile of gentle climbing we switchback moderately up a shady slope, then traverse westward to a perennial spring (5.5; 10,990), the only water along our route above the east Fork Little Colorado. Here you will find a few fair campsites in a dense spruce-fir forest, and the wrecked carcass of an Air Force jet that crashed into the mountainside above the spring in the late Forties or early Fifties.

From the spring, the trail continues gently uphill 0.4 mile to the crest of Baldy Peak's summit ridge, where, after passing a few poor, exposed campsites, it meets the signed West Fork Trail coming up from the north (5.9; 11,180). Now we join that route, turning sharply left, and follow the exposed ridgetop trail ¾ mile south to the summit (6.7; 11,403). This last stretch of trail should not be attempted if a thunderstorm appears to be brewing. (For an account of the view from the top, see Trip 75.)

Return the way you came, or via the West Fork Trail (4 mile car shuttle required; reverse the steps of Trip 75.)

See Maps 32 and 30

on the West Fork Little Colorado River trail

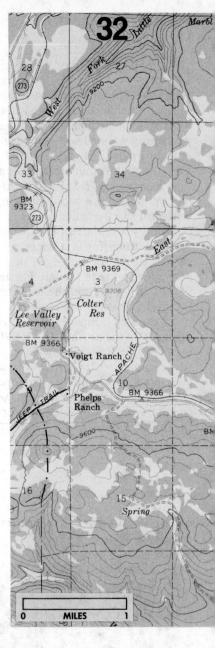

Area 4:
The Grand Canyon

Over 200 miles long, up to a mile deep, and as much as 18 miles wide, the Grand Canyon of the Colorado River is one of the most spectacular features on the face of the earth, awesome in scale yet possessed of a delicate, intricate beauty as well. It is also one of the largest unroaded areas left in the continental United States, a vast wilderness of soaring buttes, twisting gorges, and crystalline creeks beckoning to those with the skill and stamina to explore it on foot.

According to a legend of the Hualapai Indians, a tremendous flood once swept the earth, drowning all life and preventing its resurgence until a great hero gouged out a colossal gash in the ground to channel off the water. As it has been unraveled by modern geologists, the story of the Grand Canyon's creation is somewhat more complicated than the Indian version, and will be sketched only briefly here. For a more complete account, see one of the books listed under Further Reading.

In the pre-Cambrian era, some 2,000,000,000 years ago, the present Grand Canyon area contained sandstones, lavas and other types of rocks. Our knowledge of the Canyon's history essentially begins at this time, but the fact that such a variety of rocks were already present indicates that complex geological processes must have been at work for long periods before. At any rate, tremendous tectonic forces crumpled and squeezed these pre-Cambrian rock layers, buckling them into a range of mountains higher than any now on the continent. The intense pressure and heat that accompanied this mountain-building activity metamorphosed the rocks into the dark gneisses and schists which today are the oldest — and hence the lowest — rocks exposed in the Grand Canyon. Cracks in this metamorphic rock were invaded by fluid magma from below, and later this molten rock hardened into the light-colored granitic marblings for which the Granite Gorge was named.

In the course of time, erosion reduced this lofty mountain range (and others which followed it) to a level plain, which was then flooded by a succession of seas and fresh-water swamps. As the initial oceanic inundation progressed, the land was covered first by a layer of fine sea sand (today's Tapeats sandstone), then by silt and the mud of decayed seaweed (now the Bright Angel shale), and finally by the skeletal remains of billions of tiny sea creatures (the Muav limestone). The shells of the myriad inhabitants of a later sea were cemented together to form the hard, erosion-resistant Redwall limestone layer. The Supai formation, deposited on an ancient floodplain, contains fossilized plants and animal tracks. This plain was later covered by a shallow swamp, rich with plant and animal life whose fossil remains are now preserved in the Hermit shale. Following this the climate grew markedly drier; the swamps dried up, and wind-driven sand dunes wandered across a huge desert. Left behind was the Coconino sandstone layer, the cream-colored band of cliffs which is so obvious just beneath the canyon's rim. On top of the Coconino layer are more oceanic deposits — the Toroweap and Kaibab formations — indicating that the area was again inundated by sea water.

Up to 8000 additional feet of rock was deposited upon these layers, but it was all eroded away by the time the Colorado River arrived on the scene and began slicing into the earth's multilayered crust. The Colorado's erosive power was increased by the gradual, unexplained uplift of the surrounding country, which maintained the river gradient at a rushing, abrasive angle, allowing for the entire canyon to be carved in the comparatively short span of a few million years. The construction of Glen Canyon Dam has, for the time being, considerably reduced the Colorado's erosive capability.

The Grand Canyon's vast amphitheaters and coves were gradually carved outward from the trench cut by the river. The shales and softer limestones eroded fastest, undercutting the bases of the sandstone and harder limestone layers which, lacking sup-

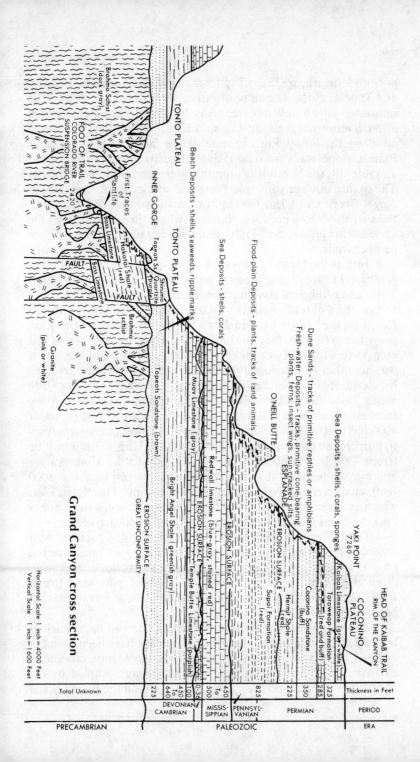

Grand Canyon cross section

Horizontal Scale 1 inch = 4000 Feet
Vertical Scale 1 inch = 1600 Feet

HEAD OF KAIBAB TRAIL
RIM OF THE CANYON

COCONINO PLATEAU

YAKI POINT 7260

Sea Deposits - shells, corals, sponges

Dune Sands - tracks of primitive reptiles or amphibians
Fresh-water Deposits - tracks, primitive cone-bearing plants, ferns, insect wings, sun-cracked silts

Flood-plain Deposits - plants, tracks of land animals

Sea Deposits - shells, corals

Beach Deposits - shells, seaweeds, ripple marks

ESPLANADE

O'NEILL BUTTE

Kaibab Limestone (gray-white)
Toroweap Formation (red and buff)
Coconino Sandstone (buff)
Hermit Shale (red)
Supai Formation (red)
Redwall limestone (blue-gray, stained red)
Temple Butte Limestone (purplish)
Muav Limestone (gray)
Bright Angel Shale (greenish gray)
Tapeats Sandstone (brown)
Shinumo Quartzite (purple)
Hakatai Shale (red)
Bass Limestone

ESPLANADE
EROSION SURFACE
EROSION SURFACE
EROSION SURFACE
EROSION SURFACE
GREAT UNCONFORMITY

TONTO PLATEAU
TONTO PLATEAU
INNER GORGE

FOOT OF TRAIL
COLORADO RIVER
SUSPENSION BRIDGE 2420

Brahma Schist (dark gray)

First Traces of Plantlife

Brahma schist

FAULT

FAULT

Bass Limestone

Tapeats Ss.

Granite (pink or white)

	Thickness in Feet	PERIOD	ERA
	325	PERMIAN	PALEOZOIC
	285		
	350		
	225		
	825	PENNSYL-VANIAN	
	450 To 500	MISSISSIPPIAN	
	0-36	DEVONIAN	
	100	CAMBRIAN	
	450 To 640		
	225		
	Total Unknown		PRECAMBRIAN

port underneath, spalled off to form the steep Coconino, Redwall and Tapeats cliffs. The amphitheaters were eroded as much by the rainwater which *fell* into them as by the stream water which *drained* into them; this must be so, because amphitheaters formed all along the South Rim, in spite of the fact that the Coconino Plateau slopes away from the canyon. Receiving both stream water and rainfall, the North Rim amphitheaters tend to be much larger. The major side canyons, such as those of Garden Creek, Bright Angel Creek and Clear Creek, have developed along fault lines. Because they often produce "breaks" where they slice through the various cliff layers, such faults generally dictate the routes of rim-to-river trails.

Just as the Grand Canyon neatly displays the chapters of its geological history, so it presents an intriguing cross section of life zones and ecological communities, ranging in elevation from 2400 feet (at the Colorado River) to 8400 feet (along the North Rim). In fact, with the nearby San Francisco Peaks extending this elevation range to over 12,000 feet, the biologist C. Hart Merriam found this area perfect for studying the effects of altitude on plant life, and it was here that he developed the idea that plants could be grouped by elevation into natural communities — the now-familiar "life zones." Ascending the south wall of the Grand Canyon, one finds three of these zones laid out in neat order. Lowest (below about 4000 feet) is the Lower Sonoran zone, with its yuccas, agaves, cacti, burrobrush and sagebrush; then comes the Upper Sonoran zone (from 4000 feet to about 6500 feet), dominated by Utah juniper and pinyon pine. Next is the Transition zone (up to about 8000 feet), characterized by forests of ponderosa pine. The North Rim, which averages about 1000 feet higher than the South Rim, pokes into the Canadian zone, with dense forests of spruce and fir.

Though more clearly displayed in the canyon than in most other regions, these zones are sometimes "mixed up" and inverted on a small scale, usually as a result of local anomalies of exposure. A good example is the occasional presence of pines and firs in shady pockets at the base of the Coconino cliff, at elevations well below 6000 feet.

The presence of humans in the Grand Canyon dates back at least 3000 years. Split-twig figurines of that age have been found in isolated caves throughout the canyon, as have some crumbling cliff dwellings. More recently, the canyon was occupied by the Havasupai Indians and their ancestors, who built the Bright Angel and other trails and raised crops along Garden Creek. Hikers frequently find chipped arrowheads, scrapers and other artifacts along the trails.

The Grand Canyon was unknown to white men until 1540, when Garcia de Cardenas, a member of Coronado's famed expedition to the American Southwest, was guided there by Hopi Indians. For the next three centuries whites showed no further interest in the area. Until 1869, in fact, when John Wesley Powell made his daring voyage down the Colorado, it was not even known for sure whether the large, sluggish river that emptied into the Gulf of California was the same as the stream to the north, known then as the Green River, which had its headwaters in the Rocky Mountains. Following Powell's expedition came a succession of geologists, prospectors, trail builders and, later, painters and photographers, whose works familiarized the canyon to an increasingly curious public. Then came the Grandview and El Tovar hotels, Fred Harvey Mule Trips, rustic resorts at Hermit and Bright Angel creeks, and the full crush of modern tourism.

It is to the credit of the National Park Service that the canyon, in spite of its worldwide popularity, remains as pristine as it is. At present, the wilderness character of the backcountry faces two major threats: the proposed Hualapai Dam and Reservoir, whose waters would inundate a substantial part of the chasm, and the "burro problem." The idea that part of the Grand Canyon should be flooded is so repugnant to most Americans that Hualapai Dam is likely to remain forever on the drawing board. The burros present a lesser but more immediate problem. Descendants of pack stock that escaped from turn-of-the-century miners and prospectors, these feral animals have prospered in the Inner Canyon, to the point where they have begun to foul springs, strip away elements of the natural plant cover, and drive out such native animal species as the magnificent desert bighorn sheep. This problem was recognized as early as 1924, and between then and 1969 about 2800 burros were either shot or removed from the Canyon. A Park Service plan to shoot the remaining 300 or so animals was vigorously opposed by "animal lovers" (who were presumably ignorant of the burros' negative impact on other animals). As a compromise measure, the Park Service now proposes a period of live removal of burros by private parties, followed by shooting and fencing as needed to eliminate whatever animals remain in the National Park.

Hiking is possible year-round in the Grand Canyon. Summer weather is generally quite pleasant on and just below the rims, but it gets quite hot at lower elevations. During the winter, the top parts of South Rim trails will usually bear a light covering of snow, but should be hikable except immediately after storms. The North Rim is closed from about October to May. The best time to hike? Spring and fall — spring if you like running water and wildflowers.

Backcountry permits are required for all overnight trips within the Grand Canyon. These may be picked up in person at the North Rim and South Rim visitor centers. The number of hikers permitted on each trail at any given time is strictly regulated; during the popular spring and summer months, you should write or call the Backcountry Reservations Office (see below) and make a reservation well in advance of your trip.

Managing Agencies

Superintendent's Office
Grand Canyon National Park
Grand Canyon, AZ 86023

Backcountry Reservations Office
Grand Canyon National Park   (permits and information about
Grand Canyon, AZ 86023   weather, water availability, etc.)
    (602) 638-2474

Further Reading

The Grand Canyon: The Story Behind the Scenery, by Merrill D. Beal (KC Publications, Las Vegas, Nevada, 1978)

The Man Who Walked Through Time, by Colin Fletcher (Alfred A. Knopf, New York, New York 1967)

Grand Canyon Place Names, by Byrd H. Granger (University of Arizona Press, Tucson, Arizona 1960)

The Grand Canyon, by Joseph Wood Krutch (William Morrow and Company, New York, New York 1968)

Grand Canyon Wild Flowers, by W. B. McDougall (Museum of Northern Arizona, Flagstaff, Arizona 1964)

Exploration of the Colorado River and Its Canyons, by John Wesley Powell (Dover Publications, New York, New York 1895)

Grand Canyon National Park, by Robert Scharff (David McKay Company, New York, New York 1967)

The Wilderness World of the Grand Canyon, by Anne and Myron Sutton (J.B. Lippincott Company, New York, New York 1971)

The Grand Canyon, by Robert Wallace (Time-Life Books, Alexandria, Virginia 1972)

Many other books and pamphlets may be ordered from the Grand Canyon Natural History Association, P.O. Box 399, Grand Canyon, AZ 86023

Approaches/Trailheads:

Bright Angel Lodge   From Flagstaff follow U.S. 180 northwest about 80 miles to the South Entrance of Grand Canyon National Park. Where Highway 64 (East Rim Drive) branches right, a little over a mile beyond the Entrance Station, continue straight ahead and go 3 miles to a parking area near Bright Angel Lodge. The Bright Angel Trail begins just west of the lodge area.

Yaki Point   From Flagstaff follow U.S. 180 approximately 80 miles northwest, then turn right onto Highway 64 (East Rim Drive). Go east a little over 1 mile, then turn left onto Yaki Point Road. About 0.3 mile later, turn left again and proceed about 300 yards to the trailhead.

Grandview Point   Follow the preceding route to the junction of East Rim Drive and Yaki Point Road. Go straight ahead here, and continue east along East Rim Drive for 8 miles to the Grandview Point cutoff. Now turn left; the trailhead is ½ mile beyond.

North Rim   From Flagstaff follow U.S. 89 north, then U.S. 89 Alternate west to Jacob Lake, 164 miles. Turn left here, and proceed 43 miles to the parking area at the head of the North Kaibab Trail.

Hermits Rest   From Flagstaff follow U.S. 180 northwest to Grand Canyon Village, about 85 miles, then proceed along West Rim Drive to its terminus at Hermit's Rest (8 more miles). From mid-May to mid-September, West Rim Drive is closed to private cars and access is provided by free shuttlebuses.

Trip 77
Bright Angel Lodge to Indian Gardens and Plateau Point

11.6 miles round trip; 3080′ elevation gain

Strenuous dayhike or backpack (2–3 hiking days)

Season all year; hot in summer

Water available all year at Indian Gardens (mile 4.5), and at resthouses (miles 1.5 and 3.0) from May 1 to September 30

Features

The Bright Angel Trail has been used since prehistoric times to cross the great gulf of the Grand Canyon, and to this day it remains the easiest of the inner canyon routes. This trip descends the upper part of the trail to lush, cottonwood-forested Indian Gardens, where the Park Service maintains a backcountry campsite, and then follows a more modern pathway out to Plateau Point, a spectacular overlook of the Colorado River.

Description

From the trailhead just west of Bright Angel Lodge (0.0; 6840) the trail immediately begins a moderate, switchbacking descent through the Kaibab limestone and sandstone formations, the youngest of the sedimentary rock layers that have been exposed to view by the erosive action of the Colorado River. A pair of short tunnels and many tight switchbacks then bring us to the base of the Coconino sandstone layer, the light-colored band of cliffs which is so prominent in most views of the Grand Canyon rims. This layer was formed from the wind-blown sands which blanketed large portions of the southwest some 300 million years ago. Fossil footprints have been found here, records of the existence of a variety of small reptiles that scurried across the ancient dunes.

Below the Coconino cliff the trail makes a long, descending traverse to the right, presently arriving at the first of three resthouses along our route (1.5; 5800). This small shelter contains an emergency telephone connected to the South Rim, and has piped water between May 1 and September 30. By the time we reach this point the forest cover has gone through significant changes — gone are the ponderosa pines that were so prevalent on the rim (though a few of the pines, and even some Douglas-firs, can still be glimpsed up in shady, cliff-sheltered nooks high on the canyon wall). In their place are a few scraggly Colorado pinyons and Utah junipers, and a variety of other shrubs and small trees, including mountain mahogany, pale hoptree and Stansbury cliff-rose.

Several landmarks are visible from this section of the trail — the bright green patch of cottonwoods visible almost directly below is Indian Gardens; the flat, dull green shelf extending just beyond is the Tonto Plateau (upon which the wide trail leading out to Plateau Point is painfully obvious); beyond that is the long gash of Bright Angel Canyon, reaching back along the line of the Bright Angel Fault deep into the high country of the North Rim. Rising high above either side of Bright Angel Canyon are clusters of steep-walled buttes and parapets, with such names as Brahma Temple, Buddha Cloister, Cheops Pyramid and Tower of Ra.

Below here, several more sieges of switchbacks bring the hiker to Threemile Resthouse (3.0; 4800) (water between May 1 and September 30). This shelter stands at the brink of the spectacular Redwall, the rust-colored limestone layer that forms the highest continuous band of cliffs in the canyon. Finding a "break" in the Redwall is generally a paramount consideration in locating any rim-to-river trail; our particular route has been made possible by lateral earth movements along the Bright Angel Fault which have broken the continuity of the precipice at the head of Garden Creek Canyon.

After switchbacking down through the Redwall, the trail eases onto the gently sloping surface of the Tonto Plateau. Presently we pull up alongside Garden Creek wash (usually dry at this point) and descend moderately a little less than a mile to Indian Gardens (4.5; 3760). Here there is another resthouse, a ranger station, camp tables, and a tiny, year-round creek, all in a magnificent setting of tall cottonwood trees. The Havasupai Indians used to raise crops here, and it is not hard for the present-day visitor to imagine how peaceful life must have been in those days. Backpackers should not camp here without obtaining the necessary permit at the South Rim Visitors Center; the ranger checks every evening for permits, and those without them have the choice of paying a hefty fine or walking back up to the trailhead.

To reach Plateau Point, turn left at a signed trail fork at the lower end of the campground and descend gently along the left side of willow-bordered Garden Creek. At the signed junction with the westbound Tonto Trail stay right, and continue across the sagebrush-dotted flats of the Tonto Plateau, until it ends abruptly at an awesome overlook of the Colorado River, foaming and swirling down the dark throat of the Granite Gorge some 1300 feet below. This is Plateau Point (5.8; 3760). The walls of the Granite Gorge, incidentally, consist mostly of schist and a variety of highly metamorphosed sedimentary and volcanic rocks — not granite. It derives its name from the thin, light-colored granitic intrusions which marble the darker rock in places.

Return the way you came. Remember to allow about twice as much time for the trip up as the trip down.

See Map 33

Trip 78   Bright Angel Lodge to Indian Gardens, the Colorado River and Bright Angel Campground

18.6 miles round trip; 4360' elevation gain

Strenuous dayhike or backpack (3–4 hiking days)

Season all year; hot in summer

Water available May 1 to September 30 at resthouses (miles 1.5 and 3.0) and all year at Indian Gardens (mile 4.5), the Colorado River (mile 7.7) (purify), and Bright Angel Campground (mile 9.3)

Features

This — the classic route into the heart of the Grand Canyon — leads the hiker past a kaleidoscope of awesome vistas, follows a splashing creek down a narrow gorge shaded by cottonwoods and overhanging cliffs, and then crosses the roaring Colorado River via a suspension bridge to a delightful backcountry campground on Bright Angel Creek. To ease the difficulty of the return to the rim, the trek is best done as a 3-day backpack, spending the first night at Bright Angel, the second at Indian Gardens. Though the route is classified as either backpack or dayhike, it is really too long and strenuous to be enjoyed by any but the strongest dayhikers — and even they should not attempt it during hot weather.

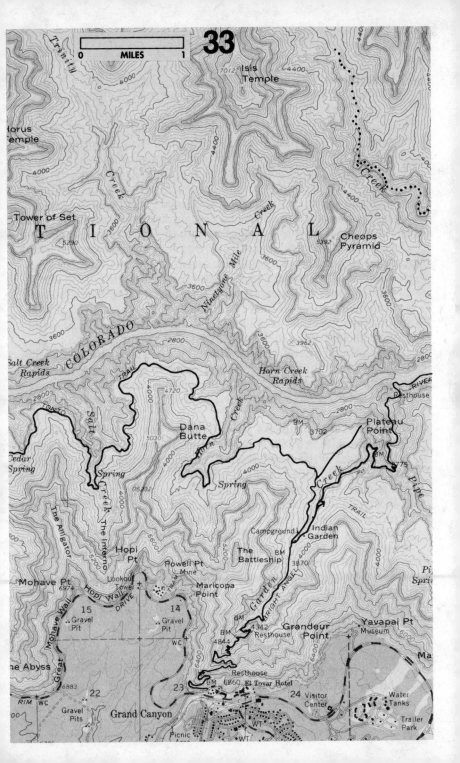

33

0 MILES 1

Trinity Creek

Isis Temple 7012

4400

4400

Horus Temple

Creek

4000

Tower of Set T I O N A L Cheops Pyramid

5290 5392

Creek

Ninetyone Mile

3600

3600

3962

COLORADO 2800

3600

Salt Creek Rapids Horn Creek Rapids

2800 RIVER

TRAIL Resthouse

TONTO 4720 2800 BM Plateau Point

Salt 4000 3702

Dana Butte BM

5030 Horn 875

Cedar Spring Spring Creek Pipe

Spring 4000 Creek

05232 Spring 4000 TRAIL

The Alligator The Interno Campground Indian Garden

Hopi Pt 5600 The Battleship BM

Powell Pt Mine 3870

Mohave Pt Lookout Tower Maricopa Point BRIGHT ANGEL Pi Spr

6974 Hopi Wall DRIVE Garden

15 14 Grandeur Point Yavapai Pt Museum

Gravel Pit Gravel Pit BM 4342 Resthouse

WC BM

The Abyss 4844

6883 Resthouse Ma

RIM WC 22 23 BM 6860 El Tovar Hotel Water Tanks

Gravel Pits 24 Visitor Center

Grand Canyon Picnic WT Trailer Park

WT

Description

From Bright Angel Lodge (0.0; 6840), follow the directions for Trip 77 to Indian Gardens (4.5; 3760). At the signed junction just north of the campground, turn right and follow the Bright Angel Trail as it passes just left of a pumphouse (which supplies water to the South Rim), then proceeds along the right-hand bank of Garden Creek. Soon the eastbound Tonto Trail branches right at a signed junction (4.8; 3680); we stay left here and continue gently downhill. As the channel of Garden Creek begins to deepen, the trail is forced to traverse a few yards above the willow-lined stream along a series of ledges cut into the Tapeats sandstone formation. Just beyond a pretty grove of cottonwoods we drop back down to creek level, cross back and forth a few times, then cut through a low saddle (5.9; 3320) just above the point where Garden Creek disappears down a steep, narrow slot. Here the trail begins a moderate-to-steep, switchbacking descent into the canyon that Pipe Creek has cut into the Vishnu schist, the deepest and most ancient of the rock layers exposed in the Grand Canyon. The light-colored streaks that marble the generally darker rock in places are granitic intrusions, the result of molten igneous rock forcing its way up into cracks in the schist layer and then hardening in place. It is these intrusions for which the Granite Gorge was named.

Several switchbacks later the trail bottoms out and crosses Pipe Creek (6.8; 2780), which we then follow down-canyon, past the bottom of the deeply recessed gorge containing Garden Creek, to a resthouse with a chemical toilet (7.7; 2440). We are now within a stone's throw of the Colorado River, which is accessible via a short side trail branching left from here. The river makes a good turnaround point for well-conditioned dayhikers. If you feel tempted to take a dip in the cold water, bear in mind that swimming in this stretch of the Colorado is both dangerous and prohibited by the Park Service.

To reach Bright Angel Campground, we turn right at this junction, climb a short distance, and traverse eastward, staying a hundred feet or so above the roaring, swirling river. Views are impressive along this stretch of trail, of the dark cliffs of the Granite Gorge, towering directly above the hiker, and of the tiered buttes and ridges around Zoroaster Temple, soaring gracefully into the distant haze across the gorge. After slogging through a deposit of shifting, windblown sand, we approach the first of two steel suspension bridges spanning the river. Those with an eye for efficient engineering will doubtless be struck by this structure's lean, elegant design, which achieves strength without bulk, stability without excess mass. At a junction by the bridge we turn left, cross the river, and proceed past River Ranger Station to clearly signed Bright Angel Campground (9.3; 2480). Here, in a grove of majestic cottonwoods alongside Bright Angel Creek, there are tables and chemical toilets. The resident ranger often gives interpretive talks in the evening — these are generally quite interesting and informative, and are announced on the bulletin board near the ranger station. Fishing is fair for good-sized rainbow trout, in both Bright Angel Creek and the Colorado River. Remember, you must have a backcountry permit to camp here.

Return the way you came.

See Maps 33 and 34

Trip 79   Yaki Point to Cedar Ridge

3.0 miles round trip; 1160 ' elevation gain

Moderate dayhike

Season all year

No water available along route

Features

This short trek out to Cedar Ridge is by far the easiest of the Grand Canyon hikes outlined in this guide. With its fine views and interesting destination, it is an excellent choice for dayhikers seeking to get the "feel" of inner-canyon hiking without having to spend an entire day on the trail.

Description

From the trailhead near Yaki Point (0.0; 7200) follow the South Kaibab Trail as it drops down several short, steep switchbacks through the Kaibab limestone and sandstone formations, then begins a steadily descending, northward-trending traverse. During winter and early spring this section of trail often lies beneath several inches of snow, but it is wide enough to be hiked safely if one is wearing lug-soled boots. A greater incovenience

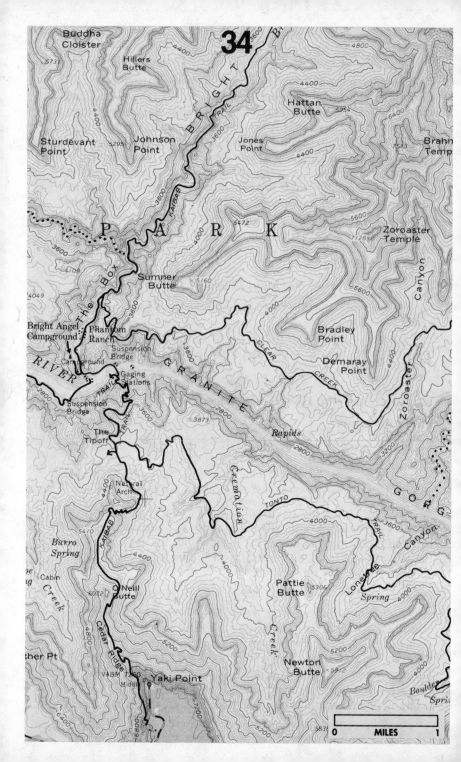

arises with the advent of warm weather, when the snow melts and the hooves of Phantom-Ranch-bound mule trains churn the trail into a quagmire.

After winding in and out of a few shady recesses, in which can be seen some tall Douglas-firs, the trail gains the upper crest of Cedar Ridge, where the switchbacking begins again. At times we are on the ridge's east side, looking across the broad drainage of Cremation Creek to Zoroaster and Brahma temples, and at times on the west flank, staring into the dizzying gulf of Pipe Creek Canyon. The switchbacks presently cease again, and we walk out onto a small flat perched atop the ridge (1.5; 6040). Here, amid a sparse growth of "cedars" (actually the familiar Utah juniper of the pinyon-juniper woodland community), the Park Service has set up a chemical toilet and an interesting display of Supai formation fossils. There is no water here.

Return the way you came.

See Map 34

Trip 80   Yaki Point to Bright Angel Lodge via Cedar Ridge, Bright Angel Campground and Indian Gardens

16.2 miles one way (4-mile car shuttle required); 4360′ elevation gain

Strenuous dayhike or backpack (3 hiking days)

Season all year; hot in summer

Water available all year at Bright Angel Campground (mile 6.9), at Indian Gardens (mile 11.7), and from May 1 to September 30 at Bright Angel Trail resthouses (miles 13.2 and 14.7)

Features

The South Kaibab Trail provides the hiker with the most direct access to the lovely Bright Angel Creek area. Since the trail tends to follow ridges rather than drainages during its descent, it also affords more extensive and panoramic vistas than perhaps any other rim-to-river route.

Since the South Kaibab is steep and waterless from top to bottom, this trip returns to the South Rim via the easier, better-watered Bright Angel Trail.

Description

From the trailhead near Yaki Point (0.0; 7200), follow the South Kaibab Trail to Cedar Ridge (see Trip 79), then continue moderately downhill to an open saddle just south of O'Neill Butte (1.9; 5800). From here the trail switchbacks down a short distance to the east, makes a descending traverse beneath the face of the butte, and then levels off again at another saddle. At a spot where one can see the bright green strip of cottonwoods lining Bright Angel Creek far below, this level stretch ends and we drop abruptly into a deep notch (3.2; 5040), just below which begins the very steep, switchbacking descent through the Redwall cliff.

After innumerable switchbacks the gradient eases a bit and the trail swings northward onto the rolling, sagebrush-dotted expanse of the Tonto Plateau. Soon we intersect the westbound Tonto Trail at a signed junction (4.6; 4000). Approximately 100 yards beyond here the eastbound Tonto branches right and we continue straight ahead on the South Kaibab, as before. Shortly after passing a chemical toilet and an emergency phone, at a point called the Tipoff, the trail begins dropping into the dark gulf of the Granite Gorge. This final descent is gradual at first, but after passing Panorama Point — which offers an excellent view of the Colorado River swirling down its steep-walled, rough-cut channel — we find ourselves once again switchbacking steeply downhill. (At this point the hiker may see the wisdom of returning to the South Rim via the less strenuous Bright Angel Trail.)

Just before the trail bottoms out at the river, we turn right at a signed junction, then walk across the Kaibab Bridge. After crossing the river the trail leads due west about 0.5 mile to a bridge across Bright Angel Creek (6.9; 2480). Bright Angel Campground is just down a well-signed, right-branching spur trail from here. The campground offers tables, toilets, interpretive talks by the resident ranger, and fair fishing for fair-sized rainbow trout in Bright Angel Creek and the Colorado River. Remember, you must have a backcountry permit to spend the night.

To return to the South Rim at Bright Angel Lodge (16.2; 6840), reverse the steps of Trip 78.

See Maps 34 and 33

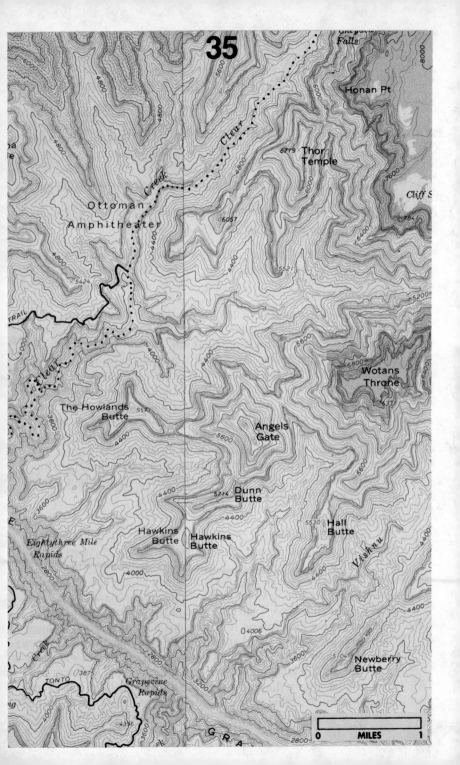

35

Falls

Honan Pt

Thor
Temple

6779

Cliff S

784

Ottoman

Amphitheater

Creek

Clear

6057

552

5200

5600

Wotans
Throne

6800

7611

5424

TRAIL

4800

6000

6400

5200

4400

The Howlands
Butte

557

Angels
Gate

5600

5600

Dunn
Butte

5714

Hall
Butte

5530

Hawkins
Butte

Hawkins
Butte

4400

4400

Vishnu

Eightythree Mile
Rapids

4000

4400

Creek

3875

TONTO

Grapevine
Rapids

4006

3600

5104

Newberry
Butte

4395

G R A

2800

0   MILES   1

Trip 81   Yaki Point to Clear Creek via the South Kaibab and Clear Creek trails; return via the Bright Angel Trail

36.0 miles total (4-mile car shuttle required); 6620' elevation gain

Strenuous backpack (4–5 hiking days)

Season October to May

Water available all season at Bright Angel Creek (miles 6.9 and 25.6), Clear Creek (mile 16.8) and Indian Gardens (mile 31.5)

Features

    This fine route drops quickly to the Colorado River, then wanders "off the beaten track" to perennial, remote Clear Creek, within whose many beautiful basins and coves hikers can find all the solitude they desire. An added bonus is the opportunity to scramble up to Cheyava Falls, a rainy-season-only cataract which, on those rare occasions when it has a boisterous flow, is the highest and most spectacular waterfall in the Grand Canyon.

    In order to avoid what would be a relentlessly steep, waterless, and shadeless hike back up the South Kaibab Trail, the return to the South Rim is made via the easier Bright Angel Trail. Most hikers prefer this routing; if you cannot handle the short car shuttle involved, it is best to begin and end your trip at Bright Angel Lodge, rather than at Yaki Point.

Description

    From the trailhead near Yaki Point (0.0; 7200) follow the South Kaibab Trail down to the bridge across Bright Angel Creek (6.9; 2480) (see Trips 79 and 80). Most hikers will want to spend the night at nearby Bright Angel Campground before tackling the waterless 9-mile trek to Clear Creek. When ready to continue, turn onto the North Kaibab Trail (it begins at the east end of the bridge over the creek) and follow it northward alongside Bright Angel Creek, past the cabins and snack bar of Phantom Ranch to the signed junction with the Clear Creek Trail (8.0; 2620). Here we turn right, and begin climbing moderately to steeply. After crossing a small drainage the trail steepens a bit, then switchbacks up to a minor saddle offering a nice view across the Granite Gorge to the cliffs and terraces that soar up to the South Rim. Next we make a short, level traverse, then climb to Phantom Overlook, a viewpoint perched several hundred feet directly above the green cottonwoods shading Phantom Ranch. Just beyond here an unsigned spur trail branches right and leads a few yards to an impressive overlook of the Colorado River. The main trail continues climbing here, then crosses another small saddle and begins traversing eastward, searching for a break in the sheer Bright Angel shale cliffs which loom — and occasionally overhang — directly above us. During the spring, in wet years especially, agaves bloom profusely in this area, their bright green-yellow flower stalks rising above the level of the surrounding sagebrush and contrasting sharply with the dark, somber walls of the Granite Gorge.

After about 0.5 mile of traversing, the trail cuts to the left and climbs steeply alongside a drainage, passing through the Bright Angel cliffs and then leveling off atop the Tonto Plateau. As we proceed eastward across the gently undulating Tonto surface, we gain a fine, wide panorama of much of the central inner canyon, as well as a spectacular, head-on view of Zoroaster Temple.

After crossing a creekbed (11.2; 3760) which drains the huge, semi-circular cove at the base of "Zoro," the trail veers southward in order to clear the projecting prominence of Bradley Point. After 2 miles (and several ups and downs) later, we cross a pair of low ridgelines and swing towards the north. As we do so, the magnificent labyrinth of canyons and amphitheaters drained by Clear Creek comes by increments into view, an inspiring sight. A rest stop here will allow you to map out enough side trips to fill a week or more of layover days.

A mile farther we cross Zoroaster Creek (14.7; 4060), then climb over a ridge and drop into an unnamed drainage. As the trail rounds a steep spur coming down from Brahma Temple it approaches the dropoff into Clear Creek Canyon, raising hopes that our lengthy traverse of the Tonto Plateau is over, but presently the path veers away again, and it is not until a full 0.5 mile later that we finally drop steeply several hundred feet down to Clear Creek (16.8; 3580). Here there is perennial water, limited fishing for rainbow trout, and excellent camping beneath a few scattered cottonwood trees.

The trail ends here, but hikers can continue cross-country either up- or down-canyon as far as they please. Clear Creek may be followed all the way down to the Colorado River, though a few sections of this route are tricky enough to make this an exploration for experienced scramblers only. (This route should not be attempted by *anyone* if a heavy storm seems imminent, as long sections of the lower canyon are narrow and sheer-walled, affording no escape from flash floods.) During exceptionally wet years, spring-season visitors are encouraged to make the rough, but not-too-difficult, side trip up to Cheyava Falls, a plume of water that emerges from a cave in the Redwall cliff and drops freely for several hundred feet, forming the highest waterfall in the entire Grand Canyon. To reach the falls, bushwack and boulderhop upstream, turning right at each major fork in the canyon. After about 4 brushy miles the cascade will appear high on the right-hand canyonside — provided it is running at all. Allow all day for this excursion.

To return to the South Rim, retrace your steps to the bridge across Bright Angel Creek (25.6; 2480), then follow the Bright Angel Trail to Bright Angel Lodge (36.0; 6840) (reverse the steps of Trip 78).

See Maps 34, 35 and 33

Trip 82   Yaki Point to Grandview Point

28.2 miles one-way (10-mile car shuttle required); 5160′ elevation gain

Strenuous backpack (allow at least 4 hiking days)

Season October to May

Water available all season at Cottonwood Creek (near mile 24.5); during rainy periods, water may be available at Lonetree Canyon (mile 10.2), Boulder Creek (mile 13.2) and Grapevine Creek (mile 19.1) (check with Park Service before leaving)

Features

After dropping into the inner canyon via the scenic South Kaibab Trail, this trip samples a long, lonely stretch of the Tonto Trail before climbing back up to the South Rim at Grandview Point. Juniper-dotted Horseshoe Mesa, with its fine vistas and fascinating mining-era relics, makes a fitting climax for this demanding trek.

Because the Tonto Trail is in many places obscure and difficult to follow, this route is recommended only for experienced
wilderness travelers.

Description

From the trailhead near Yaki Point (0.0; 7200), follow the
route of Trip 80 down to the signed junction with the eastbound
Tonto Trail (4.7; 4000). Here we turn right, abandoning the wide,
mule-trampled "highway" of the South Kaibab Trail in favor of
the narrower, harder-to-follow Tonto. For the next 20 miles or so,
our route will follow this serpentine track across the rolling
esplanade of the Tonto Plateau, winding in and out of numerous
side canyons along the way. In many places the trail will become
quite obscure, or will be confused by the lacework of pathways
"pioneered" by the inner canyon's feral burros. The confusing
sections of the trail are usually clarified by ducks or cairns, but not
always, so be prepared to spend a little extra time now and then
scouting out the route ahead. If you find such route-finding mad-
dening at times, bear in mind that the Tonto's demanding
character keeps out the hordes of strollers who would otherwise be
here, and for whose sake this wild and lonely route might otherwise be festooned with chemical toilets, ranger stations, emergency
telephones, and other Kaibab Trail-style "improvements."

After turning right at the Tonto-Kaibab junction, we climb
gently to a low saddle, then cross a shallow wash. Beyond here the
trail becomes very faint, and we follow a series of cairns steeply
down a hillside. During the spring (and to a lesser extent during the
fall) these rolling, sagebrush- and burrobrush-covered slopes are
brightened by such wildflowers as prickly phlox, wild four-
o'clock, white evening primrose, bright red Indian paintbrush,
scarlet mallow, and the blossoms of several varieties of prickly
pear. Keen-eyed hikers sometimes spot chipped arrowheads and
scrapers along the trail through here, but since collecting such artifacts is forbidden by the Park Service, it is more rewarding to keep
one's eyes on the scenery than on the ground.

After leveling off on a lower shelf of the Tonto Plateau, the
trail becomes distinct again and swings southward. About 0.5 mile
later we drop steeply into the westernmost of the three branches of
Cremation Creek; then we climb just as steeply back out again,
and repeat the process all over at the middle fork. The crossing of
the easternmost prong (7.2; 3620) is somewhat less laborious.
Those who go exploring upstream from here may spot some small

caves, within which were found some crude, 3–4000 year old figurines — the oldest evidence of humans in the inner canyon. All three forks of Cremation Creek have good, sheltered campsites, but none has any water except during exceptionally wet periods, when the easternmost branch may contain a trickle. This drainage received its name when early white visitors reported seeing Indians liberating the ashes of their cremated dead into the abyss beneath the South Rim, somewhere between Yaki and Shoshone points.

The next section of the Tonto Trail offers fine vistas across the Granite Gorge and up into the extensive basin drained by Clear Creek. These views fade as we round Pattie Butte (named for James O. Pattie, reputedly the first white American to see the Grand Canyon), and by and by we drop into Lonetree Canyon (10.2; 3640). The spring shown on the topo here is often dry, even in the springtime — check it out with the Park Service when obtaining your backcountry permit. About 2 miles beyond Lonetree Canyon the trail crosses the head of an unnamed gulch, down which there is a nice view of the muddy Colorado River in the vicinity of Eightythree Mile Rapids. A mile or so farther is Boulder Creek; again, the spring indicated on the map here may be dry, and should not be relied upon without obtaining advance confirmation from the Park Service.

After passing through a minor saddle beneath a knifeblade ridge descending from Lyell Butte, we cross a nameless drainage, then approach the brink of the Granite Gorge, where we are treated to a spectacular bird's-eye view of Grapevine Rapids. Here one can see how the bouldery flash-flood debris of Grapevine Creek bulges out into the river channel, forcing the water to ride up onto the opposite canyonside and creating considerable turbulence. (Not all Grand Canyon rapids are formed this way; others appear where the walls of the Granite Gorge pinch together to form a bottleneck, and where submerged sandbars have been deposited in the riverbed.)

In the vicinity of an oddly shaped pinnacle, the trail swings southward and begins a long detour around the deep gash of Grapevine Canyon. About 2 miles later we finally cross the western prong of Grapevine Creek (18.7; 3540); the larger, eastern branch is crossed a few hundred yards beyond. There is delightful camping hereabouts, beneath a smattering of junipers, and often a trickle of water down in the creekbed. Worthwhile side trips may be made, either upstream to the spacious amphitheater to the south, or downstream into eery, sheer-walled Grapevine Canyon.

The springs indicated on the map about a mile beyond Grapevine Creek are generally reliable (but check them out with the Park Service first, as always). Beyond them the Tonto Trail leads on, for mile after mile, back toward the brink of the Granite Gorge. Before turning away again we gain some more nice views across the Colorado River, with the graceful peak of Vishnu Temple looming in the background. Presently the route dips into the west fork of Cottonwood Creek (the spring here should not be relied upon), then climbs over a low ridge and traverses gradually downhill into the main arm of the canyon. Where the trail first hits the streambed is an obscure juntion. The Tonto Trail goes left here, while our route goes right and proceeds up-canyon, past a number of delightful, pinyon-and-juniper-shaded campsites. About 0.5 mile beyond the junction, Cottonwood Creek forks; look for water at a perennial spring just up the west branch if there is none in the creekbed below.

To reach Horseshoe Mesa, follow the trail up the drainage which branches east just below the spring. In a few hundred yards, just after passing some very large trees growing in the wash, the trail makes a quick pair of creekbed crossings, then climbs exceptionally steeply uphill to the left (east). This poorly constructed, badly eroded stretch of trail suddenly levels off atop a narrow terrace at the base of the Redwall cliff, where we cut to the right and traverse into a steep-walled, rocky-bottomed drainage. Several switchbacks up the latter (the route stays right at each major drainage fork) then bring us to a small promontory containing some old mining-camp relics. After another, shorter climb we clamber up onto Horseshoe Mesa (24.9; 4800), within sight of the ruins of Pete Berry's cabin (see Trip 83 for a description of the Horseshoe Mesa area).

To return to the South Rim from here, follow the Grandview Trail the remaining 3.2 miles up to Grandview Point (28.2; 7400) (reverse the steps of Trip 83).

See Maps 34, 35 and 36

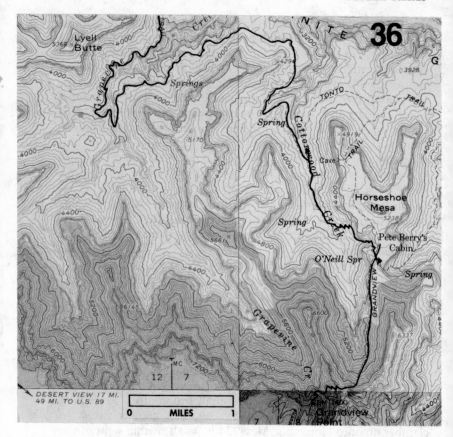

Trip 83 Grandview Point to Horseshoe Mesa

6.4 miles round trip; 2600′ elevation gain

Moderate dayhike or backpack (2 hiking days)

Season all year, except after snowstorms

No water available along route

Features

The Grandview Trail, built by prospector Pete Berry in the 1890's to service his Last Chance Copper Mine, provides an interesting and highly scenic route into the eastern inner-canyon country. A variety of fascinating relics and ruins can be found by those who take the time to explore Horseshoe Mesa, making this a fine trip for trekkers with a historical bent.

The Grandview Trail has long been unmaintained, and parts of it are rather rough. Beginning hikers should gain experience on other inner-canyon routes before attempting this one.

Description

From the trailhead near Grandview Point (0.0; 7400), follow the Grandview Trail as it switchbacks moderately-to-steeply downhill through the Kaibab limestone and sandstone formations. After dropping a few hundred feet we cut right to a deep notch, then switchback down and around a ridge to a saddle containing a few fir trees (0.6; 6840). From here the trail drops steeply to the bottom of the Coconino formation, then begins traversing eastward across the headwall of Cottonwood Creek Canyon. The trail, well defined up to this point, now begins to grow rougher and more obscure, though never really hard to follow. The entire upper part, however, may be difficult to trace following a heavy snowstorm.

This eastward traverse presently ends, and we drop abruptly down toward Cottonwood Creek. As we proceed, the steep descent gradually metamorphoses into a northward-trending, moderately dropping (with several minor ups and downs) traverse beneath the ridge leading out to Horseshoe Mesa. This section offers an interesting view across Cottonwood Creek Canyon to a curiously warped section of the Redwall. At length we sidle onto the aforementioned ridge and drop a short distance to a pile of tailings at the mouth of a deep, horizontal shaft — part of the Last Chance Copper Mine workings. (If you elect to explore this or any of the other tunnels that dot this area, use extreme caution, as many of them contain dangerous vertical dropoffs.) Several use trails branch off hereabouts; to reach the ruins of Pete Berry's cabin, follow a well-used pathway due north onto the south end of Horseshoe Mesa. After a few hundred yards the cabin (3.2; 4800) can be seen just across the head of a small ravine.

Horseshoe Mesa is thickly planted with junipers, and offers a kaleidoscope of pleasant vistas. To the north, across the Granite Gorge, one can see the prominent peak of Vishnu Temple rising beyond the shoulder of nearby Horseshoe Mesa Butte. Off to the northeast the Grand Canyon makes a mighty swing to the north, beneath the magnificent, continuous wall of the Palisades of the Desert. Almost out of sight in that direction, at the far end of the Palisades, stands Cape Solitude, overlooking the confluence of the main Colorado and Little Colorado rivers.

There is delightful camping here, but the nearest water is about 0.5 mile distant, down a steep and extremely rough trail that drops eastward into an arm of Hance Canyon from the area of the horizontal mineshaft mentioned above. This year-round spring is visible as a tiny patch of greenery at the base of the Redwall. Unless you are planning a lengthy stay, it is probably easiest to simply pack in all the water you will need.

Return the way you came.

See Map 36

Trip 84 North Rim to Roaring Springs Campground

9.8 miles round trip; 3160 ' elevation gain

Strenuous dayhike or backpack (2 hiking days)

Season May to October

Water available all season at Roaring Springs Campground (mile 4.9)

Features

As any foray beneath the Grand Canyon's rims must be, this is a strenuous excursion. Still, it serves as a fine introduction to the North Rim country, and the sight of Roaring Springs Creek bursting forth full-blown from its hole in the cliffs compensates in advance for the effort expended on the return trip.

Description

From the North Rim Trailhead (0.0; 8241), in a forest of white and Douglas fir, Engelmann and blue spruce, and quaking aspen, the North Kaibab Trail drops moderately-to-steeply southward. The aspens and evergreens quickly thin out on the steep slopes below the Kaibab Plateau, and as we swing out onto a south-facing slope they are frequently replaced by Rocky Mountain maples and Gambel oaks. Soon the trail approaches the drop-off of the Coconino cliff, which is breached via a number of tight, steep switchbacks. We cannot see much of the main Grand Canyon or the South Rim from here — or from anywhere else along this route — but there are still some nice views down the gorge of Roaring Springs Canyon to graceful Komo Point and the high bluffs of Walhalla Plateau.

Below the Coconino formation the trail switchbacks down gentler slopes into the head of Roaring Springs Canyon. After two crossings of Roaring Springs wash (usually dry here) we begin a long traverse down the south wall of the canyon, staying for the most part several hundred feet above the creekbed and passing several spectacular sections where the trail has been blasted out of the sheer, solid rock of cliffs. The forest cover becomes dominated by Colorado pinyon and Utah juniper as we lose elevation.

At length, as the trail approaches the perpendicular slash of Bright Angel Canyon, Roaring Springs come into view. You may hear them long before you see them. These springs emerge with an astonishingly powerful flow from a group of caves below the base of the Redwall limestone, and then cascade noisily a couple of hundred feet into Roaring Springs Canyon. The caves have been entered and surveyed, and contain approximately two miles of passages.

Directly across from the springs is a signed junction (4.7; 5200), where we turn left and drop a short distance to Roaring Springs Campground (4.9; 5080). Here there are tables, toilets and water. A camping permit is needed for overnight stays.

Return the way you came.

See Map 37

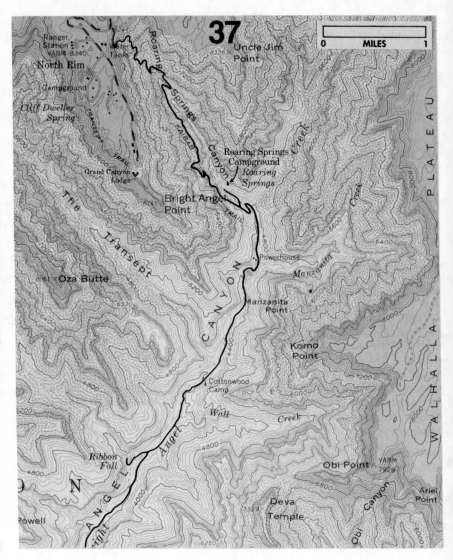

Trip 85   North Rim to Roaring Springs, Cottonwood Campground, and Ribbon Falls

16.6 miles round trip; 4560′ elevation gain

Strenuous backpack (3–4 hiking days)

Season May to October

Water available all season at Roaring Springs Campground (near mile 4.7), Cottonwood Campground (mile 6.8), Ribbon Falls (mile 8.3) and along parts of Bright Angel Creek (miles 5.3 to 8.0)

Features

    This trip descends the North Kaibab Trail to spectacular Roaring Springs, then drops into Bright Angel Canyon and follows a year-round (and trout-filled) creek to delightful Cottonwood Campground. This makes an ideal 3-day trek, as hikers who spend a layover day at either Cottonwood or Roaring Springs Campground will find themselves within convenient dayhiking range of the lush oasis of Ribbon Fall.

Description

    From the North Rim Trailhead (0.0; 8241), follow the North Kaibab Trail to the signed junction across from Roaring Springs (4.7; 5200). Roaring Springs Campground is 0.2 miles down the left-branching trail from here; with its booming, cascading springs and shady groves of hoptree, box elder, oak and cottonwood, this makes a worthwhile detour, even if you do not plan to camp here.

    To continue to Cottonwood Campground and Ribbon Falls, proceed straight ahead at this junction and drop steeply past a few switchbacks toward Bright Angel Canyon. Parts of the abandoned Old Bright Angel Trail can be seen rollercoastering up and down the far canyon wall from this area. Near the base of this descent we pass a residence that houses the keeper of the nearby powerhouse. This part of Bright Angel Canyon is comparatively lush, and box elder, singleleaf ash, hoptree and western hop hornbean can all be found growing nearby. Just below the buildings we cross Bright Angel Creek, often an intimidating, roiling torrent during the spring snowmelt, via a sturdy bridge. The trail now drops moderately through a narrow, cliffy section, then veers to the left and descends more gently for the remaining mile or so to Cottonwood Campground (6.8; 4000). Here, beneath a smattering of medium-sized cottonwoods, are tables, toilets, treated water, and a ranger station. Patient, skilled fishermen should have little trouble pulling a few fair-sized rainbow trout out of the nearby creek. You need a backcountry permit to spend the night.

Beyond the campground the trail continues down the bottom of Bright Angel Canyon, keeping well to the left of the creek. A number of wildflowers blossom hereabouts, including fleabane, delicate silk-tassel, wild buckwheat, cliffrose, sulfur flower, bright yellow snakeweed and Apache plume. Clumps of canyon live oak and scrub live oak grow on the dry, sunny hillsides, and an occasional Arizona redbud can be seen esconced in the shady mouth of a side canyon. The long, cliff-edged defile of Bright Angel Canyon frames a pleasant vista of the distant South Rim.

A little over a mile below Cottonwood Campground is a signed junction (8.0; 3700) with the spur trail to Ribbon Fall. Here we turn right, drop slightly, and cross a footbridge to the west side of Bright Angel Creek. After passing an interpretive sign pointing out an exposed portion of the Shinumo quartzite formation, the trail veers left to an unsigned fork. Here we go right (the left branch rejoins the North Kaibab Trail after making a bridgeless crossing of Bright Angel Creek). Soon we pull up alongside tiny, willow-lined Ribbon Creek, where you may hear the song of a canyon wren or spot an ouzel flitting up and down the cascading watercourse. It is now just a short walk up the rough path to the base of Ribbon Fall (8.3; 3;720). This year-round, hundred-foot-or-so-high fall has carved a deep, overhanging amphitheater out of the surrounding rock, within which the deep shade and drifting spray have nurtured thick carpets of moss and ferns. During hot weather this is an excellent spot for a layover-day picnic, or for just lounging around. Please stay on the established pathways here to avoid trampling the vegetation.

A signed pathway leaves the base of the fall and climbs, in a little less than a mile, to Upper Ribbon Fall. This makes a fine side trip, but the trail is steep and rough in places, and recommended only for experienced hikers.

Return the way you came.

See Map 37

Trip 86 North Rim to Bright Angel Lodge via the North Kaibab and Bright Angel trails

23.4 miles one way (214-mile car shuttle required); 4360′ eleva-
tion gain

Strenuous backpack (3–4 hiking days)

Season May to October

Water available all season at Roaring Springs Campground (near
mile 4.7), along parts of Bright Angel Creek (miles 5.3 to 14.1), at
Indian Gardens (mile 18.9), and from May 1 to September 30 at
Bright Angel Trail resthouses (miles 20.4 and 21.9)

Features

This spectacular route is for every hiker who has ever gazed
across the vast gulf of the Grand Canyon and yearned to measure
its breadth with his or her boot soles, to cross it from rim to rim on
foot. Once having done so, one looks back across the yawning
chasm with a profoundly altered appreciation of its true scale and
magnificence — and with a well-earned sense of pride and accomplishment.

Description

From the North Rim Trailhead (0.0; 8241), follow the North
Kaibab Trail to the signed junction with the trail to Ribbon Falls
(8.0; 3700) (see Trip 85). Here we continue straight ahead, climb a
few short, steep switchbacks, and then drop back down to a second spur trail to the falls (this alternate path makes a bridgeless
crossing of Bright Angel Creek, and may be impassable during the
high water of spring). Beyond here the trail descends gently down
the canyon, whose terraced sidewalls frame some nice views of the
distant South Rim. As we lose elevation, the oaks, pinyons and
junipers of the Upper Sonoran life zone are gradually supplanted
by a smattering of Lower Sonoran trees, mostly mesquite and
catclaw. Between these small, drought-resistant trees the ground
cover is sparse and desertlike, consisting of agave, yellow-
blossoming prickly pear, sagebrush, Mormon tea and burrobrush,
among other species. Collared lizards scamper off the trail here

and there as they sense our approach, and every now and then in this area hikers are knocked out of their walking reveries by the sharp warning buzz of a Grand Canyon rattler.

About 3 miles below Cottonwood Campground, Bright Angel Canyon's walls begin to close in, and soon we find ourselves at the bottom of a rapidly deepening gorge, passing beneath high, overhanging cliffs where the trail has been dynamited out of the sheer rock. A mile or so later we reach the first of several bridges across Bright Angel Creek. (Before the North Kaibab Trail was improved in the late 1920's, travelers had to ford the creek as many as *99 times* to negotiate these fearsome narrows.) The pipeline which dogs the trail through here carries water from Roaring Springs to the South Rim, and has an interesting history: just as the pipeline was about to be completed (at a cost of millions) in December 1966, it was wrecked by a phenomenal flood that swept down Bright Angel Canyon. Repairing the line turned out to be a longer and costlier project than the original installation.

A few crossings later, just beyond a point where a small, nonindigenous palm tree can be seen growing down by the water, Phantom Creek flows out of a narrow slot in the rock and empties into Bright Angel Creek (12.6; 2740). During low-water periods one can scramble cross-country up the exceedingly narrow gorge of Phantom Canyon to the open valley at its head (6–8 miles round trip, with reliable water all the way) — a worthwhile diversion for experienced hikers with time to spare. About 0.5 mile below this confluence, Bright Angel Canyon begins to open up a bit, and the Clear Creek Trail branches left at a signed junction. (Another interesting side trip is to climb up this path a little less than a mile to an overlook of the Colorado River.) Continuing straight ahead on the North Kaibab Trail from here, we presently arrive at cottonwood-shaded Phantom Ranch, with its guest cabins, ranger station, and public snack bar. A short distance beyond the ranch is the lowest of the bridges across Bright Angel Creek (14.1; 2480). Bright Angel Campground is just up the trail that branches right from here; most hikers will want to spend at least one night here before tackling the long climb out of the inner canyon. A layover day can be spent fishing for rainbow trout in either the creek or the river, exploring one of the side trips mentioned above, or resting one's bones beneath the rustling leaves of a cottonwood tree—a wise and popular choice. In the evenings the resident ranger often gives talks on the human and natural history of the canyon.

When ready to complete your cross-canyon journey, reverse the steps of Trip 78 past Indian Gardens to the trailhead near Bright Angel Lodge (23.4; 6840).

See Maps 37, 34 and 33

Trip 87   Hermits Rest to Hermit
Creek Campground

14.4 miles round trip; 3740 ' elevation gain

Strenuous dayhike or backpack (2 hiking days)

Season all year; hot in summer

Water available all year at Santa Maria Spring (mile 2.3) and Hermit Creek (mile 7.2)

Features

The spectacular Hermit Trail has not been actively maintained since 1931, but it is still easily passable and justifiably popular, since it affords both a variety of fine vistas and, along the lush banks of Hermit Creek, delightful camping. Except for the Kaibab and Bright Angel trails, this is probably the easiest of the rim-to-river routes, and it is recommended as an introduction to wilderness hiking in the inner canyon.

Description

From the trailhead just beyond Hermit's Rest (0.0; 6660) we drop down a hillside a short distance, then begin switchbacking moderately-to-steeply down toward Hermit Basin. The forest cover is light through here, mainly Colorado pinyon. As the trail twists down through the light-colored Coconino sandstone formation, you may spot some fossil footprints in the rock. These prints were left behind some 300 million years ago by small reptiles and amphibians that roamed the sand dunes which formed here during the Paleozoic Era.

Just before we reach the bottom of pinyon-and-juniper-forested Hermit Basin, the signed Waldron Trail branches left. We stay right at this fork, and proceed along a short, nearly level stretch to a signed junction with the Dripping Spring Trail (1.8; 5280). Here the route goes right again, to wander gently up and down to the brink of deep, sheer-walled Hermit Gorge. A few switchbacks then bring us to Santa Maria Spring (2.3; 5040), where there is a small shelter and reliable water. The trail now traverses northward along the sloping shelf of the Supai formation, negotiating several minor ups and downs and an occasional rockslide, where it is necessary to pick one's way carefully across the boulders obscuring the route.

After winding in and out of a few small drainages, we cross a minor ridge, then switchback down to a saddle behind Lookout Point. Fourmile Spring, shown on the topo map as being just below here, has long been dry. From the saddle, the trail resumes its gentle traversing, passing excellent views across the Granite Gorge to Mencius Temple, Tower of Ra, and the canyon of Ninetyfour Mile Creek. This relatively level section ends abruptly at the top of the Cathedral Stairs (4.9; 4440), a series of steep, rocky switchbacks which must have originally been linked together with much patience and ingenuity.

After descending the Cathedral Stairs past some somber-looking pinnacles, the trail makes a long, descending traverse below the ridge leading out to Cope Butte, then switchbacks steeply down onto the gentler terrain of the Tonto Plateau. At a four-way intersection marked by a pair of signless metal posts we meet the Tonto Trail (6.0; 3220). Here we turn neither right nor left but proceed straight ahead, descending gently along the surface of the plateau and swinging left as we approach the steep dropoff into Hermit Creek Canyon. Presently a signed spur trail to the Colorado River branches off to the right; those who have the time may wish to make the worthwhile side trip down to foaming, roaring Hermit Rapids (a little over 2 miles round trip). Otherwise we stay left here, and quickly reach the remains of old Hermit Camp, a way station maintained from 1912 to 1930 for the comfort of Fred Harvey mule-trip customers. It was dismantled shortly after the Phantom Ranch resort was opened.

Below here the trail crosses a small wash and then drops steeply to Hermit Creek Campground (7.2; 2920), where a chemical toilet has been installed to protect the water quality of tiny, perennial Hermit Creek. In order to protect the lush vegetation in this area, please stay on the pathways that have been outlined by the Park Service. A few overhanging rock shelves at the edge of the campground provide good shelter during disagreeable weather. Remember — you need a backcountry permit to spend the night here.

Return the way you came.

See Map 38

Trip 88   Hermits Rest to Boucher Creek

20.8 miles round trip; 3900 ' elevation gain

Strenuous backpack (2 hiking days)

Season all year; hot in summer

Water available all year at Boucher Creek (mile 10.4)

Features

This challenging trek follows the trail built by Louis Boucher (the "hermit" for whom Hermits Rest was named) to his asbestos mine and fruit orchards along spectacular Boucher Creek. Parts of his highly scenic route have fallen into various states of obscurity and disrepair since being abandoned in 1919, making this a trip for skilled, experienced backpackers only.

Description

From the trailhead just beyond Hermit's Rest (0.0; 6660), follow the rocky, switchbacking Hermit Trail down to a signed junction with the Dripping Springs Trail in Hermit Basin (1.8; 5280) (see Trip 87). Turning left onto the latter, we traverse westward for a mile or so, over a few minor ups and downs and across some easily negotiated rockslides. Across the upper canyon of Hermit Creek, the broad, sloping ledge of the Hermit Shale (just above the reddish, terraced Supai cliffs) is obvious; it is this shelf that we follow for the first half of the Boucher Trail.

Immediately after crossing a drainage in the bottom of Dripping Spring Canyon (3.0; 5200), look for a duck indicating the start of the right-branching Boucher Trail. The first part of this route is indistinct, but things grow clearer as we gain the wide ledge atop the Supai formation. For the next three miles or so the trail

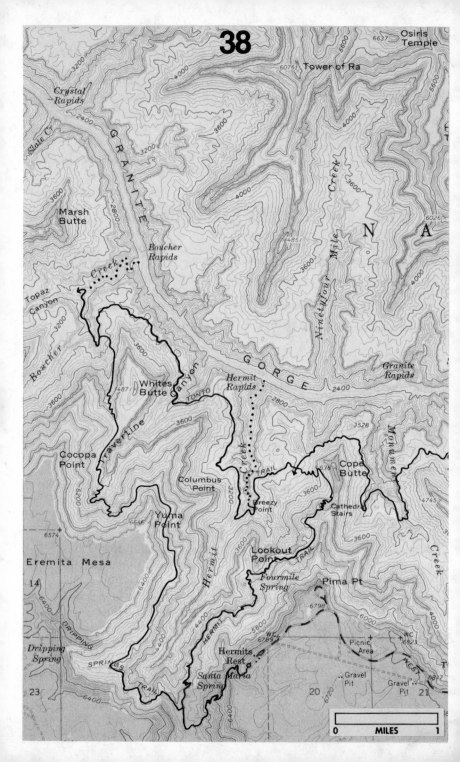

stays generally level, though it rollercoasters steeply now and then to negotiate an occasional rockslide or a steeply eroded wash. There are excellent vistas along this stretch — across the deep, dizzying gorge of Hermit Creek to the Santa Maria springhouse, down to the bright green environs of old Hermit Camp, and across the Granite Gorge to the vast, intricate array of buttes, mesas and "temples" of the north side of Grand Canyon. This view opens up even more as the trail swings left onto the ridge that drops from Yuma Point, from where one can see some distance west of Sublime Point and Sagittarius Ridge.

Approximately ¾ mile after rounding the Yuma Point ridge the wan, straggling pathway seems suddenly to end; it is no longer visible up ahead, traversing along its accustomed shelf. At this point (6.3; 5300), the route becomes very indistinct and drops steeply through a break in the Supai cliffs above slotlike Travertine Canyon. At the bottom of this rough descent, which could be dangerous when icy, we swing left and traverse along the top of the Redwall cliff to White Buttes Saddle (8.1; 4520). From here the trail drops into a narrow gorge immediately to the north and begins the bone-jarring, exceptionally steep descent through the Redwall. After dropping several hundred feet directly down a drainage channel (use caution if wet or icy) the route grows clearer, moves out to the right, and descends more moderately. Just before easing onto the Tonto Plateau we arrive at an unsigned junction, where we turn left and wind down the westbound Tonto Trail a short distance to Boucher Creek (10.4; 2760). Here, in a spectacular amphitheater, you will find the remains of Boucher's old cabin and fruit orchard, the asbestos mine he worked off and on until 1919, several good campsites, and at least an intermittent flow of water. The Colorado River, at Boucher Rapids, is a relatively easy ½-hour scramble downstream.

Return the way you came.

See Map 38

Trip 89   Hermits Rest to Boucher Creek, Hermit Creek Campground

23.5 mile semiloop trip; 4260 ' elevation gain

Strenuous backpack (3 hiking days)

Season October to May

Water available all season at Boucher Creek (mile 10.4), Hermit Creek Campground (mile 16.3), and Santa Maria Spring (mile 21.2)

Features

This route utilizes a section of the Tonto Trail to connect the highly scenic Boucher and Hermit Trails, forming a long, strenuous loop that is one of the finest 3–4 day treks in the Grand Canyon. Views are fabulous and varied the entire way, and the overnight stops at delightful Boucher and Hermit Creeks are spaced at agreeable intervals.

Since parts of the Boucher Trail are in poor condition, this route is recommended for experienced wilderness travelers only.

Description

From Hermits Rest (0.0; 6660) follow the directions for Trip 88 to the campsites on Boucher Creek (10.4; 2760). When ready to continue to Hermit Creek, the second of the two overnight stops along this loop, retrace your steps about 0.5 mile up to the Boucher/Tonto trail junction. Here we turn left, staying on the Tonto, and climb gently to a saddle atop the Tonto Plateau (11.3; 3200). You may see some feral burros grazing hereabouts, descendants of a few animals that escaped from (or were abandoned by) prospectors around the turn of the century. You also stand a rather slim chance of spotting a desert bighorn, the original and rightful inhabitant of this remote country, but local populations of these regal animals have waned steadily as the highly adaptable, highly competitve burros have continued to multiply. Plans to shoot or otherwise eliminate the burros have elicited much controversy, but their eventual removal seems essential to saving the bighorn.

Just before we reach a second saddle atop the plateau the Colorado River comes into view, and as the trail contours along the brink of the Granite Gorge it is possible to see downstream to Boucher Rapids and upstream as far as Hermit and Granite rapids. After passing below the steep cliff of White Butte, we begin working our way southward, and soon drop steeply into Travertine Canyon (13.5; 3160). At a point where a solitary pinyon is visible growing in this narrow gorge, the route proceeds up-canyon a few yards, then climbs abruptly back out the other side. Back on the Tonto Plateau, the trail swings past the base of the steep, nameless butte north of Yuma Point, then heads south toward Hermit Creek Canyon. The river presently comes back into view, but only temporarily; it is lost again as we drop slightly into a shallow gulch. Another ¾ mile of gentle traversing, interspersed with a few rough ups and downs, brings us to Hermit Creek. Here we step across the tiny creek, then continue a short distance down-canyon to Hermit Creek Campground (16.3; 2920), where there is year-round water, a chemical toilet and excellent camping. Please help to restore the lush greenery in this fragile area by staying within the established pathways and campsites.

To complete your loop trip, follow the Hermit Trail the remaining 7.2 miles up to Hermits Rest (23.5; 6660) (reverse the steps of Trip 87).

See Map 38

view from near El Tovar

Trip 90   Hermits Rest to Bright Angel Lodge via Monument Canyon and Indian Gardens

22.8 miles one-way (9-mile car shuttle required); 4200′ elevation gain

Strenuous backpack (3–4 hiking days)

Season October to May

Water available all season at Indian Gardens (mile 18.3); water almost *always available at Monument Creek (mile 8.2) (check with Park Service first)*

Features

This fine trip takes the hiker into the inner canyon via the spectacular Hermit Trail, then samples a lengthy stretch of the Tonto Trail before ascending the Bright Angel Trail back to the South Rim. If any single spot along such a scenic route can be singled out as a highlight, it is Monument Canyon, with its tiny, near-perennial creek, its beautifully sculpted cliffs and pinnacles, and its convenient location as a first night's camp.

Both the Hermit and Tonto trails are no longer maintained, but this route is travelled frequently enough that it remains in good shape, and is readily traceable by reasonably experienced hikers.

Description

From the trailhead at Hermit's Rest (0.0; 6660), proceed along the route of Trip 87 to the unsigned junction of the Hermit Trail with the Tonto Trail (6.0; 3220). If there is no running water in Monument Canyon (a possibility during dry seasons — check with the Park Service when you obtain your backcountry permit), most trekkers will want to pass their first night at Hermit Creek Campground, 1.2 miles down the trail to the left (see Trip 87). Otherwise we turn right here, climb gently a short distance to a saddle atop the sagebrush-dotted Tonto Plateau, and then traverse past the base of Cope Butte to a second saddle, just beneath a steeply rising knife-blade ridge. During the spring months a variety of wildflowers brighten the sandy spaces between the clumps of sage and burrobrush, including white evening primrose, wild four-o'clock, blue larkspur, scarlet mallow, prickly phlox and Indian paintbrush. You may see a collared lizard or a banded gecko dart off into the brush as you approach.

Beyond the saddle, the trail swings southward to avoid the steep dropoff into Monument Canyon. In places we skirt the brink of this deep gash, gaining fine views of Granite Rapids, roaring and foaming down in the bottom of the Granite Gorge. Presently the trail drops down to a fork of Monument Creek, cuts left down the streambed (usually dry) a short distance, and then moves right to a small saddle (8.1; 2920) at the base of a tall, slender pinnacle — the "monument" of Monument Canyon. Next we work our way up into the main branch of the canyon, hugging the base of a steep cliff and passing several left-branching side trails which lead down to various campsites and swimming holes along the creek. A number of fine, secluded campsites can be found in this area. The Colorado River, at Granite Rapids, is a fairly easy 40-minute scramble down the canyon from here. Another side-trip possibility involves walking a mile or so upstream, into the lovely, spacious amphitheater beneath Mohave Wall and The Abyss. The presence of reliable water attracts a variety of wildlife to this drainage: mule deer and feral burros visit every now and then, and campers will likely have their food stores looked over by the resident gang of ravens.

Just after passing beneath an overhanging rock shelf, the trail crosses Monument Creek to its east side, then clambers back up onto the Tonto Plateau and proceeds northward. As we climb gently over a pair of minor ridges, the route swings to the right, then descends gradually into the shallow gulch that contains Cedar Spring (9.5; 3320) (just down-canyon from the trail; water during rainy periods only). The next 2 miles are spent rounding a long ridge dropping down from The Alligator. (This formation's name seems inexplicable from this angle, but requires no explanation when seen from the viewpoints along the West Rim Drive.) At Salt Creek (11.4; 3380) there are a few fair campsites, but rarely any water.

For a mile and a half or so beyond here the trail stays close to the edge of the Tonto Plateau, affording a succession of interesting — sometimes dizzying — views into Salt Creek Canyon and the Granite Gorge. After we skirt the base of Dana Butte, the long aerial tram that serves the Powell Point Mine comes into view, high on the South Rim. Soon thereafter we reach Horn Creek (usually dry), and cross its two forks. Just beyond the second of these crossings, the trail dips into a minor drainage containing a spring (15.9; 3560) (water during rainy periods only).

The part of the Tonto Plateau between Horn and Garden creeks is considerably flatter than the preceding sections, and it is now an easy walk to the signed junction with the Plateau Point Trail (17.5; 3720). We turn right at this fork (unless we first wish to make the short, worthwhile side trip to Plateau Point — see Trip 77) and proceed gently uphill to the semicivilized environs of Indian Gardens (18.3; 3760). Here, in the shade of several magnificent cottonwood trees, are tables, toilets, a ranger station and year-round water. Most hikers will wish to spend at least one night at this restful oasis before beginning the laborious climb back to the South Rim. When you *are* ready to complete your journey, follow the Bright Angel Trail the remaining 4.5 miles to Bright Angel Lodge (22.8; 6840) (reverse the steps of Trip 77). Remember to carry water on this stretch, since the water faucets at the Bright Angel Trail resthouses are generally shut down during the season indicated for this trip.

See Maps 38 and 33

Grand Canyon from Yaqui Point

Area 5: The Mazatzal Wilderness

Encompassing over 205,000 acres, the Mazatzal Wilderness is the second largest of the wild areas covered in this guide, exceeded in size only by the backcountry of Grand Canyon National Park. The name Mazatzal (locally mispronounced Ma-ta-ZEL) is a Paiute Indian term; when accompanied by the gesture of pointing between spread fingers it meant "empty-place-in-between." This is an apt description of the Mazatzal, even today, for this wide-open expanse of mountains, plains and mesas which sprawls between the Verde River and the Tonto Basin remains one of the least-visited areas of the state.

The Mazatzal Mountains run along the east side of the wilderness, rearing up in a precipitous escarpment above the Tonto Basin to the east, falling away more gently toward the flat-bottomed Verde River Valley to the west. With elevations ranging from 2100 feet, at Sheep Bridge, to over 7000 feet along parts of the Mazatzal Divide Trail, reasonably comfortable hiking may be enjoyed in every season. Summer hikers should be prepared for hot weather, even at fairly high elevations, and for the possibility of heavy thunderstorms and local flash flooding. Winter travel is quite chancy in the Mazatzal Divide area, as snowstorms here are heavier, longer-lasting, colder, and more violent than in the southern ranges. Those who venture into the western half of the wilderness should remember that it is still very lonely country, far from help and with plenty of space in which to get lost and never be found. Of course, if you are prepared to handle it, this may be precisely the sort of country you are looking for.

Geologically, the Mazatzal Mountains consist of a melange of such rocks as quartzite, shale and rhyolite, locally uplifted and tilted by massive faulting. The latter two rocks are particularly resistant to erosion, and are primarily responsible for the spectacular cliffs you will see along the eastern scarp of the range, on the west face of Mazatzal Peak, and on the forks of Deadman Creek. In large areas at lower elevations, these older rocks are covered with newer volcanic deposits, evidence of some comparatively recent volcanic activity.

The Mazatzal's biota typifies that of the rest of central Arizona, with the fortunate exception that it remains more completely intact ecologically. The low flats bordering the Verde River feature a rich Lower-Sonoran-zone plant cover of saguaro, prickly pear, ocotillo, hedgehog cactus, paloverde, creosote bush and a variety of chollas. In the foothills a grassland community predominates, with agave, sotol, gramagrass and nolina replacing the lower-elevation species. Higher up you will see lots of manzanita and shrub live oak, with pinyon pine, Utah juniper and one-seed juniper appearing in sheltered areas. Higher still are dense forests of alligator juniper, ponderosa pine, and a smattering of Gambel oak and Douglas-fir. The larger watercourses are frequently lined with nice stands of cottonwood, sycamore and, at higher elevations, Arizona cypress.

Wildlife populations in the Mazatzal remain healthy, if not quite up to primal standard. Coyotes, collared peccaries and mule deer are all common, and there are still enough cougars and black bears prowling around to keep the local ranchers in a continual uproar over their depredations. (Limited cattle grazing is unfortunately still allowed within the wilderness area boundaries.) Golden eagles can often be seen here, soaring and wheeling high above the mesas and canyons; with luck, you might see a rare-and-endangered southern bald eagle as well. The usual crew of nocturnal prowlers — ringtails, skunks, woodrats and porcupines — are also up and about every night, as you may discover if you leave your camp provisions in a vulnerable place.

The ruins of several ancient Indian dwellings are scattered throughout the Mazatzal. Some of these are thought to date back as far as 2500 BC, but most are more recent than that, being remnants of the Sinagua people, who occupied the region from approximately 700 to 1300 AD. (Trips 97 and 100 pass the ruins of one such dwelling.) Considerably more recent evidence remains of white use of the area — in the form of old cabins, abandoned mines, and the overgrown, dilapidated camps of cowboys and sheepmen.

During the prolonged Indian wars of the late 1800's, some of the most feared of the "renegade" Apaches — the Tonto bands — operated out of the Mazatzal region, which was then *terra incognita* to the whites. After several bloody battles most of the Tontos were either killed or forced to surrender, but one band, under the leadership of Chief Delshay, refused to submit. At least two stories exist concerning Delshay's eventual demise, either or both of which may be apocryphal. According to one account, he and his followers roamed and raided at will until 1890, when they were invited to negotiate a peace treaty at Fort Reno in the Mazatzal foothills. Delshay accepted, but upon entering the fort he was "mistaken" for a thief and killed. The other tale has it that he remained at large until George Crook, the famed Indian fighter, offered amnesty to any captive Apache who could produce the chieftain's head. Two heads were promptly brought in, one to the Fort Verde reservation, the other to the San Carlos. Supposedly Crook later wrote, "Being satisfied that both parties were earnest in their beliefs, and the bringing in of an extra head was not amiss, I paid both parties."

One way or another Delshay met his demise, but that did not mark the end of violence in the area. Almost as deadly as the local "Indian troubles" was the internecine warfare that broke out between cattlemen and sheepmen in Pleasant Valley, east of the Mazatzals. The infamous Tewksbury-Graham Feud, immortalized by Zane Grey in his novel *To the Last Man*, broke out in 1887, when the Tewksbury clan moved their sheep onto what had previously been exclusive cattle range. The beef-running Grahams didn't think their steers needed the competition, and the shooting that ensued lasted for five years, during which time every male member of the Graham family died, as did all but one of the Tewksburys. Ironically, when the bottom dropped out of the beef market a few years later, cattlemen began to see the hated "woollies" in a rosier light; today in the Tonto Basin, cattle and sheep often graze side by side in perfect harmony, mirroring the calm that reigns in the wild, undisturbed mountains towering above them.

Managing Agencies

Tonto National Forest
P.O. Box 29070
102 S. 28th Street
Phoenix, AZ 85038
    (602) 261-3205

Cave Creek Ranger District
P.O. Box 768
Carefree, AZ 85331
    (602) 488-3441

Payson Ranger Station
P.O. Box 100
Payson, AZ 85541
    (602) 474-2269

Further Reading

To the Last Man, by Zane Grey (Harper and Row, New York, New York 1922) (about the Graham-Tewksbury feud)

Arizona's Mazatzal, by Francois Leydet (*National Geographic Magazine*, February, 1974)

Mazatzal Wilderness Management Plan, available for review at local Forest Service offices

Approaches/Trailheads:

Barnhardt Trailhead   From Mesa, drive northeast on State Highway 87 for approximately 65 miles, then turn left onto signed Barnhardt Road (Forest Road 419). (One can also reach this turn-off by driving south from Payson for 14 miles along State 87.) Follow this good dirt road (O.K. for passenger cars) 4.7 miles to the parking area at its terminus.

City Creek Trailhead   From Payson, drive west on East Verde River Road (Forest Road 406). About 10 miles from Payson, this dirt road (OK for most passenger cars) passes through a low gap, drops down to the left, then switchbacks to the right and heads due north up the floor of the canyon containing City Creek. Continue a few hundred feet past the switchback, until you see the trailhead sign off to the left of the road.

Sheep Bridge   From Carefree, drive east along Carefree Road (paved) for 6 miles to a junction. Continue straight ahead about 2 miles farther to a junction just beyond the end of the pavement. Continue straight again, following Forest Road 24 north past

Seven Springs and Cave Creek campgrounds to signed Tangle Creek Road (Forest Road 269) (approximately 38 miles from Carefree). Turn right here, and follow Tangle Creek Road past Tangle Creek Administrative Site to Sheep Bridge, down on the Verde River (about 8 miles from the end of Forest Road 24 at Tangle Creek Road). Parts of this route will prove troublesome for passenger cars. After rains, it may require a 4-wheel drive vehicle.

Before attempting this lengthy and rather involved approach, it would be wise to study a copy of the Tonto National Forest Recreation map, available for 50¢ from the Forest Service.

Trip 91   Barnhardt Trailhead to Y Bar Basin

14.4 miles round trip; 3240′ elevation gain

Strenuous dayhike or backpack (2 hiking days)

Season March through November

Water available at Windsor Seep (mile 7.2) except during dry weather spells

Features

Cradled high on the eastern shoulder of the Mazatzal Mountains, Y Bar Basin makes a fine destination for the dayhiker or weekend backpacker. The basin itself is secluded and prettily forested, and the trail leading up to it affords panoramic vistas across Tonto Basin and the rugged Sierra Ancha.

Description

From Barnhardt Trailhead (0.0; 4220), follow the signed Y Bar Basin Trail as it proceeds gently southward up a rocky, juniper-dotted slope. The first part of the trail is very faint, but frequent cairns clearly mark the route. As the hillside gradually steepens, we negotiate a few moderate switchbacks, then cut to the left and traverse across the ravine-furrowed face of Suicide Ridge. After winding in and out of 5 small drainages, the trail rounds a minor ridgelet affording a good view down a rocky bottleneck in Shake Tree Canyon, a considerably larger drainage which has opened up below. A moderately dense forest cover of ponderosa pine and pinyon pine develops as we climb along the right-hand wall of this glorified ravine. A few Douglas-firs — Canadian-zone trees that are not at all common in the arid Mazatzal Mountains — grow in sheltered pockets along this stretch.

After following Shake Tree Canyon to its head, the trail crosses an unnamed saddle (5.4; 6300), then drops steeply into Y Bar Basin. At the bottom of this descent we pass the Y Bar cattle tanks, then proceed uphill a few hundred yards to an obscure junction. Here we stay right, and continue climbing beneath the rocky southern shoulder of 7903-foot Mazatzal Peak. There are occasional good campsites along this stretch; in early spring and during spells of rainy weather, water is available from a small streamlet that parallels the trail about 200 yards to the south. As we gain elevation, breathtaking vistas open up through the pines, across the rumpled lowlands of Tonto Basin to the broad, arching backbone of the Sierra Ancha. This view can be especially pleasing at sunset, when the jagged shadow line of the Mazatzal peaks creeps silently up the flanks of the distant ranges.

The trail climbs less steeply as it approaches the head of Y Bar Basin. At Windsor Seep (7.2; 6500) there are good, ponderosa-shaded campsites, with water available except during dry weather spells. Just beyond is a saddle atop the Mazatzal Divide, which affords an excellent view of Mazatzal Peak's sheer, 900-foot-high west face, and a more limited view across the rugged, rarely-visited fastnesses of the western Mazatzal Wilderness.

Return the way you came.

See Map 39

Trip 92   Barnhardt Trailhead to Mazatzal Divide via the Barnhardt Trail

12.2 miles round trip; 1960´ elevation gain

Moderate dayhike or backpack (2 hiking days)

Season March through November

Water generally available, in early spring and following rainy periods, in Barnhardt Canyon (near mile 1.4) and along unnamed creeklets at miles 3.1 and 4.9

Features

En route to a scenic saddle high atop the Mazatzal Divide, this route winds beneath rugged cliffs and spurs, through forests of oak and ponderosa, and past pretty copses of ash and sycamore. Short sidetrips provide access to other interesting features — a spectacular "narrows" in Barnhardt Canyon and, in season, a graceful waterfall tucked away on a tributary stream. The Barnhardt Trail is one of the best-maintained pathways in the Mazatzal, making this trip a logical choice for the hiker seeking an introduction to these rough mountains.

Description

From the parking area at the end of Barnhardt Road (0.0; 4220), follow the signed Barnhardt Trail westward, through a rather sparse vegetative cover of nolina, sharp-spined sotol and agave, Emory oak, Arizona white oak, alligator juniper and one-seed juniper. The trail is rocky and quite wide at first, but its dimensions quickly narrow to those of a footpath as it works its way onto the south wall of Barnhardt Canyon. In 0.4 mile we pass a Mazatzal Wilderness boundary sign, then pass through a stock gate and climb a bit more steeply, staying well above the creek. Where a major tributary drainage branches off to the left (1.4; 4640), it is possible to leave the trail and scramble cross country a half mile or so west up the main canyon to the mouth of the spectacular narrows, visible ahead, from which Barnhardt Creek emerges. There is usually water here, and backpackers can find fair-to-good campsites nearby.

To continue on to the Mazatzal Divide, follow the main trail as it switchbacks, steeply at times, up the left-hand wall of the

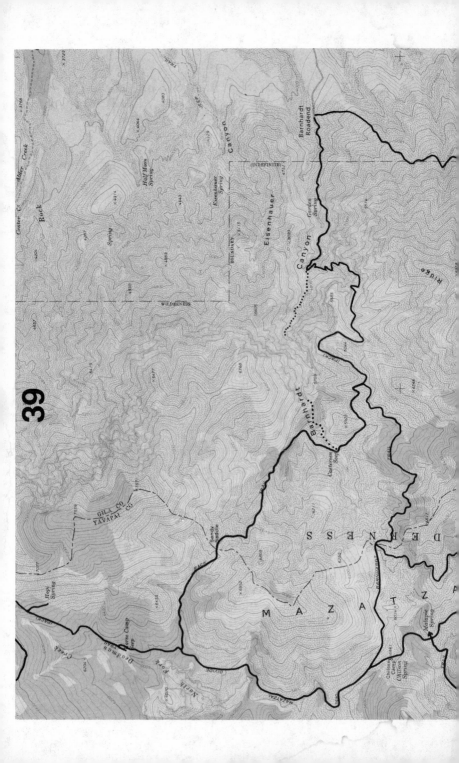

39

tributary canyon. Velvet ash, Arizona walnut and sycamore grow in shady nooks along this watercourse. After gaining 600 vertical feet the trail swings to the right, past an inviting but dry campsite atop a ridgelet with a good view, then winds past two branches of the tributary stream. The second of these small creeks (3.3; 5720) flows out of a narrow, rocky cleft; when the water is running high, you will find a spectacular, roaring cataract a few yards up in this gorge. This fall makes a worthwhile destination for dayhikers who find themselves running short of time and/or energy.

Beyond here we climb around a protruding ridge to a signed junction with the right-branching Sandy Saddle Trail (4.2; 5960). (Just 0.8 miles down the latter path, in the bottom of Barnhardt Canyon, is Castersen Seep, which may have water when the other sources along this route are dry.) Staying left at this junction, we next wind across a manzanita-covered slope into a shallow drainage featuring some nice copses of ponderosa pine. A tiny creeklet here has water in early spring and following rainy periods; camping at such times would be delightful. Castersen Seep is a 0.7-mile scramble down the drainage course.

From here the trail continues gently uphill for about 0.5 mile, then drops across a brushy slope to a signed junction in a saddle atop the Mazatzal Divide (6.1; 6020). Views are excellent from this high pass: eastward, the Sierra Ancha swells up beyond the basin of Tonto Creek, while to the west the vista stretches across the rugged Mazatzal backcountry to the Verde River Valley.

Return the way you came.

See Map 39

teddy-bear cholla on HK Mesa

Trip 93   Mazatzal Peak Loop (Barnhardt Trailhead to Mazatzal Divide, Y Bar Basin and return)

16.7-mile loop trip; 2860′ elevation gain

Strenuous dayhike or moderate backpack (3 hiking days)

Season March through November

Windsor Seep (mile 9.5) has water except during dry weather spells; in early spring and following rainy periods, water also available in Barnhardt Canyon (near mile 1.4) and along unnamed creeklets at miles 3.1 and 4.9

Features

Topping out at 7903 feet, flanked by steeply eroded cliffs, Mazatzal Peak is both the highest and one of the most prominent landmarks in the wilderness that shares its name. This route circles completely around the magnificent mountain, first climbing up to the head of rugged Barnhardt Canyon, then following a portion of the Mazatzal Divide Trail past the peak's sheer west face before dropping eastward into beautiful Y Bar Basin. Strong hikers can complete (and enjoy) this route in a single day, but most will find it ideal for a three-day backpack.

Description

From Barnhardt Trailhead (0.0; 4220), follow the Barnhardt Trail to the signed junction atop the Mazatzal Divide (6.1; 6020) (see Trip 92). Here we turn left, onto the Mazatzal Divide Trail, and traverse southward across a series of brushy, thinly forested slopes. This section of the trail is somewhat overgrown in spots, but is not hard to follow. There are occasional good views eastward, across the barren Mazatzal foothills to Pine Mountain and East Cedar Mountain, rising in the distance beyond the Verde River.

At a saddle (7.6; 6060) the signed Brody Seep Trail branches off to the right. (It is 0.9 mile down to the seep, which generally has water in winter and early spring only.) The sheer, 900-foot high western cliffs of Mazatzal Peak loom directly ahead as we continue our traverse. After winding in and out of a pair of small ravines, the trail passes beneath these cliffs, then switchbacks moderately uphill to a wooded saddle containing a signed fork. Now we turn left, onto the Y Bar Basin Trail, and drop a short distance downhill to Windsor Seep (9.5; 6500), where there is good camping beneath tall ponderosa pines (water is available except during dry weather spells). To complete your loop from here, reverse the steps of Trip 91 the remaining 7.2 miles back to Barnhardt Trailhead (16.7; 4220).

See Map 39

Trip 94   Barnhardt Trailhead to Y Bar Basin, Davenport Wash, Deadman Creek, Mountain Spring, Sandy Saddle

43.2-mile loop trip; 8900 ' elevation gain

Strenuous backpack (allow at least 5 hiking days)

Season November to May, except after snowstorms

Windsor Seep (mile 7.2), Club Spring (near mile 16.0) and Mountain Spring (mile 23.7) have water all year, except that Windsor Seep may not have water during very dry spells; in early spring and following rainy periods, water also available at Davenport Wash (mile 17.1), Deadman Creek (mile 20.0) and other points (see text)

Features

After climbing up to pretty, forested Y Bar Basin, this lengthy route crosses the Mazatzal Divide and samples a healthy chunk of the rarely visited western Mazatzal Wilderness before looping back to the trailhead via Barnhardt Canyon. Along the way it passes through some of the roughest, most pristine country left in Arizona, where one is as likely to encounter a bald eagle or black bear as another human.

Because many of the trails on this route can be hard to follow, it is recommended only for skilled and experienced hikers.

Description

From the parking area at the end of Barnhardt Road (0.0; 4220), follow the Y Bar Basin Trail to Windsor Seep (7.2; 6500) (see Trip 91). At a signed junction in a saddle 200 yards beyond the spring continue straight ahead, on the northbound Mazatzal Divide Trail now, then drop down a few switchbacks and traverse northward beneath the spectacular, 900-foot-high cliffs of Mazatzal Peak. At a second saddle (9.1; 6060) there is another junction; here we turn left and follow the signed Brody Seep Trail down into the minor drainage that contains Brody Seep (water available in winter and early spring only). The trail now traverses 0.4 mile across a brushy slope to a fork, where we turn left onto the signed Club Trail, which drops abruptly downhill (west). After following the Brody Seep drainage channel for a short distance, the trail climbs around a sunny, south-facing hillside planted with yucca, agave and some massive alligator junipers, then switchbacks steeply down into a narrow canyon and crosses South Fork Deadman Creek (12.5; 4320). There are a few fair campsites in this area, shaded by a riparian growth of sycamore and ash. The creek generally flows until midspring or so, and briefly during summer rainy spells. During very wet periods, it is worth while to walk a few hundred yards downstream to view a high, lacy waterfall formed by a small tributary streamlet.

Immediately after crossing South Fork Deadman Creek we climb, occasionally quite steeply, out of the canyon to the west. The trail levels off temporarily to cross a small, usually dry streamcourse, then climbs moderately to a broad ridgetop forested with pinyon pine and some large shrub oaks. Here we pass through a gate in a stock fence, then descend gradually, leaving the trees behind and passing into more open country. After dipping in and out of a series of shallow drainages, we drop steeply onto a low, grassy ridgetop. Here the trail bends to the left, cuts over another ridgetop, then drops across a minor streamcourse and contours southward into a small but comparatively lush, oak- and sycamore-shaded canyon. During wet weather spells, when running water is present, camping would be delightful here.

An unsigned sidepath branches to the right in this canyon, just before the Club Trail crosses the streambed; we stay left and proceed 0.4 mile farther to the site of abandoned Club Ranch (16.0; 3780), which now consists of little more than some old corrals and a pair of leaking cabins. The buildings are still used from time to time by local ranchers — please do not disturb any supplies which may be found inside. Club Spring (water available year-round) is about 200 yards up a signed spur trail to the left.

From Club Ranch the trail descends gradually to Davenport

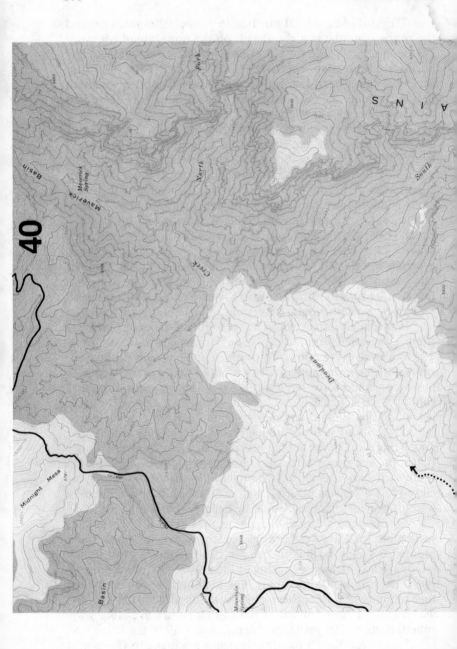

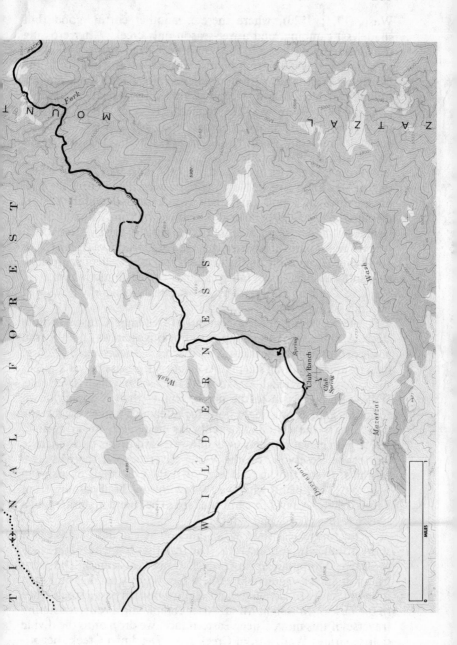

Wash (17.1; 3520), where there is another corral, good (but shadeless) camping, and a wet-season-only creek. After crossing (or fording, in wet season) the bouldery, barren wash we climb up to a trail sign, visible from below, where we turn right, onto the Deadman Trail. This path soon sidles up alongside a long, shallow ravine, which we follow, steeply at times, to its head at a saddle (18.4; 4340). Here we are treated to some fine, extensive views — both northward, across the oak-dotted Mazatzal foothills, and southward, to the distant, forested tops of Mount Peeley and Sheep Mountain.

From this gap we drop, gently for the most part, into the canyon of Deadman Creek. Near the bottom of this descent the trail passes through a pull gate, then switchbacks downhill a short distance farther to a corral near the canyon bottom. The route now swings left and runs parallel to a fence for 100 yards, after which we turn right, pass through a gate, and ford Deadman Creek (20.0; 3090) to a cairn visible on the far side. Several excellent campsites, shaded by an occasional tall sycamore, can be found in this area. The creek, one of the largest in the Mazatzals, generally flows well into the spring months.

The beginning of the ascent out of Deadman Canyon is quite steep. At the crest of a small, protruding ridge partway up, the trail levels off for awhile, cuts northward across a succession of gullies, then resumes climbing steeply. At length, after passing yet another stock fence, we reach a saddle (21.6; 4460) which overlooks Willow Spring Basin to the north. Rather than dropping down from this gap, as one might hope for after such a steep ascent, the trail turns to the right and switchbacks moderately up a ridgeline. As we gain elevation the view southwestward opens up to include Horseshoe Reservoir, on the Verde River beyond the Mazatzal foothills. Presently the trail levels off, then descends to a signed junction (23.7; 4840) with the Willow Spring Trail coming from Sheep Bridge. A few fair campsites are to be found in the area, in a sparse forest of oak and juniper.

Our route turns right at the junction here and proceeds east a short distance to another fork. The trail that branches right leads to nearby Mountain Spring, which flows year-round. The main trail switchbacks some 600 vertical feet up to a saddle, and then follows a series of ridgelines and shallow ravines past a stock fence to the base of Midnight Mesa. After completing a rollercoastering traverse of this mesa's steep eastern face, we drop onto the divide that separates Wet Bottom Creek from Deadman Creek, negotiating a few minor ups and downs before descending a short distance to cross a usually dry tributary of Wet Bottom Creek (27.2; 5210).

A steep, 1000-foot climb now brings us to a high point overlooking Maverick Basin, from where we follow a ridgeline northeastward past several ups and downs. After about a mile the trail veers off this ridge to the left, then proceeds across relatively gentle terrain to a signed junction (30.5; 5860) in The Park, a ponderosa-pine- and alligator-juniper-forested basin at the head of Wet Bottom Creek. There are several excellent campsites in this beautiful area, with water available at Pete's Pond in a nearby ravine (in early spring and following rainy periods only).

At the junction in The Park we turn right, and follow the Mazatzal Divide as it switchbacks moderately up onto a ridgetop, then traverses southward to a saddle overlooking the gently sloping headwaters of North Fork Deadman Creek. After dropping slightly across a rocky, sunny hillside, we pass the signed, left-branching spur to Hopi Spring (which flows during rainy periods only). About 1 mile beyond here, a sidetrail (35.1; 6080) branches right a short distance to Horse Camp Seep (usually reliable until late spring).

Continuing south along the Mazatzal Divide Trail, we next descend slightly, then cross a small creeklet just upstream from a steep dropoff. At a junction just across this creekbed we turn left, onto the signed Sandy Saddle Trail, and follow the dwindling watercourse to its head at Sandy Saddle (36.4; 6420). After taking in the rather limited views from this pass we traverse southward a bit, then drop steeply some 700 feet down a brushy ridge. After crossing a minor drainage, the trail climbs a bit before finally descending to the floor of Barnhardt Canyon at Castersen Seep (38.1; 5620). Camping is fair here, with water available in winter and early spring only. For an interesting side trip, scramble downstream about ¾ mile to the upper end of the steep-walled narrows of Barnhardt Canyon.

To complete your long loop trek, follow the trail as it climbs up a ravine, crosses a minor saddle, and then ascends to a signed junction with the Barnhardt Trail (39.0; 5960). Turn left here, and reverse the steps of Trip 92 the remaining 4.2 miles to Barnhardt Trailhead (43.2; 4220), just across the parking area from where the trip began.

See Maps 39, 40, 41, 42 and 43

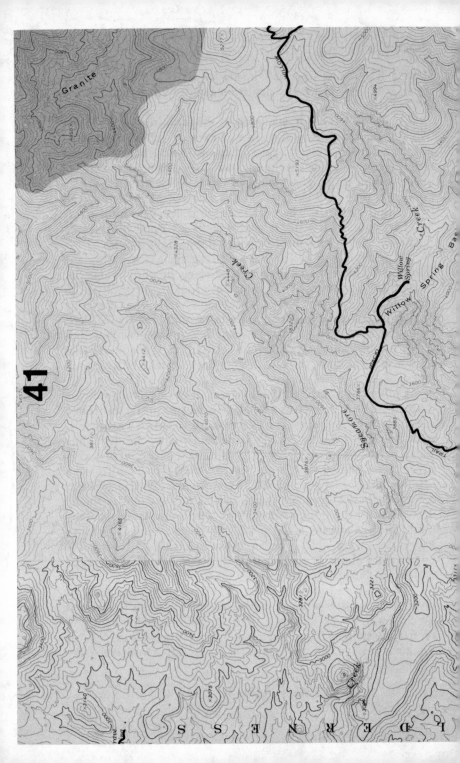

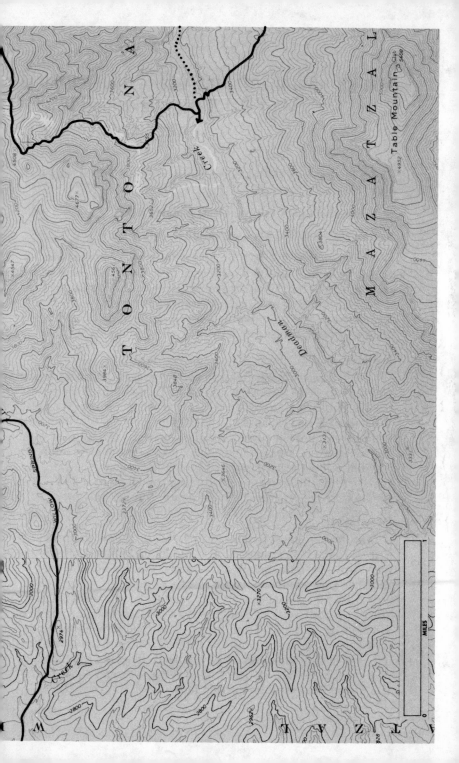

Trip 95   Barnhardt Trailhead to Sheep Bridge via Y Bar Basin, Davenport Wash, and Deadman Creek

33.5 miles one way (150-mile car shuttle required); 6700 ′ elevation gain

Strenuous backpack (allow at least 4 hiking days)

Season November to May, except after snowstorms

Windsor Seep (mile 7.2), Club Spring (near mile 16.0), Mountain Spring (mile 23.7) and Willow Spring (near mile 26.3) have water all year, except that Windsor Seep may not have water during very dry spells; in early spring and following rainy periods, water is also available at Davenport Wash (mile 17.1), Deadman Creek (mile 20.0) and other points (see text)

Features

This transmontane trek crosses the rugged Mazatzal range from east to west — from the edge of the Tonto Basin all the way to the Verde River. In between lies the heart of the Mazatzal Wilderness, a vast expanse of wild country, corrugated with peaks and canyons, populated with cougars and bears, and forested with oak and pinyon, saguaro and cholla, ponderosa and sycamore.

Reflecting the harsh nature of the country they penetrate, the trails used by this route are mostly rough and hard to follow. This is a trek for the experienced backcountry traveler only.

Description

From Barnhardt Trailhead (0.0; 4220), follow the route of Trip 94 to the signed junction near Mountain Spring (23.7; 4840), then turn left onto the Willow Spring Trail. Follow this as it descends a bit, climbs westward to a rocky point affording a good view across the Verde River Valley, and then switchbacks steeply down a sparsely vegetated ridgeline to a saddle containing another junction (26.3; 3860). From here it is ¾ mile to Willow Spring (water available year-round) via a signed spur trail that branches left. The main trail swings to the right and circles around the head of a small basin to a second saddle, where we catch a glimpse of Horseshoe Reservoir shimmering far away on the Verde River.

A short, switchbacking descent now brings us to the floor of the shallow canyon drained by Horse Creek. A lone, tall cottonwood tree down by the watercourse is probably the best campsite in this otherwise shadeless area; the creek generally has water until early spring or so. Soon the trail climbs a short distance away from Horse Creek, then follows a low ridgecrest westward for about ¾ mile before dropping back down almost to creek level. Here we leave the Mazatzal Mountains behind and descend very gently onto the creosotebush- and paloverde-dotted floor of the Verde River Valley, gaining good views back toward the high country as we pull away from the foothills. Wildflowers are abundant here in the spring — look for brittlebush, desert mallow, owl clover, golden poppy, verbena and desert mariposa, among others.

After about a mile, Horse Creek meanders off away from the trail to the south; we continue westward, and in another mile pass a Mazatzal Wilderness boundary sign (31.3; 2430) between two small hills. About 1.7 miles farther, where Horse Creek returns north from its meanderings, we drop down a short distance toward creekside to an unsigned fork marked with a cairn. Here the Verde River Trail branches right; we stay left, cross Horse Creek, then dip into and climb out of a small tributary ravine. At an unsigned junction just beyond here, we go straight ahead, and continue westward a short distance to Sheep Bridge on the Verde River (33.5; 2100). The trailhead on Tangle Creek Road is just across the bridge.

See Maps 39, 40, 41 and 44

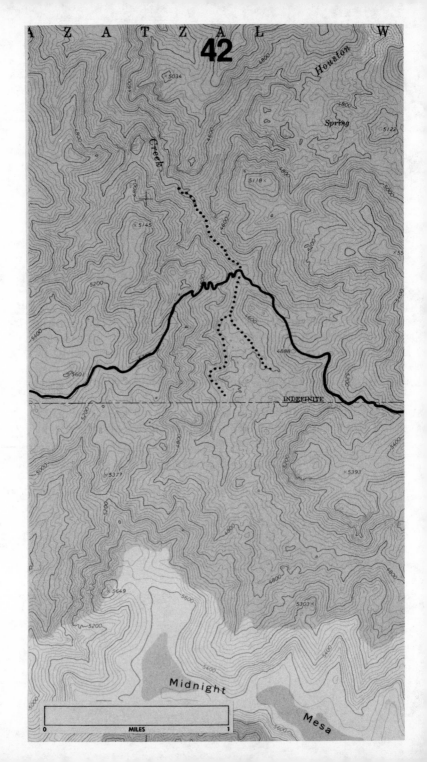

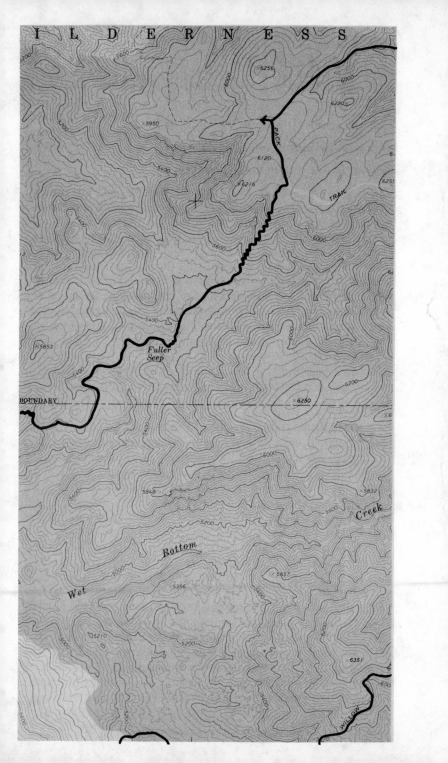

Trip 96   City Creek Trailhead to Fuller Seep

20.2 miles round trip; 4500' elevation gain

Strenuous backpack (2–4 hiking days)

Season all year, except after snowstorms

Fuller Seep (mile 10.1) has water all year; in early spring and following rainy periods, water also generally available along unnamed creeklets (mile 6.2 to mile 7.0)

Features

This route climbs stiffly up from the lowlands near the East Verde River, past the soaring, heavily timbered ramparts of North Peak, then winds for miles through the pleasant shade of the dense, mature stands of ponderosa pine and alligator juniper which cloak the northern Mazatzal high country. Fuller Seep provides delightful camping, as do a number of other forested nooks along the trail.

The second half of this route is rough, can be difficult to follow, and is recommended only for experienced hikers.

Description

At the signed trailhead on East Verde River Road (0.0; 3440), pass through a pull gate and cross City Creek (which may be dry during the summer months) to a cairn that marks the north end of the Mazatzal Divide Trail. This path stays near City Creek at first, ascending gently past another fence and signs of an old road, then swings to the right and climbs more steeply into a small ravine. There is much catclaw in this area, as well as a few small shrub oaks.

A few hundred yards after passing a Mazatzal Wilderness boundary sign, we switchback moderately uphill to a ridge, whose crest we then parallel to a saddle (2.6; 4540) overlooking the East Verde River to the north. After twisting up another set of switchbacks, the trail circles around the head of a tiny drainage planted with manzanita, mountain mahogany, and a variety of scrubby oaks. There may be a trickle of water here during rainy periods. After leaving this drainage via a small saddle we resume switchbacking moderately uphill. Many switchbacks later, a thicket of Gambel oaks heralds the end of this long, nearly shadeless climb; just beyond, the trail rounds a high ridge and traverses westward.

This section affords an excellent view across Hell's Hole and the deep gash of City Creek to the massive, densely forested crown of 7449-foot North Peak.

Soon we exit the Hell's Hole drainage via an unnamed gap, just beyond which, in a shady forest of tall ponderosa pines and stout alligator junipers, is a signed junction with the right-branching Red Hills Trail (5.5; 6080). Here we turn right, drop slightly to another saddle, then bend left and switchback down into a canyon on the west side of the Mazatzal Divide. Once on the floor of this drainage, the trail follows a creeklet gently downhill to a small cabin (6.4; 5700). This shelter is still used occasionally by local ranchers; please do not disturb whatever meager stores may be inside. A short distance beyond this cabin the trail meanders across a fairly level, beautifully forested area where three small streams come together. In early spring and during rainy periods, when the creeks run, camping is excellent here.

After crossing the third streamlet, we switchback steeply a short distance up to a minor gap, then climb more moderately along a canyonside to a signed junction (8.3; 6080) atop the flat, ponderosa-pine- and alligator-juniper-crowned mesa known as Knob Mountain. Our route goes left here, striking off southward across the plateau. About 0.4 mile later, where the mesa breaks off sharply, we swing to the right and switchback very steeply some 700 feet down to the floor of a basin. Once on the bottom of this basin we proceed a few hundred yards down its gently sloping floor, cross a creek (one of the tributaries of Wet Bottom Creek; water in early spring and during rainy periods) to its left side, and then meet a sign announcing that we have arrived at Fuller Seep (10.1; 5280) (the actual seep, with its year-round water, is apparently a few hundred feet downstream, at the confluence of a tributary drainage). Several excellent campsites, shaded by a sparse-to-moderate forest cover of ponderosa pine, pinyon pine and alligator juniper, can be found in this area. Worthwhile side trips can be made up- or downstream; hikers with enough time and energy may wish to continue on the Red Hills Trail to Wet Bottom Creek (see Trip 97).

See Maps 43 and 42

Trip 97   City Creek Trailhead to Sheep Bridge via Fuller Seep, Wet Bottom Creek and HK Mesa

29.2 miles one way (170-mile car shuttle required); 5700 ' elevation gain

Strenuous backpack (allow at least 4 hiking days)

Season November to May, except after snowstorms

Fuller Seep (mile 10.1) and Dutchman Grave Spring (near mile 23.6) have water all year; in early spring and following rainy periods, water also available at Wet Bottom Creek (mile 13.1) and other points (see text)

Features

This exceptionally rough and lonely route climbs to the Mazatzal high country in the vicinity of North Peak and Knob Mountain, then drops down to Fuller Seep and wanders across the rough-hewn, pinyon- and cypress-studded country drained by Wet Bottom Creek. After passing some ancient, enigmatic Indian ruins, the trail continues on to the Verde River via scenic HK Mesa.

Parts of this route can be exceedingly difficult to follow; those who venture onto it should bring along a compass, and know how to use it in conjunction with the maps in this guide.

Description

From the City Creek Trailhead (0.0; 3440), follow the route of Trip 96 to the Fuller Seep sign (10.1; 5280). From here we continue along the Red Hills Trail, which crosses quickly back to the right-hand (north) side of the creekbed near the seep, then passes a corral and begins climbing away from the canyon bottom. A mile and a half later this climb tops out at a saddle (11.3; 5420), from where we descend along the right-hand wall of a sparsely wooded canyon. After traversing northward past a tributary ravine to a second, smaller saddle, we drop down a usually dry drainage to Wet Bottom Creek (13.1; 4460), where there is fair camping beneath a smattering of oaks, pinyons and sycamores. Better campsites can be found a few hundred yards upstream. The creek generally has a good flow until mid-spring or so.

After crossing Wet Bottom Creek the trail switchbacks moderately up to a saddle, then bends left and continues to climb, more steeply, along a ridgeline. Soon we veer right and traverse at a less radical angle across a hillside supporting a nearly pure stand of smooth cypress, a pretty, fragrant evergreen recognizable by its smooth, fibrous bark. Beyond this grove the trail crosses another saddle, then passes a fence and winds across an open slope affording an excellent view to the southeast.

Presently we veer north and follow a ridgeline past several minor saddles before dropping into the head of a drainage. After crossing this usually dry gulch to its right-hand side, the trail traverses along the canyonside, letting the creekbed fall away below, then passes through a pull gate and switchbacks abruptly back down to creekside. We now proceed down-canyon, hopping several times across the streambed, which by this point may contain a trickle of water during the rainy season. About 0.5 mile later the trail leads up a tributary to the left, passes a good, oak-and-pinyon-shaded campsite, and climbs a short distance to a saddle (18.5; 4660). From here we traverse southward through yet another gap, then drop down a bit and walk northwestward across a relatively flat, treeless expanse. The trail temporarily disappears on this grassy mesa; look for ducks and cairns to guide you past some piles of dark stones. These piles, not particularly impressive but obviously the work of human hands, are probably remnants of structures built around 1100 AD by members of the Sinagua Indian culture. These people may have chosen to build on this particular site because of its excellent defensive properties; with its commanding view of the surrounding country, enemies would find it nearly impossible to launch a surprise attack. Other ruins can be found nearby in this area.

From the far end of the mesa, a steep descent brings us to a barren saddle containing some old mine workings. Here the trail swings left and switchbacks down a ravine to the top of a large heap of tailings piled at the mouths of three deep, horizontal mineshafts (21.0; 3900). In all probability, copper was mined at this abandoned site. A few interesting relics are strewn about. Use extreme caution if you decide to explore the shafts — they may contain hidden vertical dropoffs.

From the mine area the trail continues steeply down the ravine, which offers occasional views down to Horseshoe Reservoir and snatches of the Verde River. After dropping about 400 feet we traverse to the left, cross a minor saddle, and then descend

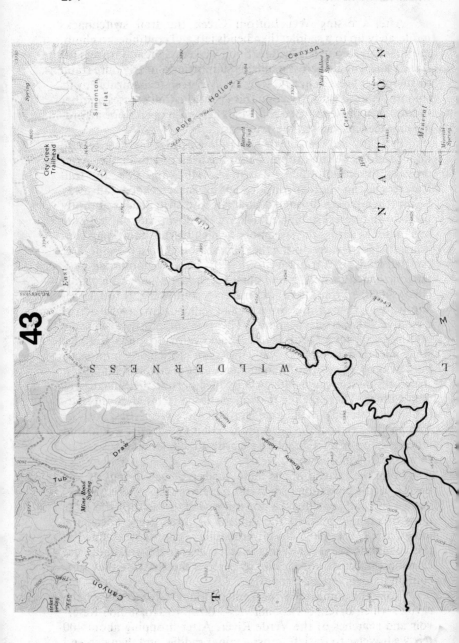

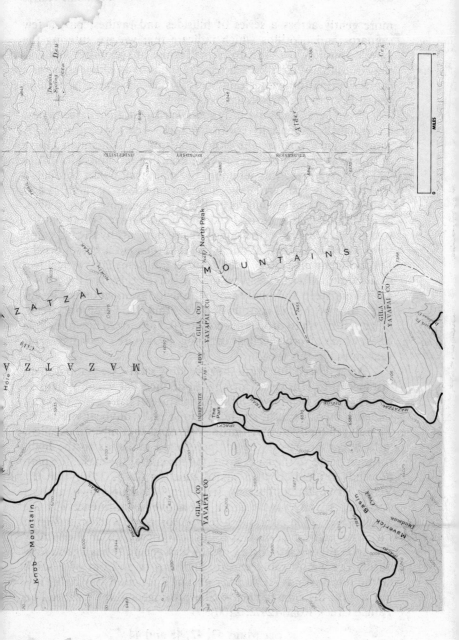

more gently across a series of hillsides and ravines, past a few saguaros and ocotillos which indicate that we are entering the Lower Sonoran life zone, to a small copse of sycamores and cottonwoods that shelter the scattered remains of an old prospector's camp. During the winter rainy season there is generally running water down in the streambed to the right.

From here we climb gently southward a bit, then descend past an unsigned, potentially confusing fork, where we turn left. A short distance farther, the short side trail to Dutchman Grave Spring (water available year-round) branches left at a cairn (23.6; 2900). Just beyond this junction, the main trail passes through a comparatively lush area shaded by cottonwoods, sycamores and some large mesquites and shrub live oaks. Camping is good here.

About 0.5 mile beyond the Dutchman Grave Spring cutoff, we ford a small creek (the same stream that runs by the old camp ruins we passed about a mile back) and then cut across a brushy flat and labor up a steep, deeply rutted trail some 200 vertical feet to a saddle. After descending the far side of this gap (the path is again very steep and badly eroded) one looks down on the bright green tops of the tall cottonwood trees that line Sycamore Creek. It is not difficult to drop cross country 0.5 mile or so down to these trees, which afford excellent camping. Sycamore Creek has water year-round in this area.

After descending from the preceding saddle we climb a slight distance onto HK Mesa, a rather ill-defined flat which is densely planted with a rich Lower Sonoran mixture of paloverde, ocotillo, saguaro, creosotebush, staghorn cholla and teddybear cholla. As we pull gradually away from the Mazatzal foothills, an excellent vista opens up across the juniper-dotted midlands to the high, forested peaks to the east. From the far end of the mesa, the path descends moderately to a signed junction (28.5; 2150) with the Verde River Trail. Turning left here, we drop down a short distance, cross Sycamore Creek just above its confluence with the Verde River, then continue a few hundred yards to an unsigned fork marked by a cairn. Our route now goes right, on the Willow Spring Trail, crosses Horse Creek, which generally has a good flow during the winter rainy season, and dips in and out of a small ravine just beyond. At another unsigned junction stay right; it is just a short distance farther to Sheep Bridge and the trailhead on Tangle Creek Road (29.2; 2100).

See Maps 43, 42, 45 and 44

Trip 98   City Creek Trailhead to Barnhardt Trailhead via the Mazatzal Divide and Y Bar Basin Trails

27.5 miles one way (30-mile car shuttle required); 4860′ elevation gain

Strenuous backpack (3–5 hiking days)

Season March through November

Windsor Seep (mile 20.3) has water except during very dry weather; in early spring and following rainy periods, water also available at The Park (near mile 9.0), Horse Camp Seep (near mile 13.6) and Chilson Spring (near mile 16.0)

Features

Utilizing a lengthy section of the Mazatzal Divide Trail, this fine route parallels the high crest of the northern Mazatzal range, from North Peak to Mazatzal Peak. Except at the trek's beginning and ending, elevations are well above 5000 feet, making this an excellent choice for backpackers seeking a measure of relief from the heat of lowland summers.

Description

From the City Creek Trailhead (0.0; 3440), follow the Mazatzal Divide Trail to the signed junction with the Red Hills Trail (5.5; 6080) (see Trip 96). This trail may be erroneously signed "Dutchman Trail." Turn left here, and continue along the Mazatzal Divide Trail as it ascends a gently rising ridgecrest to a broad saddle atop Knob Mountain. After dropping steeply back down this hill's southern flank, the trail climbs again for a short distance, then dips into one of the diminutive headwaters of City Creek, which may contain some running water during early spring and following heavy rains. We next climb around a low ridge and enter a beautiful, nicely forested area, known as The Park, at the head of Deadman Creek. Where the signed North Peak Trail branches left, we go straight ahead and continue south a few hundred yards to another junction (9.0; 5860), also signed, where the Deadman Trail goes right. There are several excellent campsites in this area, shaded by tall ponderosa pines and some magnificent, thick-

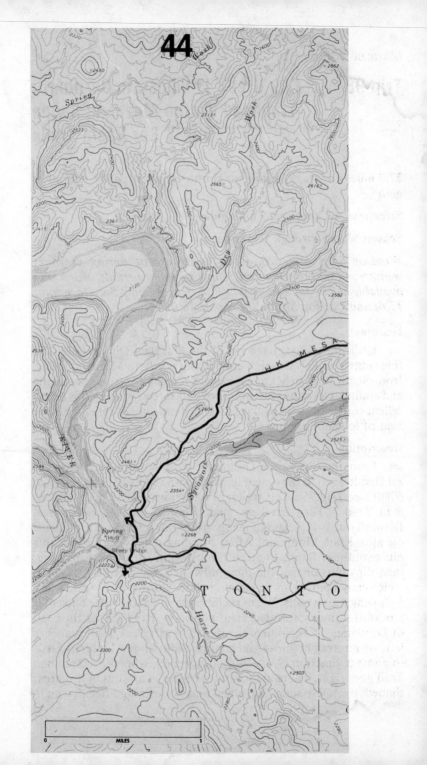

44

0   MILES   1

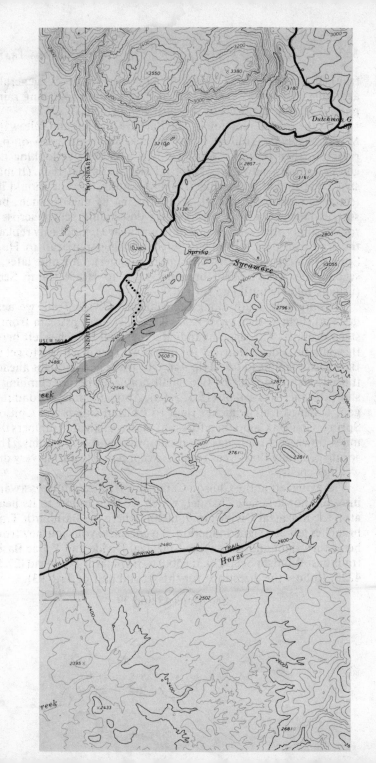

trunked specimens of alligator juniper. Water is generally available in a nearby ravine (called Pete's Pond) following rainy periods and on the heels of the spring snowmelt.

At the second junction in The Park we turn left and follow the Mazatzal Divide Trail as it switchbacks moderately up onto a ridgetop, then traverses southward to a saddle overlooking the gently sloping headwaters of North Fork Deadman Creek. (It may strike one as odd that, while traveling southward, one should intercept a creek's north fork *after* crossing its main branch, but such is indeed the case here.) After descending gently across a rocky, sunny area where manzanita and agave temporarily replace the trees, we pass the signed, left-branching spur trail to Hopi Spring (which may be dry during the summer). One mile later, a second spur (13.6; 6080) branches right to Horse Camp Seep (usually reliable until late spring).

Continuing south along the Mazatzal Divide Trail, we next descend slightly, then cross a small creeklet just upstream from a steep dropoff. The signed Sandy Saddle Trail branches left here; this path provides a shortcut for hikers who are in a hurry to get to Barnhardt Trailhead (see Trip 94). Our route goes straight ahead, then winds in and out of two small drainages before climbing a short distance to a saddle (15.5; 5690). About 0.5 mile beyond this gap, a signed trail branches right to Chilson Camp and Chilson Spring. Chilson Camp, in a forest of massive alligator junipers 0.2 miles down this trail, has good campsites and a few ruins. The spring generally flows year round, except possibly during very dry weather spells.

Staying left at the Chilson Camp cutoff, we contour eastward into a minor drainage channel, which we then follow to its head atop the Mazatzal Divide (16.9; 6020), where the Barnhardt Trail branches left at a signed junction. To complete your journey from here, turn right and follow the Mazatzal Divide and Y Bar Basin trails past Windsor Seep (20.3; 6500) to Barnhardt Trailhead (27.5; 4220) (follow the directions for the second half of Trip 93).

See Maps 43 and 39

Trip 99   Sheep Bridge to Deadman Creek

27.8 miles round trip; 5900′ elevation gain

Strenuous backpack (4 hiking days)

Season November through April, except after snowstorms

Willow Spring (near mile 7.2) and Mountain Spring (mile 9.8) have water all year; water also generally available at Deadman Creek (mile 13.9) in winter and early spring

Features

Remote Deadman Creek and its many forks reach into the wild heart of the Mazatzal backcountry. The creek's bouldery banks, dotted here and there with tall sycamore trees, afford delightful camping and provide challenging cross-country access to the tens of thousands of acres of pure wilderness country which flank them.

The trails used to reach Deadman Creek are for the most part in poor condition, and this trek is recommended only for experienced wilderness travellers.

Description

From the trailhead near the end of Tangle Creek Road (0.0; 2100), walk across Sheep Bridge and follow the Willow Spring Trail eastward. Stay left an an unsigned junction a few hundred feet beyond the bridge, dip into and out of a small ravine, and then cross Horse Creek (which generally has a good flow during the winter wet season) to its north bank. Just beyond is the junction of the Verde River and Willow Spring trails — unsigned but marked with a cairn. Now we bear right and climb gently eastward, toward the Mazatzal foothills. The ground cover hereabouts consists mostly of mesquite and creosotebush, but shortly after crossing a shallow wash we enter a more familiar, Lower-Sonoran-zone plant mixture of saguaros, gangling ocotillos, paloverdes, yellow-blossoming prickly pears, and teddy bear chollas.

Just before passing between two low hillocks we reach a Mazatzal Wilderness boundary sign (2.2; 2430). Beyond here the trail continues eastward, every once in a while swinging within a stone's throw of Horse Creek. Presently we climb gently onto the crest of a low ridge that roughly parallels the watercourse, then drop back to creek level near a solitary, tall cottonwood tree (5.5; 3000). When Horse Creek has water, this spot makes a good first night's camp.

About 0.5 mile beyond here the trail bends left, away from the creek, and sneaks up a ravine to a saddle that affords a good view back across Horseshoe Reservoir and parts of the meandering Verde River. Next we wind moderately uphill, staying just beneath the crest of a ridge, to a second saddle (7.2; 3860), where a signed spur trail branches off to Willow Spring (¾ mile down the side trail to the right; water available year-round). Beyond this junction the trail continues up the ridgeline. After touching another saddle the gradient steepens considerably, and we ascend many switchbacks to a rocky prominence (8.8; 5020) with a sweeping view of the Verde River Valley and the southern Mazatzals. From this point we proceed one mile downhill to the terminus of the Willow Spring Trail near Mountain Spring (9.8; 4840). There are a few fair campsites here, in a sparse forest of one-seed juniper, Utah juniper and shrub live oak. The spring has water all year long.

At a junction here we turn right, onto the Deadman Trail, and climb steeply uphill to the south. Some 600 feet higher the trail tops out, then drops along a ridge to a saddle (12.0; 4460) between Willow Spring Basin and the canyon of Deadman Creek. From here we traverse westward a short distance, then drop steeply past a stock fence. The angle of this descent soon eases, but only for a while; after touching a minor saddle, the track abruptly plunges straight down a ridgeline to the bouldery banks of Deadman Creek (13.9; 3090). There is excellent cool-weather camping here, and for some distance up- and downstream, among mesquite trees and an occasional tall sycamore or cottonwood. The creek generally runs throughout the winter rainy season and well into spring. Hikers with a layover day (or two) may wish to scramble up-canyon and explore the stream's rugged, cliffbound forks, or continue along the trail to Davenport Wash and the site of Club Ranch (see Trip 94).

Return the way you came.

See Maps 44, 41 and 40

Trip 100   Sheep Bridge to HK Mesa, Fuller Seep, Chilson Camp, Davenport Wash, Deadman Creek and return

56.2-mile loop trip; 11,200' elevation gain

Strenuous backpack (allow at least 6 hiking days)

Season November to May, except after snowstorms

Water available all year at Dutchman Grave Spring (near mile 5.6), Fuller Seep (mile 19.1), Club Spring (near mile 39.0), Mountain Spring (mile 46.7) and Willow Spring (near mile 49.3); in early spring and following rainy periods, water also available at Wet Bottom Creek (mile 16.1), The Park (near mile 23.8), Chilson Spring (near mile 32.3), Deadman Creek (mile 42.6) and other points (see text)

Features

Experienced backpackers looking to stretch their legs and test their skills will want to try this lengthy, challenging loop trip. Good for a week or more of hiking days, this route winds through the shrubs and cacti of the desert lowlands, climbs into the pine- and juniper-forested high country, fords icy, rushing creeks (in season), and visits ancient Indian ruins, abandoned mines, and dilapidated cowboy cabins.

Much of this route is obscure and hard to follow; do not attempt it until you have successfully completed easier trips in the Mazatzal. Carry a compass, and know how to use it.

Description

From the trailhead near the end of Tangle Creek Road (0.0; 2100), cross the Verde River via Sheep Bridge and follow the Willow Spring Trail eastward. At an unsigned junction a few hundred feet beyond the bridge we stay left, then dip into and out of a small ravine and cross Horse Creek (which generally has a good flow during the winter wet season) to its north bank. A bit beyond this crossing is an unsigned junction marked with a cairn. Our route turns left here, onto the combined Dutchman Trail/Verde River Trail, and proceeds a short distance northward to pleasantly forested, appropriately named Sycamore Creek — larger than Horse Creek, and considerably more likely to have flowing water.

After rock-hopping Sycamore Creek we walk uphill a few hundred feet to a signed fork (0.7; 2150), where we turn right, onto the Dutchman Trail. This path now winds uphill, steeply at times, toward the flat top of HK Mesa. This area supports a nice growth of saguaro, foothill paloverde, ocotillo, prickly pear, barrel cactus and teddy bear cholla. Once on top of HK Mesa the trail levels off, and as we catch our breath we can enjoy the fine view of the forested Mazatzal peaks, still far away to the east.

Near the east end of HK Mesa we pass a Mazatzal Wilderness boundary sign, beyond which the trail drops a short distance to a low, broad saddle (3.4; 2570) overlooking a refreshingly green strip of cottonwoods that line Sycamore Creek. This riparian grove offers delightful camping, and is an easy, 0.5 mile cross-country jaunt down from the saddle. Sycamore Creek is perennial in the area of these trees.

Continuing northeast from this gap, the trail crosses a small wash and climbs past a steep, badly eroded section to another, higher saddle. Following the descent of a similarly steep and eroded trail on this saddle's far side, we work across a flat, brushy area to a creekbed, which we cross at a cairn just upstream from the influx of a tributary. There may be running water here until early spring. The trail next parallels the tributary eastward to a surprisingly lush area shaded by cottonwoods, sycamores and some large mesquites and shrub live oaks — good camping. Just beyond here, at an unsigned junction (5.6; 2900) marked with a cairn, the Dutchman Grave Trail branches right and passes Dutchman Grave Spring (water available year-round) a short distance away.

From this fork the Red Hills Trail swings north and then undulates over a pair of low gaps. The section immediately beyond the second of these saddles is potentially confusing; follow the very faint, poorly ducked track as it heads across a small creekbed, climbs past an unsigned, left-branching spur trail, then drops slightly and veers northward to a small grove of cottonwoods and sycamores near the ruins of an old prospector's camp. The way soon grows clearer, and we ascend steadily up the right-hand wall of a spacious drainage to a saddle. Here the trail contours to the right, into a small canyon, and climbs very steeply past some good views across the Verde River Valley to Horseshoe Reservoir and portions of the Verde River to the top of an ugly pile of mine tailings visible from below (8.2; 3900). Copper ore was apparently taken from this mine, which is now abandoned. Be very careful if you explore any of the horizontal mineshafts from which the tailings emerge; they may contain hidden vertical dropoffs.

A short, steep climb from this mine brings us to a saddle; here we swing to the right and ascend a rocky ridgeline to an unnamed mesa. A slight rise on this plateau affords a magnificent vista across the Mazatzal midlands to the high, forested peaks to the south and east. The trail peters out temporarily as it proceeds southeastward, and we must rely on a series of widely spaced ducks and cairns to guide us to some mystifying Indian ruins — crude (but obviously man-made) agglomerations of dark stones, apparently built by people of the ancient Sinagua culture around 1100 AD. The shelters may have been occupied during a period of warfare, since the mesa on which they rest would have been easy to defend; their exposed location certainly has little else to recommend it, being many miles from the nearest permanent water supply. Other ruins can be found in the area.

At the mesa's far end the trail reappears, swings left toward the edge of a drainage, and then climbs moderately through a pinyon-pine forest to a saddle (10.7; 4660). After traversing northward 0.5 mile or so we drop into an oak- and pinyon-shaded canyon and pass a good campsite near the confluence of two minor drainages (water available during rainy periods only). The trail now follows the larger of these two creeks upstream, crossing frequently from bank to bank. About 0.6 mile later, after a tributary comes in from the left, we climb abruptly up a ridgeline, pass a stock fence, and then drop gradually back to creek level. After recrossing the drainage bottom in a small basin, the trail meanders uphill through a rocky, potentially confusing area — watch for ducks. This comparatively gentle ascent soon metamorphoses into steep switchbacks, which top out at a high saddle (13.0; 5140) overlooking the rugged canyon of Wet Bottom Creek. Here we turn right and proceed first south, then east, staying on or just below the crest of a broad ridge. Shortly after passing a stock fence the trail descends moderately through a pretty, shady stand of smooth cypress, then drops more steeply down a narrow ridge. This long descent ends at Wet Bottom Creek (16.1; 4440), which generally has water throughout the winter rainy season. A few poor-to-fair tentsites, beneath a scanty riparian growth of sycamore and oak, can be found nearby; much better ones are located about 0.5 mile up- and downstream.

After crossing Wet Bottom Creek the trail turns up a side can-

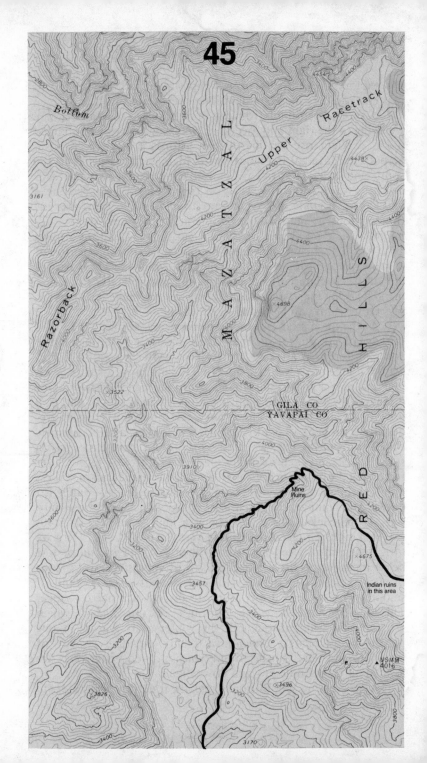

45

Bottom

Upper Racetrack

4454

4400

4438

M A Z A T Z A L

2800

3161

Razorback

3522

4200

4400

4400

H I L L S

•4698

4200

GILA CO
YAVAPAI CO

4000

3910

R E D

Mine
Ruins

×4675

3457

Indian ruins
in this area

3826

×3496

VSMM
4016

3170

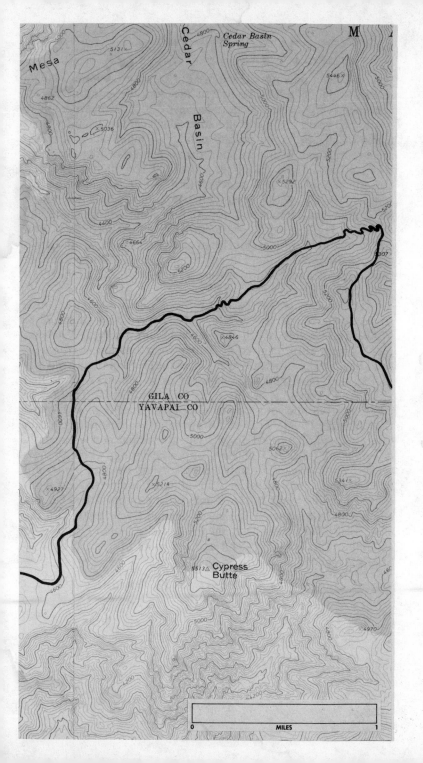

yon and, after passing a few more fair campsites, climbs along a series of ridges and hillsides to a saddle. A gentle, contouring descent then brings us to signed Fuller Seep (19.1; 5280), where there is water all year long, a corral, and excellent camping amid a smattering of alligator junipers and ponderosa pines. From the seep area we walk gently uphill a short distance, then switchback steeply up an ill-defined ridgeline. Some 700 feet higher, the trail abruptly levels off and proceeds northward across pine- and juniper-crowned Knob Mountain. At a signed junction (20.9; 6080) atop this flat mountaintop we turn right, continuing on the Red Hills Trail, and drop gently into a canyon. This descent soon steepens, and a terminal flourish of steep switchbacks lands us in a cozy, forested basin where three streamlets come together. During rainy periods and in early spring, when the creeks are likely to flow, camping is excellent here.

The trail exits this basin via the easternmost of the three streams, whose course we follow past a corral to a cabin (22.8; 5700). This shelter is still used occasionally by local ranchers; please do not disturb any equipment or food that may be stored inside. Beyond the cabin, the trail traces the creeklet to its head at a saddle, then cuts right and climbs a few switchbacks to the Red Hills Trail's terminus at the signed Mazatzal Divide Trail (23.8; 6080). To continue your loop trip from here, turn right and follow the Mazatzal Divide Trail as far as the signed cutoff to Chilson Camp (32.3; 5660) (see Trip 98). Then turn right and walk gently downhill 0.2 miles to Chilson Camp and Spring, where there is reliable water (except possibly during very dry weather spells) and good camping in a forest of stout alligator junipers. Next, continue downhill from Chilson Camp, cross a minor drainage, and climb a short distance to a signed junction (32.8; 5590) with the Club Trail. Turn right here, then follow the route of Trip 94 to Mountain Spring (46.7; 4840) and the route of Trip 95 back to Sheep Bridge (56.2; 2100).

See Maps 44, 45, 42, 43, 39, 40 and 41

Index

Agua Caliente Trail 148
Aguila Corral 126
Alligator, the 265
Alma Mesa 203
Alpine, AZ 182
Alpine Ranger District 181
Anita Park 159, 160, 162, 163, 166, 170, 177
Anita Spring 160, 163, 166, 170, 178
Apache Indians 16, 78, 85, 177, 269
Apache Junction, AZ 18, 19
Apache Lake 19
Apache Spring 118
Arizona, map of state *vi*
Armour Spring 155
Ash Creek (Blue Range) 194
Ash Creek (Rincon Mountains) 88
Aspen Trail 121
backpacking 6
Baker Canyon Trail 175
Baldy Lookout 151
Baldy Peak 180, 218, 220, 222, 223
Baldy Spring 151-152
Barkley Basin 47
Barnhardt Canyon 273, 276, 277, 278, 283
Barnhardt Road 270, 273, 278
Barnhardt Trail 273, 277, 283, 300
Barnhardt Trailhead 270, 271, 273, 277, 278, 283, 286, 297, 300
Basin Trail 177
Battleship Mountain 15, 33, 56
Bear Canyon (Chiricahua Mountains) 170
Bear Canyon (Santa Catalina Mountains) 112
Bear Canyon Trail 167
Bear Creek 112, 113
Bear Mountain Lookout 182, 196, 198, 200, 202
Bear Valley 198, 200, 201, 202
Beaverhead Lodge 182
Bellows Spring 151
Bird Canyon 98
Black Mesa 15, 23, 26, 28, 30, 32, 38, 44
Black Mesa Trail 28, 30, 31, 38
Black Top Mesa 15, 27, 28, 31, 34, 38, 44, 56
Black Top Pass 43, 44, 45, 54
Blue Camp 182, 183, 195, 196, 199, 200, 201, 202, 207
Blue Lookout 184, 185, 214
Blue Lookout Road 182, 183, 184, 213, 214, 215
Blue Lookout Trail 214
Blue Range 2, 179, 180, 202, 207
Blue Range Primitive Area 179, 182, 187
Blue River 179, 180, 182, 183, 187, 188, 206, 208, 210, 215, 216, 218
Blue River "breaks" 180, 208, 217
Bluff Saddle 38, 43, 44, 45, 53
Bluff Spring 34, 50, 52
Bluff Spring Canyon 50, 52
Bluff Spring Trail 35, 46, 47, 50, 52

Bog Springs 88, 143, 144
Bog Springs Campground 88, 143, 144
Booger Spring 159
Boucher Creek 259, 261, 262
Boucher, Louis 259
Boucher Trail 259, 262
Boulder Basin 26, 27, 28, 30, 38
Boulder Canyon 55, 56
Boulder Canyon Trail 20, 28, 33, 38, 56
Boulder Creek (Grand Canyon) 246
Boulder Creek (Superstition Wilderness) 20, 22, 31, 32, 33, 56
Boulder Peak 74
Box Camp 118
Box Camp Canyon 110, 118
Box Camp Trail 87, 111, 117, 118
Box Spring 118
Bridalveil Falls 98, 99, 101, 103, 104, 106
Bradley Point 243
Brahma Temple 243
Bright Angel Campground 234, 237, 239, 240, 242, 256
Bright Angel Canyon 228, 237, 239, 240, 244, 253, 254, 255, 256
Bright Angel Lodge 231, 232, 234, 236, 239, 240, 242, 244, 255, 257, 266
Bright Angel shale 226, 243
Bright Angel Trail 4, 228, 231, 232, 236, 240, 242, 244, 255, 264, 266
Brody Seep 279
Brody Seep Trail 277, 279
Bull Pass 28, 34
Bull Pass Trail 38, 54, 55
Burnt Stump Spring 175
"burro problem" 229, 245, 262
Burro Trail 172, 175
Buzzard's Roost 47
Cactus Picnic Ground 86, 98, 101, 103, 104, 106
Campaign Creek 19, 70, 74
Canada del Oro 86, 90
Canadian life zone 5, 115, 130, 132, 157, 167, 179, 208, 209, 228, 272
Canyon Lake Trailhead 18, 20, 32, 33, 55, 56
Cardenas, Garcia de 229
Carefree Road 270
Cashier Spring 201
Castersen Seep 276, 283
Castle Dome Mountain 77
Catalina Highway 87
Cathedral Rock 98, 99, 105
Cathedral Rock Trail 101, 105, 106
Cavalry Trail 35, 54
Cave Creek Canyon 89, 176, 177
Cave Creek Ranger District 270
Cave Trail 46
Cedar Ridge 237, 239, 240
Cedar Spring (Grand Canyon) 265
Cedar Springs (Blue Range) 207
Centella Point 157, 158
centipedes 9
Charlebois Spring 34, 35, 53
Cheyava Falls 242, 244
Chilson Camp 300, 303, 308
Chilson Spring 300, 308

Chiricahua Apache 85, 177
Chiricahua Mountains 2, 83-85, 157
Chiricahua Peak 159, 160, 162, 163, 169, 178
Chiricahua Wilderness 83-84, 89
Cima Park 159
City Creek 270, 290, 297
City Creek Trailhead 270, 290, 292, 297
Clear Creek 228, 242, 243
Clear Creek Trail 242
Clements Cattle Company 74, 77
Clifton, AZ 182
Clifton Ranger District 181
Club Ranch 279, 302
Club Spring 279
Club Trail 279, 308
Cochise 85
Coconino Cliff 228, 232, 249, 251, 257
Coconino sandstone 226
Coffee Flat Trail 57, 60
Colorado Plateau 15, 185
Colorado River 226, 228, 229, 232, 234, 236, 237, 240, 242, 243, 258, 261, 265
Continental, AZ 88
Cope Butte 258, 264
coral snakes 9
Coronado, Francisco de 229
Coronado National Forest 90, 94, 98
Cottonwood Campground 253, 254, 256
Cottonwood Creek 247, 249
Country Club Drive 88
Cow Head Saddle 130, 132, 136, 137, 142
Cremation Creek (Chiricahua Mountains) 157, 159, 160, 163, 166, 169, 170, 175, 178
Crest Trail (Santa Rita Mountains) 155
Crook, George 269
Crystal Spring 47, 50, 51, 52
Davenport Wash 278, 279, 282, 286, 302, 303
Deadman Creek 268, 278, 282, 286, 297, 301, 302, 303
Deadman Trail 282, 297, 302
Deer Spring 177
dehydration 6-7
Delshay 269
Devils Bathtub 142
Douglas Ranger District 85
Douglas Spring 126, 127
Douglas Spring Campground 130, 141, 142
Douglas Spring Trail 88, 130, 137
Dripping Spring 19, 57, 60, 61
Dripping Spring Canyon 259
Dripping Spring Trail 258, 259
Dutch Blue Creek 189, 194, 202, 203
Dutchman Grave Spring 296, 304
Dutchman Trail (Mazatzal Wilderness) 297, 303, 304
Dutchman's Trail (Superstition Wilderness) 18, 26, 27, 30, 31, 34, 38, 45, 46, 50-56 *passim*
East Boulder Canyon 27, 28, 31, 34, 38, 43, 44, 45, 55, 56

East Fork Little Colorado River 180, 222
East Fork Little Colorado River Trail 220
East Fork White River 180
East Speedway Trailhead 88, 126, 130, 137, 141, 142
East Verde River 290
East Verde River Road 270, 290
"El Sombrero" mine 16
Esperero Canyon 99, 101, 104
Esperero Creek 99
Esperero Trail 86, 98, 106
Federal Antiquities Act 67
Fire Loop Trail 131, 137
Fireline Trail 79
First Water Trailhead 18, 23, 27, 30, 31, 32, 34, 38
First Water Wash 23, 27
fishing 10, 120, 167, 213, 218, 222, 237, 240, 243, 254, 256
Flagstaff, AZ 1, 231
Florence Junction 19
Florida Canyon 89, 153, 154
Florida Canyon Experimental Range Headquarters 89, 153
Florida Canyon Trailhead 89, 153, 154
Florida Spring 153, 154, 155
Fly Peak 157, 158, 159, 160, 163, 169, 178
Fly Peak Lookout 157-158
Foote Creek 207, 208
Foote Creek Trail 182
Fort Apache Indian Reservation 181, 182, 184, 223
Fossil Springs 177
Fourmile Spring 258
Fraser Canyon 57, 60
Fraser Wash 19, 57, 60, 63
Fritz Ranch 182
Frog Tank Trail 66, 70, 77
Fuller Seep 290, 291, 292, 303, 308

Garden Creek 228, 229, 232, 236, 266
Garden Valley 23, 30, 32
Gardner Canyon Trail 152
Geronimo (see Golthlay)
Geronimo Head 15
Gila monster 9
glaciation (in White Mountains) 180-181, 219, 222
Glen Canyon Dam 226
Globe Ranger District 17
Golthlay 85
Grand Canyon 1, 2, 4, 225-230
Grand Canyon National Park 2, 10, 231, 267
Grandview Point 231, 244, 247, 248, 249
Grandview Trail 247, 248-249
Granite Gorge 234, 236, 240
Granite Rapids 265
Grant Creek 183, 209, 215, 216, 217, 218
Grant Creek Trail 183, 210
Grapevine Canyon 246, 247
Grass Shack Spring 142
Greenhouse Trail 159
Greer Allotment 219
Gray, Zane 269

Hackberry Mesa 23, 26, 32
Hance Canyon 250
Hannagan Meadow 179, 183, 208, 216
Hannagan Meadow Lodge 183

Hannah Hot Spring 189-190, 206
Hannah Springs Creek 189, 194, 202, 206
Happy Valley 88
Happy Valley Lookout 142
Happy Valley Peak 141, 142
Happy Valley Saddle Campground 138, 139, 141
Havasupai Indians 228-229, 233
Heartbreak Ridge 142
Helens Dome 127, 130, 132, 137
Hell's Hole 291
Herb Martyr Dam 177
Hermit Basin 257, 259
Hermit Camp 258
Hermit Creek 257, 258, 262, 263
Hermit Creek Campground 257, 258, 262, 263, 264
Hermit Shale 226, 259
Hermit Trail 257, 259, 262, 263, 264
Hermits Rest 231, 257, 259, 262, 263, 264
Hieroglyphic Canyon 40, 41
Hieroglyphic Spring 41
Hieroglyphics Trail 40
hitchhiking 3
HK Mesa 292, 296, 303, 304
Hohokam Indian culture 16
Honeycutt Spring 79
Hoolie Bacon Trail 62
Hopi Indians 229
Hopi Spring 283, 300
Hopkins, Mount 148
Horn Creek 265, 266
Horse Camp Seep 283, 300
Horse Creek 286, 296, 301, 302, 303
Horseshoe Pass 172, 174, 175
HU Bar Box 187, 188
HU Bar Ranch 182, 187
Hualapai Dam 229
Hualapai Indians, legend of Grand Canyon 225
Hudsonian life zone 180
Hutch's Pool 106, 107, 109, 110, 120, 124, 125

Ina Road 86
Indian Canyon 195, 196, 201
Indian Gardens 232, 233, 234, 236, 239, 257, 266
Indian Paint Mine 20, 21, 32, 33, 55, 56
Italian Spring 131, 137, 142

Jacob Lake, AZ 231
Javelina Picnic Ground 88, 134, 136, 142
JF Ranch 18-19, 57, 61, 63, 70, 78, 79, 82
JF Trail 63
Josephine Peak 152
Juan Miller Campgrounds 182
Juh 85
Junction Saddle 160, 169
Juniper Basin 88, 134, 135
Juniper Basin Campground 135, 136

Kaibab formations 226, 232, 237, 249
Kent Spring 143, 144
Kimball, Mount 95, 96-97, 103, 104
Kings Ranch 18, 40
Kings Way 40

Knob Mountain 291, 292, 297, 308
KP Cienega 183, 212, 213, 215
KP Creek 209, 212, 213, 214, 215, 216
KP Creek Trail 185, 210
KRN Trail 70

La Barge Canyon 20, 21, 22, 32, 34, 35, 47, 53, 62,
La Barge Spring 34, 35, 52, 53
Lanphier Canyon 182, 194, 196, 200
Largo Canyon 182, 196, 198, 199, 200, 202
Last Chance Copper Mine 248-249
Lemmon Creek 122, 123, 124
life zones 4-6, 228
Little Bald Mountain 163
Little Blue Box 189, 194, 203-206
Little Blue Creek 188, 189, 194, 200, 202, 203, 206
Lode Star Mine 146, 147
Log Spring 176
Lone Juniper Spring 169
Lonetree Canyon 246
Lookout Point 258
Lost Dutchman Mine 16-17, 21, 29, 78
Lower Bear Canyon Picnic Ground 87, 111, 112, 113
Lower Blue River 179, 182, 187, 189, 202, 206
Lower Sonoran life zone 5, 13, 115, 126, 130, 228, 255, 296, 301

Madera Canyon 88, 89, 146, 147, 149, 150, 155
Madera Canyon Roadend 88, 146, 148, 150, 152, 155
Magee Road 86, 94, 96, 103, 104
Manning Cabin 137, 142
Manning Camp 130, 131, 132, 136, 137, 141, 142
Manning Camp Trail 142
Maple Camp 171, 172, 174, 176
Maple Spring 198, 199
Marsh Valley 54
Marshall Gulch 121, 122, 123
Marshall Gulch Picnic Area 87, 119, 121, 122, 124
Mazatzal Divide 267, 272, 273, 276, 277, 278, 283, 291, 300
Mazatzal Divide Trail 267, 277, 279, 283, 297, 300, 308
Mazatzal Mountains 268, 271
Mazatzal Peak 268, 272, 277, 279, 297
Mazatzal Wilderness 2, 267-269, 272, 273, 278, 286, 290, 301, 304
McNary, AZ 183
Merriam, C. Hart 228
Mesa, AZ 270
Mesa Ranger District 17
Mescal, AZ 88
Mica Fire Tower 130, 131
Mica Mountain 127, 130, 131, 132, 136, 137, 141, 142
Midnight Mesa 282
Miller Canyon 88, 138, 141
Miller Creek Trail 138
Miners Canyon 47
Miners Needles 47
Miners Summit 51, 53, 63

Miners Trail 47
MM Ranch Trail 210
Mogollon Rim 180, 185, 198
Mohave Wall 265
Monte Vista Lookout 165, 166, 170
Monte Vista Peak 165, 169
Montrose Canyon 90, 103
Monument Canyon 264, 265
Mormon Ridge Trail 89, 159, 163, 166
Mormon Spring 99
Morse Canyon 165, 166
Morse Canyon Trail 89, 165
Mount Baldy Wilderness 179, 180, 181, 183, 218
Mount Lemmon Highway 87, 117, 118
Mount Lemmon Trail 124
Mount Wrightson Wilderness (proposed) 83-84
Mountain Spring 278, 282, 286, 302, 308
Muav limestone 226
Mud Spring (Blue Range) 208, 209, 215, 216, 217
Mud Spring (Santa Catalina Mountains) 114, 115
Multiple-Use policy 216-217
Music Canyon Spring 53
Musk Hog Canyon 60

Needle Canyon 31, 34, 38, 44, 45, 54, 56
Nogales Ranger District 85
North Fork Deadman Creek 283, 300
North Kaibab Trail 231, 242, 250, 253, 255, 256
North Peak 290, 291, 292, 297
North Peak Trail 297
North Rim (of Grand Canyon) 228, 231, 250, 253, 255
North Slope Trail 131, 132, 137

Oacpicagua, Luis 85
Old Baldy Trail 146, 148, 149, 151, 152, 155
Old Spanish Trail 88
O'Neill Butte 240
Onion Saddle 89
Oracle Road 86

Paint Mine Saddle 21, 33, 56
Paint Rock 166, 170
Palisade Canyon 110, 111, 114, 115, 117, 119
Palisade Ranger Station 87
Palisade Trail 111, 114, 115
Palomino Mountain 15, 30, 31, 39, 55
Papago Indians 16
Paradise Park 217
Paradise Park Trail 210
Park, The 283, 297, 300
Parker Pass 27, 30, 31, 34
Pattie Butte 246
Pattie, James O. 246
Payson, AZ 270
Payson Ranger District 270
Peralta Canyon 42, 46, 47
Peralta Canyon Trail 39, 42, 43, 54, 55
Peralta, Don Miguel 16
"Peralta Grant" 16
Peralta Road 47
Peralta Trailhead 18, 34, 35, 38, 39, 44-55, 61, 63
Pete Berry's cabin 247, 248-249
Peters Trail 35, 53

Pete's Pond 283, 300
Phantom Creek 256
Phantom Ranch 239, 242, 256, 258
Phelps Cabin 184, 222
Phoenix, AZ 2, 13, 14, 16
Phoneline Trail 109
Pima Canyon 94, 96, 97, 103
Pima Canyon Spring 96, 103
Pima Canyon Trail 96
Pima Indians 16, 85
Pine Canyon 114, 117
Pine Creek (Santa Catalina Mountains) 111, 115, 117
Pine Creek (Superstition Wilderness) 70, 71, 74
Pine Park 177
Pinery Canyon Road 89
Pinetop, AZ 183
Pinyon Camp 14, 39, 42, 43, 44, 55
Pipe Creek 236
Plateau Point 232, 233-234, 266
Pleasant Valley 269
Portal, AZ 89
Powell, John Wesley 229
Price Canyon 169
public transportation 2
Pusch Peak 94
Pusch Ridge 90, 94
Pusch Ridge Wilderness 83, 86-87, 94, 119

Rancho Romero 86, 90, 104, 105
Randolph Canyon 60, 61, 63
Randolph Creek 60
"Raspberry Peak" 166, 170
Raspberry Ridge 166, 170
Raspberry Ridge Trail 166
rattlesnakes 8
Reavis Creek 67, 74, 77, 79, 82
Reavis, Elisha 67, 68, 74, 75, 78, 82
Reavis Gap Trail 77
Reavis Grave 67, 69, 71, 75, 78, 79, 82
Reavis Headquarters 71, 74, 75, 77, 78, 79
Reavis, James Addison 16
Reavis Ranch Road 19, 75, 79
Reavis Ranch Trail 19, 68, 74
Reavis Trailhead 19, 75, 78, 79
Red Hill Road 182
Red Hills Trail 291, 292, 297, 304, 308
Red Rock Canyon Trail 169
Red Tanks Canyon 61, 62
Red Tanks Trail 35, 47, 50, 60, 61
Redwall cliff 228, 233, 240, 244, 247, 249, 250, 261
Redwall limestone 226
regulations, backcountry 9-10, 181, 230
Ribbon Falls 253, 254, 255
Rincon Mountains 2, 83, 88, 126, 130
Rincon Peak 138, 139, 141
River Ranger Station 237
Roaring Springs 250, 251, 253, 256
Roaring Springs Campground 250, 251, 253
Roaring Springs Canyon 251
Robinson Spring 154
Rock Creek Trail 157
Rogers Canyon 19, 63, 66, 67, 69, 70, 78, 79, 82

Rogers Canyon cliff dwellings 63, 66-67, 69, 70, 79, 82
Rogers Canyon Trail 66, 68, 69, 70, 82
Rogers Trough 19, 67, 68, 69, 71, 75
Romero Canyon 90, 91, 104, 105
Romero Canyon Trail 86
Romero Pass 91, 104, 105, 124, 125
Romero Spring 91
Round Park 159, 160, 163
Rucker Canyon Creek 166, 167, 168, 169
Rucker Canyon Trail 169
Rucker Forest Camp 89, 167, 168, 169, 170
Rucker Lake 89
Rustler Park 89, 157, 159, 160

Sabino Basin 110
Sabino Canyon 87, 106, 107, 109, 110, 118, 119, 120, 124
Sabino Canyon Road 86, 87, 106, 107, 109, 111, 115, 117, 119, 124, 125
Sabino Canyon Trail 109, 117, 119
Sabino Canyon Visitor Center 85, 86, 87
Saguaro National Monument 10, 83, 85, 88, 126
Salado Indian culture 16
Salt Creek 265
Salt River 13
San Francisco Peaks 228
Sandy Saddle Trail 276, 283, 300
Santa Catalina Mountains 2, 83-85, 109
Santa Catalina Ranger District 85
Santa Maria Spring 258
Santa Rita Lodge 88, 89
Santa Rita Mountains 2, 83-84, 88, 143, 150, 153
Saulsbury Canyon 163
Saulsbury Canyon Trail 89, 162, 166
Saulsbury Creek 162
Saulsbury Saddle 162
Sawed Off Mountain 216
scorpions 8
Second Water Canyon 22, 33, 56
Second Water Spring 32, 33, 56
Second Water Trail 23, 27, 32
Sentinel Lookout 175
Sentinel Peak 169, 172, 174, 175, 177
Seven Falls 111, 112, 113
Shake Tree Canyon 271, 272
Sheep Bridge 267, 270-271, 282, 286, 287, 292, 296, 301, 303, 308
Sheep Crossing 180, 181, 183-184
Shoshoni Point 246
Show Low, AZ 183
Showers Point Campground 87, 114, 115
Sinagua Culture 268, 293, 305
South Fork Cave Creek Canyon 168, 171, 172, 174, 176, 177
South Fork Deadman Creek 279
South Fork Forest Camp 89, 171, 174, 176, 178
South Kaibab Trail 237, 239-240, 242, 244

South Rim (of Grand Canyon) 2, 240, 244, 247
Snowshed Peak 169, 172, 176
Snowshed Trail 89, 176
Snyder Road 87
Soldier Camp 118
"Spanish Hieroglyphics" 29
Speedway Boulevard 88
Spencer Peak 118
Springerville Ranger District 181
Sprung Spring 149, 150-151
Steeple Creek 209, 216
Steeple Mesa 208, 210, 216
Steeple Mesa Trail 183, 208-209, 216
Strayhorse Creek 188
subalpine life zone 180
Summerhaven 87
Sunrise Road 86, 87
Supai formation 226, 239, 258, 259, 261
Super Trail 149, 150, 151, 155
Superstition Mountain 13, 15, 40
Superstition Mountains 2, 14, 15, 17, 51
Superstition Wilderness 2, 13-17, 18, 40, 46, 47, 63, 70, 75
Sycamore Creek (Mazatzal Wilderness) 296, 303-304
Sycamore Creek (Santa Catalina Mountains) 112
Sycamore Spring Reservoir 112
Sylvester Spring 143, 144
Tangle Creek Road 271, 287, 296, 301, 303
Tanque Verde Peak 88, 134, 135, 136, 141
Tanque Verde Ridge 134
Tanque Verde Ridge Trail 136, 142
Tapeats sandstone 226
tarantulas 9
Terrapin Pass 45
Terrapin Trail 45, 50, 52, 54
Telephone Ridge Trail 198, 199
Tewksbury-Graham Feud 269
Thomas Creek 188
Tina Larga Tank 127
To the Last Man 269
Tonto Apaches 269
Tonto Basin 267, 269, 286
Tonto Basin Ranger District 17
Tonto National Forest 17, 40, 270
Tonto Plateau 233, 234, 240, 243, 245, 258, 261, 262, 265
Tonto Trail 233, 236, 240, 244, 245, 246, 247, 258, 261, 262, 264
Toroweap formation 226
Tortilla Pass 19, 66, 70
Transition life zone 5, 115, 130, 167, 179, 209, 228
Trap Canyon Spring 52
Travertine Canyon 261, 263
trogon, coppery-tailed 147, 167, 171-172
trogon, eared 171-172
Tub Spring 157
Tucson, AZ 1, 2, 86-89, 101, 109
Turkey Creek 89, 162, 163, 165, 166
Two Bar Ridge Trail 71
Upper Blue River 182, 187, 188
Upper Horrell Place 19, 70, 71, 74

Upper La Barge Box 51, 61, 62
Upper Ribbon Fall 254
Upper Sonoran life zone 5, 13-14, 115, 130, 153, 167, 179, 207, 209, 228, 255
Vault Mine 148
Ventana Canyon Trail 103
Verde River 267, 286, 292, 296, 303
Verde River Trail 287, 296, 301, 303
Verde River Valley 287
Very Steep Trail 146, 147, 148, 149
Vishnu schist 236
Voigt Allotment 222
Waldron Trail 257
Waltz, Jacob 16
Weaver, Pauline 15
Weaver's Needle 15, 16, 30, 38, 44, 55
West Boulder Canyon 27, 28, 30, 31, 38, 56
West Fork Black River 180
West Fork Little Colorado River 180, 181, 183, 218, 219, 220
West Fork Sabino Canyon 105, 106, 125
West Fork Sabino Trail 105, 106, 120
Wet Bottom Creek 282, 283, 291, 292-293, 305
Whetrock Canyon 60
Whiskey Spring 50, 51, 61
Whiskey Spring Canyon 51
Whiskey Spring Trail 51, 62
White Mountain 79
White Mountains 2, 179, 180, 181, 218
Wilderness Act of 1964 15
Wilderness of Rocks 122, 123, 124
Wilderness of Rocks Trail 122
Willcox, AZ 89
Willow Spring (Blue Range) 209
Willow Spring (Mazatzal Wilderness) 286, 302
Willow Spring Trail 282, 286, 296, 301, 302, 303
Window Rock 101
Window, The 98, 99, 101, 102, 103, 105
Windsor Seep 272, 278, 300
Windy Pass 77
Wrightson, Mount 149, 150, 151, 152, 154, 155
Y Bar Basin 271, 272, 277, 278, 286
Y Bar Basin Trail 271, 278, 297, 300
Yaki Point 231, 237, 239, 242, 244, 245, 246
Yam Canyon 203
Yuma Point 261, 263
Zoroaster Creek 243

Other Books From Wilderness Press

Wilderness Press publishes many other fine outdoor books. The complete list is below. Write for a free catalog.

Arizona Trails	Sierra Nevada Flora
Backpackers Sourcebook	Sierra North
Backpacking Basics	Sierra South
Bicycling in Hawaii	The Anza-Borrego Desert Region
Hawaiian Camping	The Boundary Waters Canoe Area
Hiking Hawaii	The John Muir Trail
Hiking Kauai	The Pacific Crest Trail
Hiking Maui	The Tahoe Sierra
Hiking Oahu	The Tahoe-Yosemite Trail
Huckleberry Country	Trails of the Angeles
Lassen Volcanic National Park	The Vertical World of Yosemite
Marble Mountain Wilderness	Waxing for Cross-Country Skiing
A Pacific Crest Odyssey	Wild Food Plants of the Sierra
Point Reyes	Yosemite Climber
San Bernardino Mountain Trails	Yosemite National Park

Desolation Wilderness and the South Lake Tahoe Basin
Guide to the Golden Gate National Recreation Area
Nordic Touring and Cross-Country Skiing
Outdoor Guide to the San Francisco Bay Area
Self-Propelled in the Southern Sierra
The Cross-Country Ski, Cook, Look and Pleasure Book
The Sawtooth National Recreation Area

PLUS hiking guides to all the 15-minute quadrangles in the High Sierra, such as **Tuolumne Meadows, Mineral King** and **Mt. Whitney**.

Wilderness Press

2440 bancroft way · berkeley, california 94704